T0322267

Service Charge   24.64
(12.5%)
Tip   0.00

Ex. VAT Total   189.2
Total VAT   32.

20% VAT Sales   19
20% VAT   32.
FINAL TOTAL   222.19

Gratuity: _____

Na

A (mostly) vegan kitchen and bar

LeftField
VAT no. 405 6043 29
12 Barclay Terrace
Edinburgh, Scotland EH10 4HP
United Kingdom
Tel: +44 131 229 1394
Printed 3 November 2022 at 21:51

le: 2, 2 guests.

Crispy Squid   £9.50
Hummus   £8.00
Beef Brisket   £19.50
Hake   £18.50
Garden Salad   £5.50
Alvarinho   £38.00
                      £7.50

Sub Total   £114.00

Total   £114.00

VAT a/c Included in Total
VAT f Included in Total

Thank You,
you again soon

****
CHECK # 500
TABLE # 64
================
--
SEAT#   ITEMS ORDERED   KOI_DINE

1   -GOUGERES
       -FOIE GRAS PARFAI
       *SHORT RIB
       *BREAD
       *2 Guests
       *SCHNITZEL
       SALMON
       UFFLE FOR 2
       TSCHINKEN
       BB20

                         £7.25
                        £11.75

OTAL

270.
23.9

29

00%=£22.80

Nights Out at Home

Jay Rayner is an award-winning writer, journalist and broadcaster. He presents *The Kitchen Cabinet* for BBC Radio 4, is a judge on *MasterChef* and has been the restaurant critic for *The Observer* since 1999. He plays piano and leads the Jay Rayner Sextet. He lives in London.

Nights Out at Home

Recipes and Stories from Twenty-Five
Years as a Restaurant Critic

JAY RAYNER

With illustrations by Jack William Martindale

FIG TREE
an imprint of
PENGUIN BOOKS

FIG TREE

UK | USA | Canada | Ireland | Australia
India | New Zealand | South Africa

Fig Tree is part of the Penguin Random House group of companies
whose addresses can be found at global.penguinrandomhouse.com.

First published 2024
006

Copyright © Jay Rayner, 2024

Illustrations copyright © Jack William Martindale, 2024

The moral right of the copyright holders has been asserted

Set in 13.5/16pt Garamond MT Std
Typeset by Jouve (UK), Milton Keynes
Printed and bound in Great Britain by Clays Ltd, Elcograf S.p.A.

The authorized representative in the EEA is Penguin Random House Ireland,
Morrison Chambers, 32 Nassau Street, Dublin D02 YH68

A CIP catalogue record for this book is available from the British Library

ISBN: 978–0–241–63958–0

www.greenpenguin.co.uk

For Taiga

Advice for Readers

This is now your book. You can read it as you wish, but I do want to help you get the most out of it, so let me offer you some advice. Just off Kingsland High Road in north London is a scuffed and neglected service road bounded on its north side by an industrial loading bay, and on the south, by a 1960s office block which at ground level has enjoyed the attentions of the area's many talented graffiti artists. It's the kind of street you wouldn't choose to walk down, but if you're in the area, you really should. At its far end there's an alley. It leads to a wide yard which is home to the 40FT Brewery, the Dusty Knuckle Bakery and more importantly for our purposes, a grill restaurant called Acme Fire Cult. You can read more about both it, and its Vikingesque co-head chef Andrew Clarke, on page 221 of the Vegetables section.

Among the many lovely things on the snack menu there is a distinctive Bombay Mix. Usually with Bombay Mix I find myself hunting through the toasted, spiced rubble for the few prized nuts. That's not an issue at Acme Fire Cult because their version is full of them. It's a nut jamboree. I have no idea how they make theirs but it inspired me to make my own. Here's what you do. Put 100g of shop-bought Bombay Mix into a plastic box with a lid. Add 75g of salted peanuts and 75g of salted cashews. You can add any salted nut of choice, but these work for me. You'll need a few extra spices for the increased volume, so add a quarter teaspoon of ground cumin, a quarter teaspoon of smoked paprika and half a teaspoon of caster sugar. Put the lid on the box and give it a good shake. And there you are: a pimped and exceedingly satisfying Bombay Mix. You can make your own adaptations if you fancy. There are flavoured roasted nuts on the market now, including cracked black pepper cashews. They work very well in this. If you want to go the extra mile, you could fry a few curry leaves in oil, crumble them up and throw those in too. It's up to you.

Why am I giving you these instructions? Because *Nights Out at Home* is a collection of stories about restaurants, the fabulous meals eaten in them and recipes emerging from them. If I've done my job properly, reading it will make you hungry. I've found in the past that advising people to get a bowl of snacks to eat alongside a reading of my books can be helpful. I'm just being a little more prescriptive this time. Of course, you can eat what the hell you like: roasted pistachios prised from the shell, Japanese rice crackers, the ultra-high processed wonder that is Tangy Cheese flavour Doritos, which will stain both your fingers and therefore the pages orange, as you turn them. But my Bombay Mix, inspired by the version at Acme Fire Cult, will properly get you in the mood. Or just put the book aside and give that a really good seeing to, until your appetite is properly sated. Then start reading the book. Your call.

I hope that helps.

Contents

List of Recipes

Introduction

It is a midweek lunchtime, somewhere back in the last decade, and I am sitting by myself in a bare-bones café just off the main drag of London's Chinatown. It's called Baiwei, and is the spartan sibling of the more ornate Barshu, the ground-breaking Sichuan restaurant a few streets away in Soho. I have not written about Baiwei. This isn't because I want to keep it to myself. Restaurant critics aren't generally in the business of keeping secrets. I have simply never felt there was quite enough about this stack of tiny dining rooms with their uncomfortable metal stools and cramped canteen tables for a whole column. Instead, I come here alone every now and then, for a couple of plates of chilli and Sichuan peppercorn-boosted food; perhaps the double-cooked pork, like the best chilli bean sauce-smeared bacon, or the dry-fried green beans. Or both together. Hold the rice. I'm off the carbs, thank you.

Today I have ordered something I have not tried before. Now I am staring down at it, my chopsticks poised in the air above the dish. I am lost in thought. It is a bowl of chopped-up and spiced pork spare ribs, in a massive heap of shiny dried red chillies. I like it very much. Scratch that. I adore it. I feel, as I occasionally do in my solipsistic way, that it is food cooked specifically with me in mind. Right now, I am analysing it. The meat is crisp, which means these mini ribs, sections of baby backs, were deep-fried. But the bones are soft and chewable. Therefore, prior to hitting the boiling fat they surely had to have been pre-cooked? Which almost certainly means they were braised in one of those deep, dark, soy and star anise-boosted liquors that are used again and again in Chinese kitchens. Those 'master sauce' braising liquors become enriched with pork fat, their flavours deepening, over months and even years. So they've been braised and deep-fried. But what about the spicing? There's a lot of cumin in there. I associate that with Xinjiang province rather than Sichuan. There's salt and a fair dusting of chilli but something else too. It takes me a minute or so to clock it: sugar. That's what's making these ribs so damn addictive. It's a killer combination of salt and sweet, of heat and aromatics. The heaped red chillies, which you are not meant to eat but merely to hunt through, add a certain depth and flavour, but do not add to the burn. I recognize that sort of fun from Chongqing chicken, in which the bird is broken into deep-fried nuggets both on and off the bone. This dish feels like a bit of a culinary mashup, both Sichuan and Xinjiang. I know I want to eat it again. And I now have the vital intelligence with which to do so, whenever I want. Give or take a bit of trial and error back in my own kitchen, I am ready to attempt it myself. It won't be exactly the same as eating at Baiwei. I am not a trained Chinese chef. But it will be a dish inspired by my deep love of the place.

I became the restaurant critic for the *Observer* in 1999. It means that, at time of writing, I have been wielding my cutlery professionally for a quarter of a century. That's over 1,500 restaurants reviewed, not just in the UK but across the world. Plus, there are so many more places that I have eaten in but which, for whatever reason, I have not written about. I have surfed the breaking wave of modernist gastronomy, of farm-to-table and live-fire cookery. I have tried dishes representing the culinary traditions of Thailand, the Indian subcontinent, the Americas and South East Asia, as well as every obvious nook and cranny of Europe, and so much more besides. The vast majority have been very good indeed. I have experienced some brilliant cooking, executed by hugely skilled professionals. When it comes to chefs, I am a bit of a fan boy.

Throughout that time, as a keen home cook, I have also been taking the very best ideas back home with me. I have been reverse-engineering engrossing restaurant dishes, to create food in my own kitchen inspired by all those places in which I have been lucky enough to eat. It has become something of a hobby, this knotty business of unpicking the food on my plate; one which only accelerated during the enforced confinement of the Covid lockdowns, when a stint in the kitchen became the best way to bring a bit of colour to a featureless day. Mostly, I've been successful. Sometimes, less so. I once spent days dwelling on a dish by the late über chef Joël Robuchon. It was a single fat scallop, in a mess of morels and veal jus, baked beneath a puff pastry shell. I couldn't work out how it was cooked so that the pastry was crisp and flaky and bronzed, but the scallop was not overdone. Eventually I cracked it. At every stage of the process everything had to be seriously chilled before going anywhere near a hot oven. I enjoyed the mental process of unlocking the method almost as much as I did eating the dish at home. It wasn't Robuchon's scallop with morels. I would once again use the word 'inspired' to describe its relationship to Robuchon's original. But it was definitely bloody delicious.

This book is the result of all that restaurant-going, of all that heroic eating and of all that home kitchen experimentation. My selflessness knows no bounds. It's a collection of recipes inspired by the glorious food that has stayed with me from the job I've been privileged enough to do for all these years, alongside the stories of the restaurants and chefs that

3

served it to me. It isn't, however, a set of restaurant kitchen recipes. What would be the point of that? Professional kitchens are complicated places, often housing multiple people working together to achieve a dish. Cooking that food is literally their full-time job, while you probably have a different full-time job, thank you very much. Plus, the recipes they use are also often extremely complex, highly technical and therefore useless to a home cook. Very few of us have someone standing in the corner of our kitchen at home ready to knock up the pastry, or another fretting over the stock pot for us. Just getting the original recipe from the chef wouldn't be helpful at all. Indeed, it would be profoundly annoying.

I too am a home cook, albeit one who has been given access to professional kitchens an awful lot over the years. Occasionally I've worked in them. Chefs love giving me really menial jobs to do in their kitchens: here, turn these three crates of girolles; now pin-bone these ninety-six red mullet fillets. It's been tiresome work, but it has given me the opportunity to observe what's going on in those kitchens, to understand how they function. That in turn has helped me get to grips with the fundamentals of so many restaurant dishes. Often, for the ones in this volume, I've had the help of the chefs themselves. Certainly, where appropriate, I've sought their blessing. What matters is that they work for the home cook. Most are very simple. Some are a little more ambitious, but that can be fun too, if you're up for it.

These are not the dishes of the grand, big-ticket restaurants with hugely recognizable names. Those restaurants have already published their statement cookbooks. They can be vital documents, a record of the work of chefs who have made a significant difference to the way we cook and eat. But to get to grips with them you need to clear a few weeks in the diary. They are more for drooling over and staring at, rather than for feeding yourself from. That said, there is still space in this book for the stories of a handful of dishes from those sorts of gastro-palaces, the ones I've come to love over the years, as much for the fun of the challenge as anything else. There are also a few versions of high street favourites. You will note that I offer you the chance to nail a version of the cultural treasure, the edible triumph, that is the Greggs Steak Bake.

Generally though, both the stories and the recipes represent the joyously smaller and lesser-known places. It's the dark crusted lamb chops from the legendary Pakistani grill house Tayyabs in London's Whitechapel, and the grilled leeks with pistachio romesco from Acme Fire Cult in Dalston. It's the crispy duck à l'orange from the shamelessly old-school Oslo Court in St John's Wood where it is forever 1977, the extraordinary blistered and bubbled flatbreads from self-taught chef Patrick Withington at Erst in Manchester, glistening with molten lardo and crushed garlic, and, from the delightful Persian Cottage in Middlesbrough, the fesen-jan, a dark Iranian stew of chicken, walnuts and pomegranate. It's the taramasalata with radishes and boiled eggs at Rosie Healey's Gloriosa in Glasgow. It's the distinctive chopped liver from Russ & Daughters in New York and a sardine-based take on the soused herring and potato salad from Chez Georges in Paris. Although British restaurants and their dishes dominate, my restaurant-going has always been global. So is this collection.

I've given these examples to make a clear point about the kinds of dishes that aren't included. There are great kitchens which, working together, can serve you, say, a perfectly cooked duck breast, pink within, golden brown without, with a beautiful tangle of wilted cavolo nero, bronzed fondant potatoes and one of those glossy, lip-smacking sauces with serious depth and attitude which brings everything together. Such a plate of food may well be an expression of the presiding head chef's great taste and technique and their ability to transfer skills to their brigade. But from my time hanging around those restaurant kitchens I can say that replicating these at home is a fool's errand because they are partworks; the product of three or four cooks working together. They are lovely plates of food, but not quite identifiable dishes. Every recipe in this book is for a self-contained item.

Most of all, this collection is a celebration. In recent years I have published two volumes of my most negative reviews, available from all good booksellers, because people do adore reading the brutal take-downs. This is because people can be horrid. They love the product of the sharpened pen, dipped deep in blood. Those horrid people might be you. Enjoy yourselves. But I don't publish negative reviews lightly. I know what the impact can be and make a point of punching up, at the over-capitalized and under-performing; the places that seem to be laughing at their clientele even as they separate them from their money. I stand by every one of those reviews.

But even as I have published those collections, I have been aware that they have emphasized the most negative aspects of my job. The fact is I adore restaurants. *Nights Out at Home* is my love letter to the places that have been the cornerstone of my working life for so long. Sometimes, of course, the recipes for these dishes are all that remains of the restaurant, because it is no longer with us. Over a restaurant-going career lasting twenty-five years that's inevitable. Baiwei closed during the pandemic, to be replaced by a rather good noodle shop, and I have never seen the cumin and chilli ribs they served there on any other menu. Recreating the food of long-gone restaurants is a sweet act of greedy remembrance. But most of them are still very much trading.

It's therefore important to say this: the recipes in this book are not a replacement for a visit to the restaurant itself. This volume is not an extended version of the words: 'I could make that at home.' Of course, when we go out to eat, we want to be fed, but restaurants are about so much more than just the food that comes out of the kitchen. That's one of the reasons I adore writing about them. They are not just about appetites, sated. They are about the room and the buzz and the service and the staff and the fact that you don't need to do your own washing up. When you cook these recipes, someone in your home will definitely have to clean up. It may even be you. At the end you will find a list of all the restaurants that are still trading, whose dishes I've been inspired by, along with their addresses. Please consider going to them.

Inevitably, this collection is a direct reflection of the restaurant sector which has been my journalistic beat these past twenty-five years: the restaurants that were available to review; the ones from those that I chose to review; and the ones in turn with dishes which were suitable to be transported back to the home kitchen. That means it's not always as representative of the world or wider society as I would like it to be. For example, there are many recipes drawing on the food of Europe, the Americas and Asia but there is very little from Africa. While there have long been beloved and highly regarded restaurants serving African communities in the UK, only very recently have they started to enter the mainstream, courtesy of places like Chishuru and Isibani, both of which I liked very much when I reviewed them. But I am still getting to grips with the fundamentals of those culinary traditions. Every cook is a work in progress and I am no different.

Equally striking is the imbalance between men and women. There have, of course, been some very successful, high-profile women leading restaurant kitchens in the UK, including Ruthie Rogers and Rose Gray, Sally Clarke, Angela Hartnett, Clare Smyth, Monica Galetti and Hélène Darroze. But all of them have their statement cookbooks, which, as I said earlier, means none of the recipes in this collection are inspired by their dishes. More generally, though, the restaurant world remains shockingly dominated by men. There are recipes here inspired by dishes created by superb women including Ravinder Bhogal, Amoul Oakes, Esra Muslu, Mary-Ellen McTague and Christine Yau. But there are nowhere near enough of them. Change is happening, but it is still painfully slow.

I was fortunate to become a restaurant critic at a point when great food and eating out was moving from being a relatively niche interest, to a mass pursuit, to arguably a way of viewing the developing culture of our great cities and beyond. In the digital age, when anyone can express an opinion on anything, and anyone else can read it, the job of the restaurant critic can look ludicrously antiquated. Who is this over-fed, over-privileged fop, declaring himself an arbiter of taste when we can all be one of those? It's a good question, and one I've only ever been able to answer by putting my back into it; by taking the job seriously, by writing as entertainingly as possible, and hoping that my arguments give my reviews enough authority so that people keep reading and, in turn, I keep being allowed to go out for dinner. But people are still interested in what it is that restaurant critics do. So scattered throughout the recipes, and the accompanying memories of the restaurants, is a series of short essays about the thrilling and glamorous life of the restaurant critic. Think of them as intercourses. Perhaps you want to know what happens when a restaurant critic goes out for dinner. Or how I deal with the fact that, courtesy of a career prancing around on television occasionally, I am less than anonymous. Or what impact all this championship-level eating has on this too, too solid flesh of mine. You're in luck. I'm going to tell you everything. I may even overshare. Sorry. (Not sorry.)

This is very much a cookbook written by a writer, rather than a chef. If you just want to read it rather than cook from it, go right ahead. It's now your book. (You can use it as a doorstop if you like; I won't judge you.) But it is designed to be a functional cookbook. You may be a little surprised therefore to see that it doesn't include lots of big colour photographs of the food you're being invited to cook. This isn't accidental. It wasn't an oversight because we were all down the pub celebrating the fact that I got it written in time. It's a deliberate choice. In the lockdown of early 2021, with restaurants closed, I wrote a dozen-strong series of articles for the *Observer* celebrating a personal selection of the greatest cookbooks of the past forty years or so; the ones that had made a significant difference to our food culture. Reading and cooking from these great works very much focused my mind on what makes a successful cookbook. A few of them were the big glossy editions, full of drop-dead gorgeous colour photography, because there is always a place for those. I have a number that I love. But sometimes, I worry that overly art-directed imagery becomes an invitation to both the reader and the cook to fail, because what you make in your own kitchen can never hope to match what you see in the pictures. Instead, the volumes which really spoke to me were the smaller, more compact ones: books like Simon Hopkinson and Lindsey Bareham's *Roast Chicken and Other Stories*, or Nigel Slater's *Real Fast Food*. If ever I'm asked to choose between taste and presentation, taste wins every time.

If it looks pretty or, more to the point, like something invitingly edible, then all to the good. But deliciousness wins out every time. That's why we have not included lots of food porn.

I recognize that some people will find this frustrating; that they like some form of visual reference for what they're aiming at. Fair enough. Throughout the writing of this book I took photographs of almost all the things I cooked, mostly as an aide-mémoire for myself. Anybody who follows me on Instagram, where on Sundays I post my own photographs of what I ate during that week's review, will know some of my photography can be awful. I don't apologize for this. I refuse to stop dinner to get a ring light up or stand on a chair. There's more than enough alluring food photography elsewhere on Instagram, without me adding to it. So be warned: some of my pictures are less than encumbered with professionalism. Nevertheless, I have created the *Nights Out at Home* photo galleries on my website, if you do want to have a look at my version of the dish. For that, just visit https://www.jayrayner.co.uk/noah, or use the QR code which you will find on page 361.

I never expected to be a restaurant critic for a quarter of a century. No journalist should ever expect to hold down any column for that long. But as I hit that milestone, with my napkin tucked firmly into my collar in an attempt to save yet another white shirt from sauce splashes, it's a delight to be able to celebrate the very best dishes it has been my privilege to eat, eat again and then rework at home. Now I get to share them with you.

The First Drink

A daiquiri

Inspired by the cocktail served at the American Bar of the
Stafford Hotel, London (and many, many other places)

It doesn't always start like this. It doesn't always begin with
me filling a well-upholstered chair in a corner of the American Bar of the Stafford Hotel in London's St James's, nursing
a potent, invigorating cocktail served so cold it could frost
the glass. If I'm reviewing lunch at a Desi pub in West Brom-
wich or a Cantonese roast meats café in Preston, that really
isn't part of the deal. But sometimes it's dinner and sometimes the restaurant is in the centre of London. There is an
old friend to be met beforehand. There is the vital business
of emotional intelligence to be shared, which is to say, the

gossip. That means a cocktail. Which for me means a daiquiri, that virtuous interplay of rum, lime and sugar syrup.

Where cocktails are concerned, I've almost come full circle. As a youth, sodden with bad taste, my drink of choice was vodka and lime: a cheap, blunt white spirit drowning in sugary lime cordial. In 1989, on my first trip to New York as a very young journalist, I asked for this at the bar of the Algonquin Hotel. The head barman of the Blue Bar asked if I meant a vodka gimlet. I was thrilled to discover that my frankly trashy drink of choice had a name and a classier, sharper iteration, for there shouldn't be sugar in a gimlet. Over the years I worked my way through various drinks, as if trying on versions of myself until I found one that fitted. For a while I thought I might be a whisky sour man, until I realized I didn't like whisky quite enough. I flirted with the old-fashioned and the sazerac, but I missed the acidity. I tried one negroni and, while recognizing that a taste for them was a mark of sophistication, quickly concluded that I couldn't fake that level of sophistication. I find negronis too bitter; they are like punishment for a crime I wasn't aware I had committed.

Eventually I found my way to the Cuban wonder that is the daiquiri, and it felt like coming home, only as an adult version of myself. The word does appear in the names of other cocktails. There are strawberry daiquiris and banana daiquiris, watermelon daiquiris and banana and honey daiquiris and so much else. Like civil war re-enactments and S&M, I know this sort of thing goes on. I just want no part of it. I want my daiquiri to be simple and crisp and if somebody else is making it for me, I want it to be one of the skilled professionals at the American Bar of the Stafford. The small boutique hotel is hardly obscure, but it is very much tucked away. It can be reached from one side by a narrow lane off St James's Street, and on the other by a discreet alley just off the easternmost path through Green Park. Turning into that dark, shadowed, albeit beautifully appointed alley is like knocking on a secret door. The dimly lit bar at the back of the hotel is part of a 1930s vogue for bars across London's West End named 'the American' to draw in wealthy customers from the US. Only two remain: the one at the Savoy and the one here. Its ceiling is famed for being hung with ludicrous American souvenirs donated by wealthy hotel guests. They bring baseball and rowing caps, university ties, and the odd carved wooden eagle. The narrow space is extremely comfortable and it really is extremely expensive. But they do good bar snacks for free, so there's that. None of your dry disappointing pretzels here. You get a trio of well-filled silver bowls containing mixed nuts, seasoned rice crackers and olives. I do love a generous bar snack, even if the cost is barely hidden in the ludicrous price of the cocktail.

The daiquiri comes in a long-stemmed coupe, which means your hand never need get round the bowl of the glass and warm it up. Early one evening I am invited to go back behind the bar to watch head American Bar mixologist Salvatore Megna do his thing. Megna, who is dark-eyed, intense and from Naples, started as a barman when he was fifteen. He is now thirty-five, and has been at the Stafford for six years. Before that he was at the Bulgari Hotel in Kensington. 'The head barman there got every potential new recruit to mix him a daiquiri as a test,' he says. 'I now do the same. When there are just three ingredients, we tend to underestimate how complicated it is. The balance of sweet and sour is the most complicated thing you can do.' Is it popular? 'It is popular, just not as popular as a negroni or martini.' Megna says he likes his made with dark rum, aged in oak barrels. I've tried dark rum daiquiris and find the caramel tones a little distracting. I prefer a white rum. 'We use Bayou rum from Louisiana,' Megna says, showing me a tall, squared-off, frosted glass bottle. He offers me a neat shot. It is rounded and deep, with a lovely balance of alcohol to sugar.

Now Megna performs the barman's dance. Ice goes in the shaker. The three ingredients join them. He clamps the shaker shut and lifts it close to his cheek. 'How long you shake is very important. It should be ten or twelve seconds.' The rattle of ice on metal is the sound of a night beginning. Finally, he uses two strainers to make sure there are no chips of ice allowed into the glass.

He invites me to try my drink. At this point I should, I suppose, say something reverential about Ernest Hemingway and how he fuelled himself on daiquiris at the bar of El Floridita in Havana, during his years in Cuba. But I'm not convinced the old soak is a good advert for anything, apart from beards, fishing and short sentences. So let me tell you instead that the daiquiri in this tall coupe glass is crisp and brisk. It is sweet and sour. It is boozy and light. It is the beginning of my night. It is everything.

INGREDIENTS

Ice
60ml white rum of your choice (choose one with a number in the title; it refers to the years it's been aged)
25ml freshly squeezed lime juice
15ml sugar syrup

METHOD

1. Fill your chosen, tall-stemmed glass with crushed ice so it chills. A shaker really is ideal for the next part. If

14

you have one, fill it with more ice, add the ingredients and shake. The drinks expert Alice Lascelles says in her book *The Cocktail Edit* that you should 'shake until the tin's so cold it hurts your hands'. I love the image and it sounds like very good advice, but you could just go for Megna's 10 to 12 seconds. Chuck away the crushed ice that was chilling your glass, and strain your daiquiri into it.

2. If you don't have a shaker, put a lot of ice into a measuring jug, then put the jug in the freezer for 15 to 30 minutes. Take the jug out of the freezer, add the rum, lime juice and sugar syrup, let it stand for 15 seconds, stir for 10 to 15 seconds, then strain into the chilled glass.

Unless you don't drink, in which case fair enough; turn the page.

Sauces

It has not always been the most intricate or flashy dishes that have stayed with me from a meal out. Sometimes it's been the incidentals, the small things which are designed only to operate as punctuation marks or edible scaffolding: a slab of the now ubiquitous sourdough, but with an especially crisp crust, like vegan crackling; the fattest of olives, stuffed with pieces of orange and flavoured with fresh thyme.

At the Green Street Seafood Café in Bath, which I visited in March of 2000, it was a bowl of what I described in my review as a 'herb dipping oil', which was waiting for me on the table in the upstairs dining room when I got there. The fact that it was only six months after I'd started doing the job full-time is relevant, because there were clearly some huge gaps in my basic knowledge. I explained in detail what was in it: 'a few handfuls of basil, chives and any other green herbs you fancy, a clove of minced garlic, a tin of salted anchovies, chopped, a squeeze of lemon juice and enough good olive oil to cover.' It was probably the first dish eaten in a restaurant professionally that I then reverse-engineered at home. What I hadn't noticed, because I was clueless, was that I had described the exact ingredients for a classic salsa verde. It turns out that I wasn't alone in this. Green Street was an early venture from the great fish and seafood chef Mitch Tonks, who would later go on to set up the trailblazing Fishworks group, before opening the rather glossier Seahorse in Dartmouth and a bunch of other flourishing businesses besides. That 'dip', he said, 'became a thing. I also didn't realize in those early days of starting out that I had made a salsa verde.' It was only when he saw Rick Stein make one on an episode of his TV show that he realized what he'd 'invented'. It's nice to have company in youthful ignorance.

I'm a big fan of accessories at the table. I especially love condiments, as the top shelf of my fridge will bear witness. It is a clutter of flavour bombs, of sticky umami-rich pastes and jellies, some more beloved than others. All the recipes below are for condiments inspired by my restaurant-going. Some of them evolved out of a specific restaurant experience; others are more general. All of them turn up on my table at regular intervals.

Dim sum dipping sauce

Over the years I've been offered a variety of options to go with my siu mai, har gau and the rest: perhaps a simple dish of light soy or another of dark Chinkiang rice vinegar, with its deep caramel notes. Sometimes I've been offered a bottle of each and been invited to mix my own. This dipping sauce recipe emerged out of my experiments at home, and it goes beautifully with dumplings, both steamed and grilled. I use a simple white wine vinegar because I find it a little lighter. I also often put in far more of the ginger than is strictly necessary because it pickles quickly, and I love delicately picking it out with my chopsticks and eating it neat. No, I don't care if you're appalled.

INGREDIENTS

60ml light soy
30ml white wine vinegar
A splash of water
3 tsp caster sugar
A thumb-size piece of ginger, peeled and cut into matchstick
  batons

METHOD

1. Mix all the liquid ingredients in a small bowl, add the sugar and stir to dissolve.

2. Add the ginger and leave to steep for an hour or two.

Pickled red chillies

In the many Vietnamese restaurants that crowd along north London's Kingsland Road, there is often a glass jar of lightly sweetened pickled chillies and garlic on the table, known as ot ngam giam toi. It's to be sprinkled on to steaming bowls of pho or clay pot stews or just to perk up rice with an extra punch. I've always enjoyed the idea of it more than the experience of eating it because those kitchens tend to use sliced bird's-eye chillies, which for me are just too bloody hot. I use generic red chillies, the sort sold by supermarkets in bags of three, which have the advantage that you can eat loads of them. But feel free to use something much fiercer, and then boast about it. Though I'd advise against using Scotch bonnets, because the flavour is so distinctive.

INGREDIENTS

60ml white wine vinegar
30ml water
1 tsp sea salt
2 tsp caster sugar
4 fresh red chillies, finely sliced (deseed if you want it milder,
   otherwise leave them in)
1 clove of garlic, very finely chopped

METHOD

1. Mix the liquids with the salt and sugar in a bowl and stir until dissolved. Add the chillies and garlic, and leave to steep for a couple of hours.

2. Once you've eaten all the chillies, you will have an excellent chilli vinegar which is great on chips.

3. You can also blitz all these ingredients to make a terrific red chilli relish, which I suggest as one of the accompaniments to the sweet soy-braised pork shoulder on page 157.

Coriander relish

It's a completely arbitrary distinction on my part, but I separate out British high street Indian restaurants depending on what chutneys and relishes arrive with the poppadoms. The standard places will serve a mango chutney of varying quality, lime pickle and perhaps a tomato-based chutney. Some, however, will also serve a coriander relish. I tend to think better of the place when that turns up. My version is 'proudly inauthentic', to adopt a phrase I first saw used by the chef Ravinder Bhogal. Which is to say, I made it up, but it has a winning zing and freshness and goes very well with a whole bunch of things including, as with the blitzed chillies in vinegar above, the sweet soy-braised pork shoulder on page 157.

INGREDIENTS

80g fresh coriander, including stalks
4 spring onions, roughly chopped
100ml vegetable oil
1 tsp caster sugar
½ tsp sea salt
Juice of 1 lime (or more)
White wine vinegar (optional)

METHOD

1. Put all the ingredients into a food processor and blitz. Add a little more lime juice or white wine vinegar if you think it needs to be sharper.

Salsa verde

Inspired by the version at the short-lived Green Street
Seafood Café, Bath

This is a recipe book, so you want volumes don't you and you
will get them. But in truth I just get a bunch of the ingredients listed below and keep mixing it up until it tastes right.
The original version was roughly hand-chopped and it's terrific like that, but you can also blitz it in a blender briefly to
turn it into more of a rough sauce.

INGREDIENTS

1 bunch of fresh basil
1 bunch of fresh flat-leaf parsley
1 bunch of fresh chives
(tarragon and chervil can also work very well)
2 cloves of garlic, crushed and finely chopped
Juice of 1 lemon (and the zest, if you're feeling fancy)
1 tin of salted anchovies, drained, roughly 50g (or 50g chopped
    pickled capers, to make the salsa verde vegan)
Enough olive oil to eventually cover (it doesn't have to be the
    good stuff)
White wine vinegar (optional)

METHOD

1. Coarsely chop all the herbs and put them into a bowl.
   You can remove the heftier stalks if you like, but
   generally I use almost all of it, and I definitely do if
   I'm blitzing it to a sauce.

2. Crush and finely chop the garlic and add that.

3. Zest the lemon if you want to add it, then juice the lemon and add both.

4. Drain the anchovies, finely chop and add them. (Or chop the capers.)

5. Pour in enough olive oil so you can see it just below the surface of the herbs. Leave for 10 minutes and give it a mix. The herbs will slump down and eventually be covered by the oil.

6. If you want it saltier, add more anchovies or capers. If you want it more acidic, add extra lemon juice or perhaps a little white wine vinegar.

Anchovy mayonnaise

Inspired by the anchovy hollandaise served at the
Hawksmoor steakhouse group

In my 2012 review of the then newly opened Hawksmoor Air Street, from the group which now operates in New York and other places in North America as well as in the UK, I swooned over their anchovy hollandaise. 'You could easily slip into a hotel room with a sauce boat of that and a consenting adult,' I said, 'and lose a whole afternoon.' It's that good. If that's your definition of a jolly afternoon. It is just a perfect accompaniment to grilled meats of all kinds, and quite a lot of grilled vegetables too. If you want to whip up your own real Hawksmoor anchovy hollandaise, you will find a recipe for that in the *Hawksmoor* cookbook, and may god have mercy on your soul.

This is not that. It's shop-bought mayonnaise with anchovies blitzed through it, because I love salted anchovies and they improve many of the things to which they're introduced. Also, I'm quite lazy. You can make your own mayonnaise if you like, if you're bored. Or trying to prove something. There are lots of recipes online. But I've always felt it was one of those things, like tomato ketchup, that the industrial manufacturers have nailed. If you glance at the ingredients below, you'll see it's in a ratio of two salted anchovy fillets per 50g of mayonnaise. Simply multiply in that ratio to make more. But below 150g it becomes a little difficult to blitz it properly, because there's not enough volume.

INGREDIENTS

6 salted anchovies, roughly chopped
150g mayonnaise

METHOD

1. Put the anchovies and mayonnaise into a small food processor. Blitz. Chill. By which I mean both put it in the fridge until you need it, and go watch something on Netflix. And talking of anchovies . . .

Anchovy sauce

Inspired by the sauce served at Le Relais de Venise l'Entrecôte, which has outposts in Paris, London, New York and Mexico City

Le Relais de Venise l'Entrecôte has been operating in Paris since 1959, and is hugely popular, especially among people who really don't like having to make too many decisions.

This is because it only serves a small number of things: a walnut salad, a steak, chips and their 'special' sauce. When I reviewed the London outpost, which opened in 2005, I criticized the chips, which were a bit flaccid, but I did very much like the special sauce. This is because at base it involves anchovies and butter, two of my favourite things. The original also involves a few green herbs, particularly tarragon and chervil. Add them by all means. Pop some capers in there too if you fancy. But I prefer to keep this simple, and knock it up in a couple of minutes when I'm serving grilled lamb chops and the like. It also goes extremely well with grilled fish and charred vegetables. The volume below is just about enough for a couple of lamb chops each for four people. In reality, you may want to double or triple it, but decency held me back from starting a recipe with '200g unsalted butter'.

INGREDIENTS

100g unsalted butter
6 good salted anchovy fillets
2 tsp Dijon mustard
A squeeze of lemon juice
A couple of tablespoons of finely chopped fresh flat-leaf parsley
    (optional)

METHOD

1. Gently melt the butter in a small saucepan. Add the anchovy fillets and bosh them about with a wooden spoon until they crumble and dissolve into the butter.

2. Take the pan off the heat and whisk in the Dijon mustard, the lemon juice and the finely chopped

flat-leaf parsley if using. Leave the pan in a warm place on the hob but do not reheat it or the sauce will separate.

3. Serve warm and serve quickly.

Thick vinaigrette

Inspired by the version served with globe artichokes at
Oslo Court, London

Vinaigrette is very personal. For example, my wife doesn't like my version. Pat thinks it's too mustardy and too thick. Fair enough. The joy of long marriage is that you can disagree on things like vinaigrette without getting divorced, because divorce involves far too much admin, unlike vinaigrette. The thickness is deliberate. This version is designed more as a dip than a dressing, although it can be used as one. It's perfect for asparagus and more specifically for the fat ends of globe artichoke leaves, which is how it's served at the marvellous Oslo Court in London's St John's Wood. (For more on Oslo Court, go to the recipe for duck à l'orange on page 150). Some people will be bemused by the complexity of my version. They'll argue that vinaigrette is basically oil and vinegar in a ratio of three to one. Go discuss that with Pat. She'll probably agree with you. I throw in other things. The small amount of light soy, which adds a bash of umami, is a trick I picked up from Henry Harris of Bouchon Racine. (Go to the recipe for chicken in a mustard sauce on page 138 for more on him and his restaurants.) The mix of vegetable and olive oil and the addition of half a teaspoon of honey comes from Felicity Cloake, whose 'How to Make the Perfect' columns in the *Guardian* are essential reading for any cook, as are the 'Perfect' books arising from them. I also use two preparation techniques, which is annoying because it creates more washing up. But it's worth it.

INGREDIENTS

A clove of garlic
1 tsp sea salt
I fat tbsp Dijon mustard
2 tsp light soy
40ml white wine vinegar
100ml vegetable oil
70ml extra virgin olive oil
½ tsp honey
1 tbsp (shop-bought) mayonnaise
A grind of black pepper

METHOD

1. Grind the clove of garlic with the sea salt in a pestle and mortar to make a paste. If you don't have a pestle and mortar, you can do this with the back of a spoon in a bowl.

2. Add the mustard to the paste, then the soy and vinegar, and mix to incorporate.

3. Pour all that into a processor, making sure not to leave any behind. Add the oils, the honey and the mayonnaise, and blitz on high for 20 to 30 seconds. The result will be a thick, almost frothy vinaigrette which will hold without separating for at least a couple of days. Add a good grind of black pepper and stir that in.

Snacks

What constitutes a snack is very much in the eye of the beholder. A snack is what ravenous teens have when they get home from school, even if the groaning plate they've put together looks very much like dinner, just two hours before you serve them actual dinner. A snack really might just be a small thing eaten because you fancy it, or it can be another, unnamed meal between the ones that already have names. When I started reviewing in 1999 it was a word reserved for the offering across the bar in pubs. It was nuts or it was pork scratchings. In the more aspiring corners of the pub estate it was olives, the good ones flecked with herbs. Meanwhile in fancier restaurants, they had another word. They were called canapés. They were tiny, fragile tart cases dolloped with the lightest of fish mousses topped with shiny beads of caviar, or spongy blinis heaped with curls of smoked salmon. They were finger food, only with the little finger very much up and out of play.

In 2009 Brett Graham, chef-proprietor of the Michelin-starred Ledbury in London's Notting Hill, was one of those involved with opening the Harwood Arms, a food pub in Fulham. It reinvented the idea of the pub bar snack. There were sausage rolls as thick as your wrist made with buttery pastry, slabs of terrine with toast, cauliflower croquettes with piccalilli, and a Scotch egg made with spiced venison, served warm, its yolk still running. The latter was an ocean away from the bright orange golf ball with a green-tinged and sulphurous yolk from overcooking, which had long been a staple of motorway services. You could easily form a full and delightful dinner from this list of 'snacks'. Around the same time, at the revered Noma in Copenhagen, I was served salty, oily lumpfish roe between two crisped slices of fried chicken skin, which raised the notion of snack to god-tier. In 2012 at the Soho bistro 10 Greek Street, it was chunky cubes of roast pork belly with spiced quince, while a couple of years later at Hoi Polloi, the restaurant of the Ace Hotel in East London, it was deep-fried rings of pickled onion served with a take on taramasalata made with salt cod. The humble snack had both come of age and come into the fancy restaurant dining room.

Some of my snack recipes are very much for nibbles; for things you pick at before the main event. Others might work as a small meal between the big meals. Or you can just ignore the word 'snack' altogether and make them your dinner.

Smoked mackerel sandwich with horseradish cream

Inspired by the smoked eel sandwich served
by Jeremy Lee at Quo Vadis, London

We love to celebrate the technical skill of great chefs. We coo over their knife skills and their precision and their ability to pair flavours. We talk less often about an even more vital quality: simple good taste; the innate ability to know when a plate of food is right. It depends I think on the chef also being an eater. It's assumed that all great chefs like their food, that appetite is a part of who they are. It's not always so. Some are absorbed more by craft and technique than the greedy joys of the table.

Jeremy Lee is an eater. He also has exquisite good taste. His menus, now served at the venerable Quo Vadis in London's Soho where he has been head chef since 2012, are the sort you could take to bed and read. There is always a pie of the day, because something under the best glazed and flaky pastry simply makes things better. How about asparagus vinaigrette when they are in season? Or turbot with artichokes and gremolata? Finish with something from what is always referred to as 'pudding': an almond tart with strawberries or a gooseberry crème brûlée or, best of all, what he likes to call, with a writer's sense of language, a 'tumble' of perfectly made snowy meringues, with various citrus curds and creams?

Lee grew up in Dundee in the early 60s, with a mother who taught domestic science and a father who was an illustrator at DC Thomson, legendary publisher of the *Beano* and the *Dandy*, one of the biggest employers in the town. For a while Lee considered studying art, but both parents loved their food and that led him in another direction. He moved from working in a Scottish country house hotel to London, eventually finding his way to the brigade of Simon Hopkinson at Bibendum when it opened in 1987. There is a direct line from Hopkinson back to the food writer Elizabeth David, and her deep interest in the ingredients you start with and doing the most sympathetic things with them. That influence can be found in Lee's cooking. Elizabeth David does often come across in her writing as an insufferable snob, but in a post-Second World War Britain, where the enjoyment of good food had come to be seen as something of an insult to the puritan values that had got the country through a war of national survival, her good taste was invaluable. She brought back an understanding of robust French country cooking, and of the essentials of the best of the Mediterranean and so much more besides. All of that is there in the way Lee both cooks and eats.

In 2012 he became the head chef-patron at Quo Vadis, a restaurant in London's Soho that had been trading since 1926 through numerous owners. His many fans were delighted. For eighteen years prior to that he had been cooking at the Blueprint Café out by Tower Bridge, a serious schlep from the centre of London. Now Lee and his food were right at the heart of things. Quo was ready for a new lease of life. That's what he gave it. His smoked eel sandwich quickly became one of those things that people talk to each other about in hushed tones: the sweet gentle oiliness of the smoked fish, the sharp nose-tickling horseradish cream to cut through it, the crisp lightly fried toast that kept the various ingredients enclosed. Perhaps a little tangled pile of sharp pickled ribbons of red onion on the side. I once told Lee how much I loved it. 'Oh, I know,' he said, as if it was something outside of himself rather than his idea. 'It's meant to be a starter but sometimes people come here and order two of those and a bowl of chips and they are done.' I very much liked the sound of that.

My version uses mackerel rather than eel, because the latter is damned expensive, as it should be. There really aren't that many sustainable sources of smoked eel, and what might work cost-wise for a rather spendy central London restaurant is not necessarily going to fly at home. It could also work, I think, with hot smoked trout or salmon, although the saltiness of the mackerel is what we're after here. I always find formal recipes for sandwiches a bit odd: it's a bloody sandwich. It's stuff between bread. But this one does have a few wriggles.

INGREDIENTS

75g finely grated fresh horseradish
75g crème fraîche
Juice of ½ a lemon
Sea salt
Pre-sliced sourdough or country loaf (or slice it reasonably
    thinly yourself, if you like a challenge)
A little vegetable oil, for frying
Mayonnaise mixed with Dijon mustard at a ratio of three to one
1 mackerel fillet per sandwich, skinned (try to pull the skin off in
    one piece. It's not important to the recipe. It's just very
    satisfying if you can do it)

METHOD

1. First make the horseradish cream. I'm firmly of the view that there's no such thing as mild horseradish cream. Either it's really punchy, or it's not horseradish cream. These quantities will make a serious,

nose-tickling horseradish cream which will work just as well with roast beef as it will with this sandwich. Which helps because this will make enough for at least 4 sandwiches, or a whole Sunday lunch. Mix the horseradish with the crème fraîche, add the lemon juice and the salt to taste.

2. Lightly toast the bread.

3. Heat the vegetable oil in a frying pan. Once hot, fry the toast in the vegetable oil for 30 seconds each side.

4. Square off the fried toast and make the sandwich: a thin smear of the mayonnaise on the bottom, then the mackerel fillet, broken up to fit the toast, and then on top of that, a good layer of the horseradish cream, according to taste. And because recipes have to be complete, even those for sandwiches: top it with the second piece of toast.

5. Bliss.

Another related idea, if smoked fish isn't quite your thing. I was a student at Leeds University in the 1980s, and back then the famous Kirkgate Market on Vicar Lane was very much the place you went for essentials. It retains that function. You can still buy cheap fruit and veg there, along with meat and fish, a new bed and – the defining quality of any British covered market, this – big knickers. However, it has also mixed that up by bringing in various street food traders. In the relatively new shed addition at the back is a Turkish grill stand offering grilled kofta, chicken shish, chips and so on. It's called Mr Mackerel, and for a very good reason. For a few quid they will sell you a grilled fresh mackerel fillet in a soft white bun, with crunchy red cabbage salad, yoghurt dressing, pickled chillies and chilli sauce. It's terrific and recalls for me the fresh mackerel sandwiches that are sold off boats moored along the Bosphorus in Istanbul. Frying a well-salted fresh mackerel fillet skin side down, then slapping it in a bun with salads and sauces, strikes me as a very good idea indeed.

Chopped liver

Inspired by the version served at Russ & Daughters,
New York

It's just after 9am on a damp January morning on New York's Lower East Side. Courtesy of jet lag, I have been awake for hours. No matter. I'm an old hand at this. I know the rhythm of these days. I also know the hunger. It doesn't matter what you ate on the plane over or what you ate last night when you got into town. You need food now, and significant amounts of it. Hence the tradition of the first morning's breakfast at Russ & Daughters on Orchard Street. Russ & Daughters is what's known as an 'Appetizing', an adjective-turned-noun in the service of a particular kind of diner, celebrating a particular aspect of the food of the Ashkenazi Jews who arrived in New York from Eastern Europe and Russia, from the mid to late nineteenth century onwards. Where a deli serves cured meats, like pastrami and salt beef (or, in local parlance, corned beef, after the corns of salt), an Appetizing serves mostly cured fish or, as they put it, 'anything that one eats with a bagel'.

The business was founded in 1904 by Joel Russ, a Jewish immigrant from Strzyżów, Poland, who made a living selling herring from a pushcart. By 1914 he had enough money to open a shop here on Orchard Street, before moving it in 1920 to 179 East Houston Street, ten minutes' walk away, where it still trades to this day. In 1933 he brought his daughters, Hattie, Ida and Anne, into the business, made them partners and changed the name to reflect that. The company percolated down through various arms of the family until, in the early twenty-first century, it was taken over by cousins Nikki Russ Federman and Josh Russ Tupper, the fourth generation to be at the helm.

In 2014 they added the café back on Orchard Street. It's a clean, white modern space, with wipe-down tables and banquettes, and glass cabinets full of salmon, smoked to their own recipe, alongside tins of caviar for those feeling expansive. There are signs at the front encouraging you to 'be a mensch' and wait to be seated. I come here for the chopped liver, that hugely comforting coarse grind of chicken livers, caramelized onions and eggs to be eaten on a bagel or with matzoh. I also come for the noise and the buzz. But mostly I come for the chopped liver. I have always found it deeply soothing, when my internal clock is playing havoc with my sleep patterns. It roots me to that significant, secular part of New York's Jewish story.

This, I recognize, is odd, because it's not as if the London I grew up in does not have a ready supply of chopped liver. But in London we Jews are a relatively tiny minority and, perhaps because the Jewish community is so small, most of the activity seems to be focused around religious observance. There is no god in my universe. I do not observe anything. I am very much secular, and that secular Jewish tradition is so much stronger and so much more obvious here in New York, which is estimated to have a population of 1.6 million Jews, as against just over 145,000 in London. You see it in the names on the businesses in the garment district, and in the culture of delis like Gottlieb's or Katz's, where the pastrami sandwiches come airport-novel thick. You hear it in the incorporation of a few words of Yiddish into the general vernacular. I once joked that if my Eastern European great-grandparents had just been blessed with a little more staying power and not got off the boat for a few more days, I would have been a noisy New York Jew, rather than one of these London ones, forever navigating the mucky business of being very much part of a minority.

So I come to New York and order the chopped liver at Russ & Daughters and feel rooted and at ease. One morning I come back and eat their chopped liver with Josh Russ Tupper, a late entry to the business who gave up a career in chemical engineering to join the world of hospitality. His mother was a hippy, he tells me, who absented herself from the family trade, and raised him on an ashram in upstate New York. His rebellion was to send himself to boarding school when he was ten and then into the reliable certainties of science. 'It was the events of 9/11 that made me think about this family and what it was all about,' he says. He decided to join them despite having no experience in or knowledge of the hospitality business. I tell him that I am what the British newspaper columnist Bernard Levin once called a 'pantry Jew'. I worshipped at my mother's fridge; understood my identity through what I ate. Josh smiles in recognition. 'We call them lox and bagel Jews.' He says he came to his identity through this food. 'I became Jewish twenty years ago when I joined the business.'

I had assumed that chopped liver had always been a part of the Russ & Daughters repertoire. Josh says not. While Russ & Daughters has never been kosher, it long kept meat off the menu as a way of managing the issue. It made things simpler. However, they did offer a vegetarian version made with mushrooms. Chopped chicken livers only started being sold at the shop in the mid-1980s. If you've not tried the Jewish way with chopped liver, it should not be confused with a pâté. It is denser, crumblier and ideally just a little sweet. Historically, however, it is said to be at the root of the French pâté de foie gras, because it was the Alsatian Jewish community which first perfected the now reviled method of fattening the liver of geese through force-feeding. I very much like the fact that the rustic, peasant food of chopped liver, and the aristocratic smooth-as-silk foie gras, may have started in roughly the same place.

Like all traditional foods, chopped liver has changed over the decades and centuries. Once upon a time the onion was grated and added raw. Others would fry the onion but not let it colour. I am used to the version in which the onions are fried to golden, which is what Russ & Daughters do. To my mind, it's the best.

Where did the recipe come from? 'I'm guessing from my aunt Maria,' Josh says. 'She was always the recipe maven. She was a Columbian immigrant.' So not Jewish? 'Hah. No.' They sell 400–500lb of it a week, upwards of 180kg. Very obligingly they give me a copy of the recipe they use in their production kitchen. Perhaps less helpfully, it's all in imperial measurements and is designed for enormous quantities of the stuff. It involves five 30lb boxes of chicken livers, 10 quarts of caramelized onions, 150 eggs and so on.

For many Jews the oracle on such recipes is the food writer Claudia Roden. Her magisterial *Book of Jewish Food*, first published in 1997, is an extraordinary work of both anthropology and recipes, covering the traditions of the Ashkenazi Jews of Eastern Europe and the Sephardi associated with the Mediterranean and the Middle East. Often, she comes across far less as the originator of a recipe than its custodian, simply passing it along. That's certainly the case with her chopped liver recipe, which she says is 'classic' and is very simple: caramelize onions, grill the chicken livers, boil eggs. Blitz them together and season to make chopped liver.

The Russ & Daughters version includes the equivalent of chicken stock cubes and a little sugar (although Josh is clear that's only included if the onions are less sweet than expected). To turn away from Claudia Roden feels to this pantry Jew like an act of secular heresy. The Russ & Daughters large-volume method also calls for the boiling of the livers for 80 minutes, which just sounds wrong to this home cook and is, I imagine, something to do with what happens when you put 150lb of chicken organs in a very big pot. One afternoon, I tested an adapted Russ & Daughters recipe against the Roden recipe. The New York Appetizing version won out. It was just deeper, richer, more savoury. And courtesy of the sugar, a little sweeter. I can guarantee that certain aspects of this method will drive some Jewish cooks absolutely nuts. You added a bit of stock cube? You added *sugar*? That's fine. I understand. Just go find the Claudia Roden recipe and use that.

INGREDIENTS

1 large onion, chopped
Olive oil, for frying
250g chicken livers
1 tsp caster sugar
½ a chicken stock cube
Sea salt and ground black pepper
2 eggs, hard-boiled

1. Gently fry the chopped onion in a couple of tablespoons of olive oil until soft and golden. Let it cool a little in the pan while you rinse the chicken livers and pat them dry.

2. Sprinkle the sugar on to the onions, and crumble over the half stock cube.

3. Gently fry the chicken livers in the same pan as the onions, until coloured on all sides, mixing them in with the onions. If there are any crumbs of stock cube visible, bosh them with a wooden spoon until they melt in the fat. Season with a little salt and pepper. When the livers are cooked through, let the contents of the frying pan cool.

4. Blitz the eggs in a processor. Reserve a quarter of the blitzed egg.

5. Add the livers and the onions to the egg in the processor and pulse a couple of times. As the name says, you want a rough, crumbly chopped texture, not a smooth purée. Add a little extra salt and pepper to taste.

6. Scoop into a bowl and top with the rest of the crumbled egg. Place in the fridge for a couple of hours to firm up.

One of the particular things about the Russ & Daughters chopped liver is that it is served with the most gorgeous, bronzed, burnished and salty matzoh, the unleavened bread associated with Passover. This delightful cracker has always taken me aback because generally matzoh is dry and tasteless. It's meant to be, because it is designed to represent the privations of the exodus from Egypt. The bread was unleavened because there simply wasn't enough time before the Jews fled Egypt to make bread properly. During my breakfast with Josh, I told him I was going to buy some of their matzoh from the shop to take home. 'Oh, you can't,' he says. 'We just sell standard, dull matzoh. When we were opening this place in 2014, I said we couldn't serve the boring stuff. We experimented and came up with a method of buttering, salting and baking it.' The presence of the butter with the chicken livers obviously breaks the Jewish dietary prohibition of mixing dairy and meat. Then again, they make no claims to being kosher and neither do I. It turns a food of privation into something truly delightful.

Buttered, baked matzoh

INGREDIENTS

Matzoh
Salted butter, at room temperature
Table salt

METHOD

1. Heat the oven to 180°C/350°F/gas mark 4. Put an oven pan below an open rack to catch excess dripping butter. It will save you having to clean your oven.

2. Put the matzoh on a flat surface (not a plate) and butter both sides of each piece liberally. Take it right up to the edges. You will have to do this carefully to avoid breaking it, especially so when you turn it over

and butter the convex side. Sprinkle both sides with table salt.

3. Place in the oven directly on the rack so it's open to the heat on all sides. Keep an eye on it. Depending on your oven, it should take 3 to 5 minutes to turn golden brown. Remove and let it cool.

Louisiana cracklins

Inspired by the version served at Toups South,
New Orleans

This story starts on one coastline and ends a few thousand miles to the west, near another. In 2002 I went, on a whisper of good things, to Whitstable on the north Kent coast. I had been told that a self-taught chef called Stephen Harris was cooking amazing food in a blocky old pub by the sea. The whispers were true. The Sportsman sits on a flood plain just beyond the village of Seasalter, a mile or two outside of Whitstable in a location with food and eating embedded deep in its story. The pub gets its name from the sporting game shoots that would take place on these saltmarshes. Seasalter gets its name, rather literally, from the practice of harvesting salt from the sea. It was a perfect location for Harris, who had run away from banking to join the culinary circus. He was obsessed by hyperlocality, but also by picking up ideas from all the best places. During my first lunch there I was served an asparagus soup with a dippy egg and soldiers, an idea which had come to him from eating a similar if much more refined dish in the Michelin three-star restaurant of Alain Ducasse in Paris.

There were rounds of braised pork belly, stuffed with black pudding, drawing on something he had eaten at Marcus Wareing's Pétrus. He put popping candy with a rhubarb sorbet, a trick he had learnt while eating at Heston Blumenthal's Fat Duck. Over time he has very much found his own voice and devised his own dishes: cured trout with apple granita and seaweed, crab and carrot with hollandaise, a mushroom and celeriac tart. Ever the artisan, he turned to making his own ham from the legs of local pigs, fed partly on the vegetable peelings from his own kitchen and cured in salt made by boiling the sea water that all but lapped at the kitchen's back door.

Word got around. Big-name chefs from all over the world made the pilgrimage. Awards were bestowed, including a Michelin star. Eventually I was asked by the then prestigious (now closed) US food magazine *Gourmet* to write about Stephen and his restaurant. I spent a couple of days with him, during which he inculcated me into his way with pork belly. Back when I started reviewing in 1999, pork belly was still an item that certain bits of the population rolled their eyes at. Once it had been the cheapest of cuts, they said. It was what you bought when money was tight. But now look at it. Like lamb shanks, it had been re-discovered by the gastropub movement, and was highly prized and so rather less than cheap. With pork belly, I always found myself travelling hopefully, but not always arriving. At its best the meat would be tender, the fat properly rendered leaving just enough to lubricate everything else, and the all-important crackling would shatter beautifully, so that you could feel the crunch in your cranial cavities. Too often, however, it was a disappointment: dry meat, too much fat and, worst of all, chewy rather than crunchy skin. Failed pork crackling is the greatest broken promise in food.

Stephen's was perfect: soft, flavourful meat, just the right amount of fat and extraordinary crackling. During that time spent in his kitchen for *Gourmet* I found out why. He confited the portioned belly in pork fat first, letting it bubble away in a bath of seasoned lipids at low temperature for 12 hours. He would then press and chill it. When the order came in, he would flash it through a very hot oven for only 20 or so minutes. The final stage was the most delightful: in the depths of a British winter, which was when I was there, he would take the oven pan and stand outside for 30 seconds. (In the summer he might depend on a gust from the opened fridge.) 'The cold air makes the crackling firm up,' he told me as I stared on, baffled. He wasn't wrong. It had an almost glass-like quality. I used his method at home a few times, and it always produced a terrific result.

Roll forward to early 2018. I am in New Orleans, this time on the edge of the Gulf of Mexico. I am researching a chapter about oysters for my book about my last meal on earth. One night I am despatched by a knowledgeable friend to a restaurant called Toups South (now closed). It is a big airy space, attached rather fittingly to the Southern Food and Beverage Museum, and belongs to a big-shouldered, bald-headed beardy chef called Isaac Toups. He has a particular way with the New Orleans repertoire. He attends to the essentials but often finds a lighter way into dishes like ham braised greens and couvillion (or Cajun fish stew). I sit at the counter as he fires gutsy southern dishes at me like one of those machines that serves tennis balls at players working on their return. Early on, he slides a bowl of pork cracklins across to me and advises me not to scoff too many because I'll get too full too quickly. What was he thinking? How was I supposed not to eat these golden, highly seasoned, crisp-skinned, melting pieces of pork belly? I am but a man. And a greedy one at that. They were everything.

I wanted to understand how to make them. The recipes I looked up were grossly intimidating in a good ol' boy ultra-macho sort of way. They all described a two-cook process, involving a first fry at low heat to render the fat and then a second that's much faster. They mentioned using a huge cauldron, preferably outside, like this is some modern-day witch's ceremony. Perhaps it is. They measured ingredients in vast weights, suggested you use a wooden paddle to get everything moving, and advised donning safety gear.

It took me a few readings to clock that what they were describing was exactly the same process Stephen Harris used in Kent. You chopped the skin-on pork belly up into pieces, then confited them in fat, rendering out more of the fat as you went. They did the confiting bit quite fast, but I could see there would be a slower and tidier way to get the job done. Then you chilled it, before deep-frying it at high heat and adding seasonings. Those recipes specify pork fat as the first cooking medium, but I think that's impractical and unnecessary. Hence, here I suggest using a neutral vegetable oil. On one point, however, those recipes were spot on. When you plunge the rendered pieces of pork belly into the boiling fat at the end, they really do cause it to bubble and spit, like tectonic plates are moving deep in the depths. Long sleeves are a must. A full-body Hazmat suit wouldn't be over-kill. Step away once you've submerged each batch. Be prepared to have a long cleaning job ahead of you. I did find myself thinking that I should have taken my small standalone deep fat fryer outside. At least then I wouldn't have been mopping the floor afterwards.

A note on the seasoning. There are many variants. Isaac Toups now sells his own commercial brand. It's called Isaac

Toups Thunderdust Cajun Seasoning. We should all have a little thunderdust in our lives, shouldn't we. His contains salt, arbol chilli pepper, sugar, garlic, white pepper and celery seed. You will find many different versions online. If you like a bit of chilli heat then by all means add some cayenne. Seriously, add what you like. Mine is based on a seasoning mix I came up with a while ago which, while covering all the bases, makes everything it touches taste like that corn snack Frazzles, on account of the smoked sweet paprika. Basically, the mix is a vegan way to make fried foods taste of smoky bacon. Put it on these decidedly unvegan pork cracklins, and oh boy.

The volumes look sizable, and you can reduce it all if you fancy. But it's a messy job and these are addictive. You might as well cook a lot.

INGREDIENTS

2kg skin-on pork belly, first cut into 3cm wide strips and then cut again into 3cm pieces (if a slab of ribs comes with the belly, take those too. You can always prepare them in the same way)
Around 2 litres vegetable oil (enough to cover the pork belly in an oven pan)
3 cloves of garlic

For the seasoning mix
1 tbsp table salt
1 tbsp garlic powder
1½ tbsp smoked sweet paprika
2 tbsp caster sugar
½ tsp ground black pepper

METHOD

1. Heat the oven to 140°C/275°F/gas mark 1.

2. Put all the pork belly into an oven pan in a single layer. Pour over enough vegetable oil to completely submerge. Peel the garlic cloves, cut them in half and throw those in too. Put any ribs on top and push down into the oil. Cover the surface with a piece of greaseproof paper, and put into the oven for 2½ hours.

3. Remove from the oven. Let it cool for 10 minutes. Take off the greaseproof paper. Remove the pieces of pork to another oven pan with a slotted spoon. If it's winter and dry, pop it outside to chill quickly for 10 minutes, then put it into the fridge for a couple of hours.

4. Strain the oil into whatever vessel you are using to deep fat fry, to remove any pork solids and garlic pieces.

5. When it comes time to cook, heat the oven to 170°C/325°F/gas mark 3. Put a rack in an oven pan and put it into the oven. You'll be using this to drain the pieces of pork belly as they come out of the fat in batches.

6. Heat the oil to 190°C. If not using a purpose-built deep fat fryer, get a kitchen thermometer. When at temperature, put the pieces of pork belly into the fat. Don't be tempted to overfill it. Due to the moisture in the skin, it really will bubble fiercely. Step back and let it do its thing.

7. Wait for the pork to go a serious golden brown. It should take about 3 to 5 minutes. Drain and move to the rack in the oven. Repeat until all the pieces of pork belly are done. Any ribs, if you have them, will only take a couple of minutes to deep-fry. Give yourself to the terrible mess you are making of your kitchen. Curse me if you like. It's fine.

8. Mix all the seasoning ingredients together. Transfer the pieces of pork belly to a sizable bowl. Sprinkle the seasoning mix over generously and toss all the pieces in it. Don't worry about excess seasoning. It will all fall to the bottom.

9. Serve with a good vinegary coleslaw.

Ultimate cheese toastie

Inspired by the XXL stovetop three cheese and mustard toastie served at chef Michel Roux's Wigmore Pub, London

Shockingly, sometimes people disagree with me. This comes from various directions. There are those who read a negative review of mine, and feel the need to tell me that I am completely wrong; that I have no taste, no knowledge and probably none of my own teeth. This was at its most intense after my less than obliging review in 2017 of Le Cinq, the Michelin three-star restaurant of the fancy Georges Cinq Hotel in Paris. My meal there was a grim experience which cost €600 for two, and left me pondering the very point of the luxury restaurant. I decried the waiters, who gave my female companion a menu without prices, as if it was still 1974. I decried the room, which I described as being decorated in 'shades of taupe, biscuit and fuck you'. Most of all I decried the food, which was clumsy, dated and extraordinarily bad value for money. That review, which to date has been read over three million times and is still available online, became a bit of a thing. There were headlines in newspapers all over the world. Most of them were gleeful; those from France, less so. As French daily *Libération* put it, 'This isn't criticism, it's entertainment. It's very excessive to provoke laughter.' On that festering online review site TripAdvisor, one contributor simply called me 'an idiot'. Other French people got in touch by email to question the mere concept of a British restaurant critic, given their perception of how poor the food in the United Kingdom is. There was no point explaining the realities. The review was brutal. Those who objected to it were entitled to be brutal in return. That's part of the job.

The more complicated disagreements come from people who have visited a restaurant to which I gave a positive review, only to find it lacking. Occasionally, they have had a point, in that my positive review was the cause of their negative experience. Inadvertently, it had damaged the restaurant I so liked. I learned this in my very first year in the job when I gushed effusively about a small French bistro in Brighton. When I had lunch there, only about a dozen other people were in the restaurant. To my astonishment, my positive review resulted in a massive boom in trade. It turned out that people not only read my reviews. Some of them acted upon them. It might be a tiny proportion of the overall readership. Over 95% of people who read my reviews do so for vicarious pleasure or displeasure. But happily, that readership can still be a pleasingly large actual number, which means a tiny proportion can still amount to a lot of bookings. It had genuinely not occurred to me that this might be the case. Sadly, neither the kitchen nor the front of house team could cope with this influx of trade. Both the cooking and the service suffered. It was all my fault. This being pre-email days, various people wrote letters telling me so.

At other times, people have simply disagreed with my assessment of the restaurant, or perhaps something happened to them during their meal which didn't happen to me. In that situation there is nothing else for me to say except that I could only report as I'd found, that I was sorry they hadn't enjoyed themselves and really, there was no need for language like that.

And then there are the lovely messages; the ones from people who have followed one of my positive reviews and want to let me know that the restaurant I had said such great things about was every bit as good as I said it was. Hurrah. Receiving messages like that is both extremely gratifying and, to be totally honest, a blessed relief. Be in no doubt: I am confident of every judgement I make. I don't reach an opinion lightly. I am not casual about it. (I was not casual about giving Le Cinq a kicking. It deserved everything it got.) But I am aware that restaurants have many moving parts, and things sometimes really do go wrong. If I've done my job properly, I will have identified the essentials and what's good about them. It's lovely when people get to experience the good stuff for themselves.

Sometimes they get in touch about a specific dish. Perhaps it was the charred lamb chops at Tayyab's (see page 163) or the deeply spiced Malaysian chicken curry at Bugis Street Brasserie (see page 133). The dish I have received the most emails, tweets, direct messages and all-round general reflected glory about is the spectacular XXL stovetop three cheese and mustard toastie served at the Wigmore. It's a kind of pub attached to the fancy Langham hotel just north of

GLORIOSA

Homemade Ginger Beer	4.5	Boulevardier	9.5
MUZ Spritz	9.5	Bergamot Old Fashioned	10
Spicy Margarita	10	Black Manhattan	11.5

Focaccia & olive oil	6
Gordal olives	5
Salted Marcona almonds	6
Boquerones, orange & burnt chilli	6
Taramasalata with radishes & soft-boiled egg	7

Roast Scottish langoustines with chive butter	16
Trout pâté on toast with pickled cucumber	8
Beetroot, almonds, pomegranate, mint & goats curd	9.5
Grilled leeks, vinaigrette & chopped egg	9.5
Roast carrots, shallots, parmesan, bitter leaves & herbs	9.5
Roast muscade pumpkin, farro, chestnuts & rosemary dressing	10

Paccheri rigati with broccoli, chilli, garlic & parmesan	16
Tonnarelli with Shetland mussels, tomato, white wine & parsley	16
Roast sea trout with brown shrimp, fennel, kohlrabi, apple & dill	24
Wild sea bass with blood orange, nocellara olives, shallot & parsley	28
Denver steak, spring greens with anchovy & sage butter	26

Clementine sorbet with frozen vodka	6
Panna cotta with burnt caramel & a nut biscuit	9
Meringue with whipped cream, passion fruit & orange	9
Choux bun, vanilla ice cream, cream & chocolate sauce	9
Chocolate and chestnut cake with pouring cream	8
Brandied prune & almond clafoutis with crème fraîche	14

Clafoutis is baked to order, please allow 15 minutes

Calvados	35ml	7
Manzanilla Sherry	75ml	6
Oloroso Sherry	75ml	8

Gloriosa, Argyle Street, Glasgow.
2023 / chef: Rosie Healey

Healey first caught my attention in 2018 at Alchemilla, her first Glasgow
restaurant, a short walk away down Argyle Street from her current location.
It was her superb focaccia which won my heart. And it was just as good
at Gloriosa.

:000 72476400

Tayyabs

Whitechapel, London

JOE ALLEN

TUESDAY
22 AUGUST 2000
NOON TO 3:00PM
SPECIAL MENU

(CHOICE OF ONE)
BROCCOLI SOUP WITH SOUR CREAM
MARINATED ANCHOVY SALAD WITH MARINATED CHERRY
TOMATOES, BLACK OLIVES AND GREEN BEANS
SMALL CAESAR SALAD

*

(CHOICE OF ONE)
POACHED SALMON WITH ASPARAGUS, NEW POTATOES
AND BEARNAISE SAUCE
GRILLED CHICKEN SANDWICH WITH GRILLED BACON, LETTUCE,
TOMATO, SCALLION MAYONNAISE AND THIN FRIES
WILD MUSHROOM AND SPINACH OMELET WITH HASH BROWN
POTATOES AND TOASTED MUFFIN

*

(CHOICE OF ONE)
PASSION FRUIT AND ORANGE MOUSSE WITH RASPBERRY COMPOTE
STILTON OR CHEDDAR CHEESE WITH OATCAKES AND GRAPES

*

FILTER COFFEE OR TEA

THREE COURSES: £14.00 (INCL VAT)
TWO COURSES: £12.00 (INCL VAT)

13 Exeter Street London WC2E 7DT
Tel: 020 7836 0651 Fax: 020 7497 2148

*Joe Allen, originally Exeter Street, London WC2.
2000*

In its pomp Joe Allen, which first opened in 1977, was practically the club room for West End theatreland. This special lunch menu from 2000 includes what was, for a very long time, the best Caesar salad in London. The restaurant moved around the corner from its original location to Burleigh Street in 2017.

London's Oxford Street, which I reviewed in October of 2021. Pilgrimages have been made, solely for that one item. Orders have been placed. Melted dairy fat joy has been unbounded. The appeal lies, I think, in the notion of the humble and the domestic, of what could easily serve as excellent hangover food, being raised to great heights by the application of cheffy technique and nerdiness. It helps that it's not just any chef that is involved. The Wigmore is a side project of Michel Roux, once the chef-patron of Le Gavroche in Mayfair, just as his father Albert was before him, before he closed it in January of 2024. (You can read more about Le Gavroche on page 294, when I write about my adventures with the restaurant's soufflé Suissesse.)

Michel Roux's understanding of the British pub food repertoire is as deep and profound as his knowledge of classical French cooking. Alongside familiar London bistro dishes like slow-cooked pork belly with chorizo and sea bream in a pesto broth, the menu includes both a Scotch egg and a pie. Plus this cheese toastie, which is the size of my foot. You should know that I have size 12 feet. It involves a mix of three cheeses, spun through with finely chopped red onion and gherkins, with a smear of Dijon mustard for an extra slap of flavour. Each of the cheeses is chosen for a specific function. There's Raclette for its stringiness, Ogleshield for its meltiness, and Montgomery Cheddar for its sharpness and acidity (both of the latter being made by the same dairy). Do not fret about these very specific choices. Each one is part of a family of cheeses and as you'll see from the recipe below, I've suggested very serviceable and possibly more available alternatives.

As to the bread, the Wigmore uses specially commissioned long loaves of an onion seed sourdough, which they cut lengthways to produce the maximum number of long slices, with very little wastage. Chris King, head chef of the Wigmore, believes the pop of the onion seeds adds an extra layer of texture to the experience and I get the point. If you can find an onion seed sourdough or something similar, go for it. Otherwise, I would suggest using middle slices from a standard round sourdough loaf. The volumes here produce one big, long Wigmore-style toastie, which, if you are of normal appetite, is something you will want to share with a friend. Or you can make two more normal-sized toasties, which is helpful because at the Wigmore they cook it on a plancha, pressed down with an iron, and you probably don't have either of those. It would be hard to fit the full Wigmore toastie into a frying pan. A toastie made from the middle slices of a standard sourdough loaf should fit.

INGREDIENTS

160g Raclette cheese (substitute with Emmental, Appenzeller, Fontina or Gruyère)
80g Montgomery Cheddar (it does not have to be Montgomery, unless you are keen to match the Wigmore kitchen product for product; use any strong mature Cheddar)
80g Ogleshield cheese (substitute with Taleggio or Fontina)
20g finely chopped red onion
30g finely chopped cornichon
Dijon mustard
4 slices of sourdough bread
Salted butter (the Wigmore uses clarified butter, but I rather like the caramelization you get from the dairy solids; you could always use vegetable oil)

METHOD

1. Grate the cheese, and mix thoroughly in a bowl with the finely chopped red onion and cornichon.

2. Spread a thin layer of Dijon mustard on one internal side of each sandwich.

3. Layer generously with the grated cheese mix, and press down with the second slice of bread. Hilariously, I now appear to be explaining how to use two pieces of bread to make a sandwich.

4. Heat a non-stick or, better still, a well-seasoned cast iron frying pan over a medium heat and add a good knob of the butter. As it melts swirl it around to cover the base of the frying pan. Add the first sandwich and cook over a medium heat for about 4 minutes. Press it down forcefully into the butter with a spatula every now and then. (The Wigmore uses a sandwich press.)

5. After 4 minutes, carefully turn it over on to the other side. The cheese will have started to melt, bonding it all together. Add another knob of butter, and lift the toastie it has now become so you can swirl the newly molten butter in underneath. Cook for another 4 minutes, again pressing it down occasionally.

6. Put on a plate or board and leave to cool for a couple of minutes, as you start to cook the second. At the Wigmore they cut it into 4cm wide slices, which does make it easier to eat.

Seaweed and sesame crackers with anchovy mayo

Inspired by the crackers served at the Suffolk-sur-Mer,
Aldeburgh

The Suffolk, a once-abandoned pub a pebble's skim from Aldeburgh's glowering sea, served very little that surprised me. This is a good thing. God knows, there are enough surprises in life. Often what we want are the good, familiar things done right. And here they all were: rock oysters at a good price, dressed crab, skate wing with caper sauce, and a whole garlic-butter-grilled lobster with rustling chips. It was the last offering which sealed the deal for me. As I explained in my review in 2023, lobster and chips was what I had eaten with my old mum on a night out, a few days before she went into hospital for a mastectomy to treat what she called 'a touch of breast cancer'. She did not want to dwell on mortality that night; she wanted to suck the very meat from the lobster-leg of life. The combination of the high luxe of lobster with the high street joys of well-made golden chips was a complete winner. Now, more than a dozen years after her death (from something other than cancer) I could quietly relive that night.

It helped that the Suffolk had squashy banquettes, sweetly familiar wines, lovely service, and the promise of a restorative walk back to my hotel along the pebbled shore. A good restaurant should be able to take you somewhere else, whatever your mood when you went in. That's what the Suffolk did.

It was a project by a young restaurateur called George Pell, who I knew from his involvement with the doughty old stager L'Escargot back in London's Soho. During the pandemic,

Pell had moved his team to the then crumbling Suffolk to open a kind of L'Escargot by the sea. He loved the experience so much, he eventually raised the money to buy the building, renovated it and moved out to East Anglia permanently. The enfolding nature of the menu at his new place didn't surprise me, because it matched the offering back in London, which is to say, they served classics done well: Tournedos Rossini, lobster bisque and of course snails in the shell, with lakes of bubbling, green, parsley-flecked garlic butter.

Which is, I think, why these crackers caught my attention. They were part of the bar menu and represented an outbreak of quiet innovation. In the best way of quiet innovation, they are also a very simple idea. Sheets of toasted nori seaweed, to express the briny seaside location, are given heft by the application of the thinnest of pastry sheets, to which are glued a big heap of sesame seeds, for nuttiness. Then you spark up the deep fat fryer, because that helps most snacks along. They reminded me of those bags of tempura-ed nori you can find in Asian supermarkets, alongside the beguiling, ramen-flavoured crisps. At the Suffolk they add whorls of an oyster mayo, but the anchovy mayo on page 23 does the job beautifully too. A gentle warning. They're both straightforward to make but also a bit of a drawn-out affair. You have to be methodical, which explains the length of the method. They are very much worth it.

Serves 4 to 6 people as a nibble before dinner

INGREDIENTS

2 eggs
5 sheets of spring roll pastry (generally sold in big packs
    measuring 25cm x 25cm; perhaps make spring rolls with the
    rest – *The Vietnamese Market Cookbook* by Van Tran and Anh
    Vu has a couple of great recipes)
5 full-size sheets of toasted nori seaweed (generally sold in
    packs of 5 or 10, measuring 20cm x 20cm)
75g sesame seeds
Vegetable oil for deep-frying
Anchovy mayo from page 23

METHOD

1. You will need two metal baking trays or baking sheets
   and some baking parchment.

2. Separate the first of the eggs into yolk and white.
   Look at the yolk and wonder what you're going to do
   with it. There will be another one along in a couple
   of hours. Perhaps add them to a whole egg to make a
   yolk-enriched omelette.

3. Lay a piece of baking parchment on the first baking
   tray or sheet. Place the first sheet of spring roll pastry
   on that and then, with a pastry brush, paint the egg
   white on to the smooth side of a sheet of nori. (The
   sides are different. One is smooth and one is rough.)
   Stick the nori squarely on to the pastry, leaving a
   border. Cover with another piece of baking parchment
   and repeat until all the pastry and nori is used up. Place
   a final piece of baking parchment on top. Put the

second tray on top to press, weigh it down with a heavy bowl or jar, and place it all in the fridge for 1 to 2 hours.

4. Remove from the fridge. Take the top tray off and move the top sheet of baking parchment over to it. Separate the white from the second egg. Paint it on to the exposed side of the top sheet of nori, then press on a generous amount of the sesame seeds. Put that sheet of nori and pastry on the newly prepared oven tray, place the next piece of baking parchment over the top, and repeat with the remaining sheets. What was the bottom tray, now goes on to the top. Weigh it down again and put it back in the fridge for at least 4 hours. Perhaps make that yolk-enriched omelette.

5. When it's time to finish them, take the trays from the fridge. Lift each pastry-nori sheet up over the tray and give it a gentle shake. (The pastry edge may stick to the baking parchment, but it can be peeled off.) A fair number of sesame seeds will fall off. It's up to you whether you attempt to save them. As the pastry sheet is bigger than the nori sheet, use a pair of scissors to trim the sheets to get rid of the excess. Then cut each sheet into 4 roughly equal pieces. You can do them as squares, or you can make them vaguely irregular shapes. Your call.

6. Heat the vegetable oil to 160°C/320°F. Once it's hot drop 3 or 4 pieces into the oil at a time, starting sesame seed down. Flip them after about 15 to 20 seconds. Beware. They fry very, very fast. Think 30 to 45 seconds at most. You want the pastry to go light golden brown and no further. Watch them like a hawk. Fish them out and drain them on kitchen paper, on

both sides. Repeat with the rest. These crackers can
hold for a good hour before you want to eat them.

7. Top with dots and whorls of the anchovy mayo. You
   can do this with a piping bag if you're feeling posh
   and know your friends will be impressed by such
   things. Or you can just dollop it on from a teaspoon
   if you know the people you're feeding really don't
   give a toss. If it's the former, get new friends.

8. Alternatively, you can dust them with a little salt, or a
   seasoning mix of your choice, like that used for the
   Louisiana cracklins on page 42.

Sage and anchovy fritters

Inspired by the snack served at Bocca di Lupo,
Soho, London

I once got into a lot of trouble for writing a column in which
I said you could eat better Italian food in London than you
could in Rome (and, while we're at it, better French food than
in Paris and better Spanish food than in Barcelona). It was a
provocative thing to write, though not, I'd say, without cause.
Each of those cities obviously has terrific restaurants, but a
food culture of great depth, of the sort with which Italy,
France and Spain are blessed, can also lead to culinary conser-
vatism; a conviction that to tinker even slightly with either the
classics or the range of those on offer is to commit a heinous
food crime. London, indeed the UK as a whole, uses its distance to great effect. It is far less constrained by tradition, but
still attends to the details. That can of course result in some
crimes against dinner. But it can also result in some superb

restaurants. I made my argument. People shouted at me. Some Italians agreed with me. Some didn't. It was a great Sunday.

The piece was partly inspired by a deeply disappointing trip to Rome, where I discovered that an almost religious commitment to the culinary canon resulted in almost every restaurant serving exactly the same menu. The parade of antipasti and pasta dishes might be done reasonably well, but there was little flair or excitement. I found a few diverting things. There was the offal restaurant Checchino dal 1887 in the old slaughterhouse district, where they offered a plate of grilled lamb sweetbreads, liver, intestine and testicles listed on the menu, in a clear and direct translation, as a plate of 'lamb entrails'. Elsewhere, in the Jewish quarter, I found deep-fried globe artichokes in the Jewish style, a crisp and friable wonder of crunchy, golden foliage. But mostly it was an endless parade of cacio e pepe and the like. It turns out you can have too much of that, however delicious it might be.

During that trip I found myself thinking wistfully of Bocca di Lupo, the lovely Roman restaurant of chef Jacob Kenedy on Archer Street in London's Soho. Kenedy has had a strong connection to Italy in general and Rome in particular going all the way back to childhood, because he visited often. His grandparents Ginny and John, a one-time actress and a gallerist, lived in Rome for many years. They were friends with the legendary film director Federico Fellini. His movie *La Dolce Vita* was partly inspired by them and the parties they held in their apartment on the first floor of the Palazzo Caetani, which thronged with the literati, the actors and singers, the very elite of Roman society. Kenedy's take on the Roman repertoire, based on his experience of the city, is famed for its robustness. He makes his own sturdy, rugged sausages, and peppery tripe stews and yes, some lovely pasta dishes. Then you can cross the road to Gelupo, the gelateria he also owns, where he sells the ice creams he learned to make during an apprenticeship in Bologna. Oh, the hazelnut. Oh, the ricotta sour cherry.

The menu at Bocca di Lupo starts with a list of snacks, including golfball-sized olives stuffed with ground pork and veal, then breadcrumbed and served hot from the deep fat fryer. There are crisp bruschetta piled with whipped ricotta and pistachio, and these completely irresistible sage and anchovy fritters. There's no reverse-engineering with the recipe I offer here. Kenedy literally gave the recipe to me as he did to 180 or so other people. My friends Alex Fane and Chloe Burrows are, quite rightly, huge fans of Bocca di Lupo. They had asked whether I might be able to convince Kenedy to cater their wedding. They love their food and wanted to serve the good stuff. Kenedy, however, had always been reluctant to do weddings because he had never found a catering company that could execute his food en masse. It is very hard to do quality pasta dishes at volume. Happily, I had a solution. The chef Sophie Wright is a panellist on *The Kitchen Cabinet*, the food panel show I have presented for BBC Radio 4 since 2012. She also has a top-flight catering company. If anyone could pull this off it would be her.

At this point I'm aware that this just reads as me boasting about all my wonderful friends, and how terribly well connected I am. (Look, at least I didn't name-drop Nigella. She's a friend of Alex and Chloe's, as it happens, and was also at the wedding. Feel for the caterers.) Our splendid wedding dinner included platters of ricotta ravioli with butter and sage, a chicken and pumpkin panzanella salad, and tiramisù served in huge family-style bowls down the table.

It began with various canapés, including these fritters. I was standing next to Jacob, also a guest at the wedding, when the first of these came round. We were both a little tense. We both felt responsible for how the food element of this party would go. They were the first bite we ate, and we knew immediately that everything was going to be fine. Indeed, more than fine. Sophie's team had done a bang-up job. And when we finally sat down to eat, there, at each place setting, was a card printed with the instructions for how to make the fritters. How could I not pass this on to you? They are a fabulous combination of crunch and salt and sweet, lofty aromatics from the sage.

Two things to note. I found it very hard to source large sage leaves from shops. Retailers don't expect you to want to eat them whole and so don't prioritize size. If you can find somewhere to buy them, good for you. But my advice is to ask around among friends and family to see whether they have a sage bush in the garden. They tend to grow at furious speed and will be heavy with the big 'uns. You also get to pretend you're a rustic foraging peasant while picking them. You'll enjoy that. Also, the lacy, tempura-style batter recipe makes much more than you'll need, but the depth is required for dredging. Have a look around to see if there are any other veg you fancy deep-frying.

Makes 12 fritters, which is apparently enough for 3 to 4 people as a snack, though frankly I could demolish that many single-handed if nobody was watching. I'd say I'm not ashamed, but clearly, I am, if only a little.

INGREDIENTS

For the batter
100g plain flour
50g cornflour
20ml extra virgin olive oil
250ml beer (non-alcoholic beer is fine for this)

For the fritters

24 large fresh sage leaves
6 anchovy fillets, halved horizontally; the higher quality the
   anchovy, the better
Black pepper
Vegetable oil, for frying

METHOD

1. Whisk together the ingredients for the batter until smooth.

2. Separate the sage leaves into matching pairs. Season each halved anchovy fillet generously with cracked black pepper.

3. Place each anchovy fillet lengthways on the base sage leaf, then press on the top leaf.

4. Put at least 2cm of the oil into a frying pan and heat to 170°C on a thermometer (or use a deep fat fryer with a thermostat). Any hotter, and they will scorch very quickly.

5. Dredge each fritter through the batter, drawing them over the edge of the bowl to remove any excess. Then fry for roughly a minute, until crispy. Drain on kitchen paper for a couple of minutes and eat immediately. Possibly just stand at the cooker, frying them and handing them out.

Intercourse: Call this a job?

Restaurant reviewing, and how it is done

I was once asked by a television producer whether he could film me in the process of reviewing a restaurant. He sounded like one of those dogged wildlife TV people, who was determined to get rare footage of Polar bears shagging, or lions downing a giraffe on the Serengeti. Apart from the fact that I thought a producer, alongside crew with a camera and sound equipment and perhaps a runner, might make for a less than chilled lunch, I had to tell him there was nothing to see: just a large man, with a big arse and too much hair, eating and occasionally frowning a bit. And then going home, sliding that large arse into his office chair and typing a bit, while also frowning.

But surely, he said, you have a process? Well yes, I do. But very little of that process takes place at the table. The fact is that mine is a writing job, not an eating job. I do have to eat the food to be able to write about it, but lots of people can do the eating. Every time I visit a restaurant to review it, there will be lots of other people there doing the eating. I, however, need to have something compelling and readable to say about the experience, and it has to go far beyond 'the lamb was overcooked; the hispi cabbage was pleasingly charred'. Each time I choose a restaurant to review I ask myself the question all journalists ask themselves when faced with a deadline: what's the story here? Or to put it another way: 'what is this restaurant column, another in a long line of said columns, actually going to be about? It doesn't matter how unique the chef or restaurateur think their establishment is. It always comes down to this: a table, a chair, and a plate of food. There is a list of dishes. It might be on paper or a blackboard or a QR code. It's still just a list. My job is to choose from that list. Theirs is to cook the food and bring it to me. None of this changes. And none of this is interesting.

For the majority of my time as a restaurant critic I have been able to access the vital information I need by going online to consult the menu long before I push through the door. Before that, restaurant PRs posted me hard copies of menus, plus information on chefs and restaurateurs and their thrilling new concepts. This did mean that in the early years, there really was a built-in bias towards the shiny and the new over the venerable and established, or even just those places that had been making their way in blessed obscurity for a couple of years. In the digital age there is much more of an opportunity to check out restaurants without big-ticket PR representation. Even if they don't have a website, they will have left digital footprints; enough by which to judge whether it looks worthy of the readers' time.

I study the menu in advance. Even if it's only a sample menu it gives me enough clues. Perhaps they only use ingredients foraged from motorway verges, or they love fermenting stuff. Maybe this is a place which cooks only over fire. There must be a piece on the utter hell of getting the smell of smoke out of your clothes, because you were seated too close to the open kitchen? Surely I can get 1,100 words out of that? I may clock a reference to a pork belly dish I know I can't order because I've ordered too many of those over the years. I dismiss those items that simply won't be ordered because of cost. That means no caviar with the scallops, no lobster, and who the hell still thinks foie gras is okay? Please chefs, let it go. I will scan the menu for something which sounds a bit odd or even ludicrous. If the kitchen thinks a dish of, say, cod with blackberries and kumquats is worth putting on the menu, then the least I can do is attempt to eat it. Indeed, the odder a dish sounds the more likely I am to order it. I will do this so that, if it's disastrous, you don't have to.

I don't eat by myself. In the early days, I did occasionally. I am forever aware that my reviews cannot just be in London. Sometimes I would take a train out by myself and sit alone over as many dishes as I could order without looking disgraceful. It was not something I much enjoyed. I could only justify this sad spectacle on the grounds that it was my job. These days I have more friends scattered about the UK and abroad, and more work reasons for being all over the place anyway. The point is that there is always someone with me, usually just one person, sometimes two. They just have to know that while I treasure their company, and their gossip, I'm not massively interested in their opinions. I'm the one writing the column, not them. For that reason, my companions are told that, when asked how everything is, which will happen repeatedly, they must answer 'fine'. Yes, it can come across as terribly passive aggressive. Yes, it can even seem rude. But it gives me room to manoeuvre. If my companion says everything is terrific, wonderful, delightful thank you, and I then write a column which is less than positive, the restaurant would be justified in being extremely confused.

Just eat your dinner. That said, if you say something witty and insightful about the food or the room or the experience, I will steal it and pass it off as my own. This is the price you pay for a free meal. Oh, and I get to taste everything. I might even suggest we swap halfway through each dish. I will also have a say in what you order. Unless it is specifically a steak restaurant, no, you can't have the steak and chips. That's only on the menu for the people who didn't really want to go out to eat in the first place, the ones who are desperately searching the menu for a plate of safety.

Yes, there will be dessert. We have a job to do here. (For a while my dear wife fell out of favour as a regular dining companion, because she didn't really like desserts and would roll her eyes when told we had to order a couple. It really took the fun out of all those unnecessary calories which I could justify to myself on account of the job.) Yes, there will be wine, but don't get excited, for this is not my money we are spending. It is the newspaper's money and there are limits. Not that those limits have ever formally been set. On one occasion I had to step out of the job to have surgery on a degraded hip. We appointed a trio of stunt doubles, people invited to write an appreciation of a restaurant they already loved. My editor rang me in a state of some agitation. 'What's our expenses policy?' she said. I was gratified by that. She clearly hadn't had cause to question my expenses up to that point. I told her my expenses policy was: 'don't take the piss'. That means a single bottle from the lower reaches of the list and if I really do decide to hit the daiquiris at the start that's coming out of my own pocket.

In the early days, having been a reporter covering everything from crime and politics to public services and the arts, I took studious notes in the little notebook forever wedged in my back pocket. The notebook is still there; I am still a reporter, in mind if not always in deed. But over the years it became clear to me that a copy of the menu is a solid aide-mémoire. The name of the dish quickly reminds you of the experience of eating it. A few years ago, I also started photographing every dish on my phone. Again, these are an aide-mémoire. I then started posting those pictures to Instagram, so readers could compare what I was served with the artfully shot images provided by our photographer, who always arranges to go in after me. But I am determined not to be the infuriating diner, disturbing every other table with a burst of flash. The pictures are taken quickly, almost casually. As I explained in the introduction, some of them are awful; not out of focus, but perhaps less than Instagram pretty. I have no problem with this. As I always say to the people on Instagram who complain about the quality of my images, and a few do, they are welcome not to look at them. These pictures really are there simply to help me when it comes to writing the review. I just happen to be sharing them.

We eat, I fire off a few shots, and then we go home. For a long while I would try to set my features in some parody of one of those Easter Island sculptures, determined not to give anything away until the big reveal of publication two or three weeks hence. But in recent years, encouraged by the traumas for the hospitality industry of the Covid-19 pandemic, I have given up on that. Now, if I think it's basically a good restaurant, if I know I'm going to write a generally positive review, I will make a point of telling the staff I had a nice time. I don't necessarily assume anyone cares what I think. Then again, why should me coming to their place for dinner be needlessly traumatic? It is possible that, in my older age, I have become a nicer person.

That's my process. It's not much but it is mine. And I'm absolutely certain it would make lousy television.

Starters

As with snacks, the way we define how certain dishes sit within a meal can sometimes feel a little arbitrary. All the recipes in this section do work particularly well as starters, but you could obviously make them main courses. By the same token, within the sections on meat, seafood and vegetables, you'll find some dishes which really work best as mains, and some which equally could be starters. The decision is yours. I know, I know. I'm offering you a shocking amount of freewill.

Caesar salad

Inspired by the Caesars served at both
Joe Allen and Hawksmoor

Before we get to this greatest but most abused, violated and traduced of all salads, we must first deal with one of the greatest red herrings in food: the cult of authenticity. When people talk piously about a dish being authentic, they are insisting that it is right or correct. There are two problems with this. The first is that all recipes are at some point invented. None of them is holy scripture. They all start the same way: with somebody cooking something for the first time. Or perhaps a group of people cook a dish regularly based on the ingredients that are available to them, and then somebody writes down what it is they've been doing. That becomes the recipe. But of course, it is only a version of the recipe, put together by the person who happened to be holding the pen at the time.

In 1954 the social historian Dorothy Hartley published a book called *Food in England,* which drew together traditional recipes based on her experiences of travelling across the country as a journalist for the *Daily Sketch.* It is an impressive work of oral history, which remains in print to this day, and which serves as a significant document of a certain kind of English cooking based upon what was available from the fells, fields and rivers. If you want a recipe for oxtail pot or tongue or ox-cheek brawn or marrow butter, this is the book for you. But it is only *a* recipe rather than *the* recipe. It is the product of Hartley's investigations and more importantly her biases and tastes. This was brought home to me early on in the life of *The Kitchen Cabinet.* Each episode we visit a different place in the United Kingdom, where we take questions from a live audience. We always have a couple of site-specific themes, often based around a local food or dish. In the first few series we featured a lot of meaty stews: Lancashire hot pot, say, or Monmouth stew or Liverpool's scouse (or lob scouse). Two things became clear. First, despite the different names, all of them had roughly the same antecedents regardless of what they were called. They were a way to stretch relatively expensive meat further by adding vegetables, even when utilizing the cheaper cuts. And second, there was no agreed recipe. During our first episode from Liverpool, we discussed scouse, generally a stew made with lamb neck and root vegetables. There was much argument among our audience as to whether, say, peas should be in there or not. Each household made it a different way. Which was the authentic recipe for scouse? Honestly, I'm not getting into an argument with a bunch of Liverpudlians over something as important as that. It's their culture. I can't get involved.

I first tackled the question of authenticity in one of my very earliest reviews in 1999, when I went with my wife Pat to a venerable Swiss restaurant called St Moritz in London's Soho. It's still going after half a century. Pat's mother was Swiss and so we have eaten cheese fondues unironically for years, obsessing over the balance of the correct cheeses and the correct booze, and the interplay of heat upon them. That review includes this sentence: 'When I say that it is good, I mean it is authentically Swiss, by which I mean, in turn, that it is unbelievably cute – verging on the naff – in a grossly pretty "slap my thigh and call me Heidi" kind of a way.' Worryingly, I am clearly equating authentic with virtue. I would now excuse myself as being terribly young and ignorant at that point, were it not for the fact that honour is saved a couple of paragraphs down. 'We were brought a basket of bread which Pat declared authentically Swiss,' I wrote. 'The Swiss are the only nation on earth who can bake bread which tastes stale the moment it comes out of the oven. God knows how they do it.'

Here then is the second point. Even if there is such a thing as authenticity, authentic is not the same as good. I made this argument a few years later in a piece on the various tribes of foodie holidaymaker: the Dordogne Bores, who insist that eating confit de canard and tarte aux pommes for fourteen days flat is utter bliss, the Gastro Tourists who choose their destination according to how many nineteen-course tasting menus they can reach easily, and the Authenticity Addicts. When it was published my glittering prose was cut to shreds by an editor with a lack of good taste and probably, to be fair, a lack of space. So now I get to unleash my brilliance on the world here.

Authenticity Addicts

The members of this particular AA group regard eating not as a pleasure, but as a contact sport, which will make them feel better about themselves. The Authenticity Addict is convinced that everything they have ever eaten at home is in some way a fake – apart from the snot and gristle concoction that is jellied eels – and that only by travelling the world and eating exactly what the locals eat can they really connect with the culture they are visiting. This means they end up consuming some of the nastiest food items ever devised, although they will always claim to really, really, like them: stews made from goat intestines, with the bitter tang of bile and urine; braised cow's udder in gravy; pressed pig's ear in vinegar.

What the Authenticity Addict fails to recognize is that renowned local dishes like these are almost always the product of poverty, and that poor people's food is generally more a matter of necessity than tastiness. Why do poverty-stricken Chinese people eat pig's ear? Is it because they really like chewing through the flavourless, rubbery slices of porker lobe? Perhaps some of them do. But it's also the case that in cash-strapped communities, nothing can go to waste, even the ear. In short, while claiming to be rejecting the usual conventions of tourism, Authenticity Addicts are really just patronizing poor people.

Over fifteen years on I still very much agree with myself.

Which brings us all the way back to the dear Caesar salad. It should surely be possible to say that there is an authentic, which is to say, right way to make one because it has a relatively recent origin story. It was said to be invented by restaurateur Caesar Cardini, an Italian immigrant to the US, at his restaurant just over the border with Mexico in Tijuana on 4 July 1924, when a rush of custom caused the kitchen to run out of ingredients. To feed the customers he came up with his salad of Romaine lettuce with croutons and an emulsified dressing involving olive oil, egg yolk, garlic, Dijon mustard, Parmesan cheese and Worcestershire sauce, prepared tableside. It was such a success that Cardini eventually moved to Los Angeles, where he started a business selling a bottled version of the dressing.

However, over the years a number of competing claims have emerged. It was said that it was actually Alex Cardini, Caesar's brother, who invented the salad, or that it was not the Cardinis at all but a member of staff. And that it was originally called the Aviator salad. Plus, there are arguments over whether it should include anchovies, or whether the anchovy content in the Worcestershire sauce should do the trick.

None of the original recipes include dry chargrilled chicken breast, with the texture of desiccated cotton wool. None of them demand spongy prawns or floppy bits of grilled salmon leaking white albumin over the leaves or, I dunno, spit-roasted Dalmatian puppy. I'm not going to claim that any of these versions of the Caesar salad are wrong. I'm just saying that I have never been served a good one, or one as great, as thrilling, as the unadorned version I first met at Joe Allen, the delightful American brasserie which I first went to shortly after it opened in London in 1977, when I was ten. I have often referred to Joe's, as it was known to its regulars, as one of the first places where I learnt to eat out. The original opened in New York in the 60s, just off Broadway, and quickly became a hangout for actors straight off the stage. If anything, the London sibling was even more of a starry joint. It had a piano player, Jimmy Hardwick, originally hired so they could have a late licence, but who eventually became an integral part of the experience. He knew the Great American Songbook inside out, and made sure to learn the score of each new musical as it opened, so he could segue into whichever tune the star who'd just walked through the door was famous for performing.

The food was American classics. The ribs came with black-eyed peas and a corn muffin, before such things had ever been heard of in London. There was a chilli bowl. And there was the Caesar salad. No, it was not made tableside, but it was delivered in its own thick heavy wooden salad bowl, with servers so you could toss it yourself. (Eventually the wooden bowls were retired on the instructions of environmental health.) The leaves were kept whole. There was the creamy, pokey dressing. There were drifts of freshly grated Parmesan at a time when Britain associated the cheese with a pre-ground dust smelling weirdly of vomit (literally; both have a shared aroma compound, accentuated in the Parmesan as it dries). Best of all there were the extremely garlicky croutons, made with cubes of fried white bread. It was a strangely exciting experience to discover, as a ten-year-old with an absurdly developed appetite, that I was the kind of kid who would not just willingly, but enthusiastically order a salad.

This led inevitably to huge disappointments over the years as I ordered Caesar salads from other places and got something which was a ninth-generation photocopy of a shadow of a whisper of the real thing. Why had the leaves been shredded like that? Where was the hit of garlic? Why had marinated anchovies, or boquerones, been used instead of salted anchovies? And what the hell was all the stuff on top? Joe Allen has survived in various guises for decades and a Caesar salad is still on the menu, although it has changed a little. The closest I have found over the years to the original and, to be fair, it is very close indeed, is that served at the steakhouse group Hawksmoor: whole leaves, a proper punchy dressing, lots and lots of grated Parmesan. They include the recipe in their 2017 *Hawksmoor* cookbook. Mine is based on theirs, although they do not include anchovies in the dressing. They add them after. I bloody love salted anchovies and so I do throw a few into the processor. You can choose to do otherwise. And there is no raw egg yolk, which, given the state of egg production, is probably for the best. Also, the Hawksmoor croutons, made with torn sourdough, are, well, just a little too fancy for my liking. I talked to the chef Rowley Leigh who, as well as being the chef-patron of Kensington Place, was head chef at Joe Allen for a while, admittedly a long time ago. He said it was so far back in the past that he could remember very little about it, but thought garlic powder was involved. After a bit of experimentation, I concluded he was right; that, to get the Joe Allen Caesar salad garlicky hit, a bit of that was definitely the way to go. So here it is.

If, having made this, you feel the need to put a grilled chicken breast across the top, you are dead to me.

Serves 4

INGREDIENTS

4 slices of white bread, crusts removed, cut into 2cm squares
4 tbsp vegetable oil, for frying
A knob of butter (optional)
1 tbsp garlic powder
½ tsp kitchen salt
2 Romaine (or Cos) lettuce, broken up into whole leaves, the root discarded
6–8 salted anchovy fillets, chopped, depending on taste (optional)
20g grated Parmesan
Ground black pepper

For the dressing
(You will need about 50ml per person, so this will make a little more than necessary)
100g Parmesan, finely grated
40ml white wine vinegar
20ml fresh lime or lemon juice
1 tbsp Dijon mustard
4 anchovy fillets
120ml sunflower oil
40ml good olive oil

1. Fry the cubes of bread in the vegetable oil until golden brown. If you're feeling especially indulgent, add a knob of butter halfway through. Drain on kitchen paper.

2. Mix the garlic powder and salt. When the croutons have almost cooled, toss them in the seasoning mix in a bowl. Remove, leaving any excess seasoning in the bowl.

3. Make the dressing by putting all the ingredients apart from the oils into a food processor. Start to blitz, adding the oil in a gentle stream so it emulsifies.

4. Toss the whole lettuce leaves with the dressing (ideally in a mixing bowl), so every leaf is coated. Arrange the leaves on a large serving plate.

5. Sprinkle over the pieces of chopped anchovy, if using, and then the croutons, shuffling the leaves around so it's all properly mixed. Sprinkle over the grated Parmesan, and add a good grind of black pepper.

Here's one adaptation, to prove that I am not committed to false notions of authenticity. In Cervo's, a Portuguese-accented restaurant on New York's Lower East Side, I was once served a dish listed on the menu as 'Treviso' – known in the UK as radicchio – 'with anchovy'. It immediately struck me as a clever take on a Caesar salad, but using the bitter hit of different leaves. It was delightful, and would also work very well with the equally bitter hit of puntarella.

Butternut squash 'cappuccino'

Inspired by soups served as an amuse-bouche
at Pétrus and many other classy joints in
the early 2000s

Magazine food and drink editors tend to circle around the familiar. If it's Easter there must be new ways to talk about roasting lamb. Let's have a thousand words on a stress-free Christmas, or insightful ideas for how to cater a picnic so not everyone is utterly miserable. That's not a criticism. Journalism is as seasonal as the first snowdrop and the last leaf fall. Readers may be able to sniff a lack of originality, but they do also like a certain familiarity. Some notions, however, never really fly. Regularly over the years I have been sounded out about a feature roughly framed as: 'How to cook like a Michelin-starred chef'. It didn't ever work because underlying it was some false idea of 'fanciness'; some shared version of high end, which was a bit weird. With just a few tricks, involving tweezers, squeezy bottles and an interest in things which had nothing to do with eating well, the pitch went, you too could mimic the cookery and plating of the finest chefs in the world at home. Or perhaps not.

I have never been a huge devotee of Michelin stars. I don't have a problem with anybody doing anything for prizes and gongs. There are awards recognizing achievements in car park management. There are awards celebrating the laundry and dry-cleaning sector. There are even, believe it or not, awards for people who get paid to go out for dinner on someone else's dime and write smartarse things about it. I

78

keep mine in the downstairs loo, thank you for asking. We all like a bit of recognition.

So why shouldn't there be awards, badges and certificates for great chefs? My problem with Michelin stars is that, by design or not, they celebrate a particular aesthetic. If you end up in a Michelin three-star restaurant, there will be battalions of suited and booted waiters. There will be hush and reverence. There may be edible flowers and outbreaks of fluttery gold leaf. If you ask directions to the loo, they will take you there, like you're still a toddler. And somewhere under all of that guff, if you have the patience, you may well find some sublime cookery, executed by people whose skill and talent has been honed over many, many years. That food simply cannot be replicated at home through the application of a few gimmicks.

Or at least, not much of it can.

Whatever big-name chefs say about exploring their imaginations and pushing the limits of what can be done with prime ingredients, the very highest levels of gastronomy are particularly susceptible to the entreaties of fashion. This is because a lot of its clientele, the people who can afford the large price tag, like to think of themselves as having exclusive tastes. Which means they want to be bang up to date. One restaurant puts a certain dish on its menu and it quickly proves popular. People talk about it, and that chatter reaches the ears of other chefs, who think they'll give it a go. Quickly it spreads and soon it has become a cliché. We move on. But just because it's familiar doesn't mean it's in any way bad. We're just a little bored with it because we are fickle and shallow. We crave something else.

The savoury 'cappuccino' is a case in point. This became a very big thing in the early noughties. It was basically a soup. No, not even 'basically' a soup. It was just a soup. But it was a soup lifted into the world of luxurious soft furnishings and velvet tasselled cushions courtesy of a good dollop of cream and a device which, with a bit of imagination, could double as a sex toy. The dairy fats would be whipped to a froth, perhaps with one of those battery-operated, hand-held cappuccino beaters. Hence the title. That said, the froth was rarely stable enough to maintain itself for long, because of everything else that was in the soup. Still, it was always very nice indeed: rich and mouth-coating. Sometimes it was served as a starter. Occasionally it was the sauce element of a dish. Most often, however, it arrived as an unexpected amuse-bouche, a tiny flavour bomb at the very start of the meal to get you going.

At the restaurant of the Grand Hotel in Eastbourne in November of 2002 it was a wild mushroom cappuccino. In 2004 at a London restaurant called Patterson's, overseen by the former head chef of the Garrick Club, it was a seafood cappuccino, while at Morgan M in Islington it was a shellfish cappuccino. Over in New York at Per Se that year Thomas Keller, of French Laundry fame, had yet another mushroom cappuccino. At some point in 2004, a very big year for the dish, I went with my then young family to the Center Parcs holiday village in Sherwood Forest, where the air smells forever of industrial chlorine, introduced to keep the massive tropical swimming dome from turning into a festering petri dish of virulent infection. Next to the pool they had attempted (and failed miserably) to open a fancy restaurant. There on the menu, with the roasted seabass, was a horseradish cappuccino. When a restaurant trend reaches Center Parcs, it's probably time to move on.

They weren't all called cappuccinos. Sometimes the fancier places, which didn't want to sound like they were aping

Starbucks, called them veloutés. This translates from the French as velvety. The grandest of cookbooks, like *Larousse Gastronomique*, will tell you that a velouté soup, like a velouté sauce, has to begin with a roux of flour and butter cooked out together, then let down with stock (instead of the milk used in, say, the making of a white sauce). Study a few more modern recipes, however, and you'll see that quite a few cooks use the word merely as a description of a thick and, yes, velvety soup. The very first of these that I recall, the one that stays most sharply in my memory, is a frothy pumpkin velouté served to me in 2002 at the original Gordon Ramsay-owned Pétrus on London's St James's Street (now home to Angela Hartnett's original Café Murano). The head chef was a young Marcus Wareing, who was making his name with an unapologetically French classical menu. A lot of butter was involved in his food back then. Sauces were deep. Cream was whipped. And at the start there was a thimble-sized serving of that soup. After the salsa verde from the Green Street Café in Bath it was the next restaurant dish I went home and attempted to reverse-engineer, pretty successfully as far as I was concerned.

The frother of choice in the Wareing kitchen at that time was the Bamix stick blender. You can indeed use a cappuccino beater if you have one to hand but you don't really need one. Just give it a light whipping in the pan by hand with a bell whisk. You will see that I've added a couple of extras to really zhuzh it up, which were often a part of the experience. None of this will turn you into a Michelin-starred chef. And nor should you want it to. But it will make you a really nice soup.

Makes enough for 6 portions

INGREDIENTS

550g butternut squash, peeled, deseeded and chopped into 4cm
   pieces (roughly half an average sized squash, after it's been
   peeled and deseeded)
1 large onion, roughly chopped
3 or 4 cloves of garlic, unpeeled
2 tbsp balsamic vinegar
3 tbsp olive oil
Sea salt and ground black pepper
A couple of knobs of salted butter
1.2 litres vegetable stock (with extra if needed)
200ml double cream
Truffle oil
A small bunch of fresh chives, finely chopped

METHOD

1. Heat the oven to 200°C/400°F/gas mark 6.

2. Put the butternut squash, onion and unpeeled garlic
   cloves into a high-sided oven tray. Drizzle on the
   balsamic vinegar and olive oil, season liberally with
   salt and pepper, and then turn it all with your hands
   so everything is coated. Add the knobs of butter.
   Bake in the oven for between an hour and 75
   minutes, moving all the ingredients around every now
   and then, until the pieces of squash are starting to
   brown and the onions are beginning to caramelize.
   Leave it in for longer if your oven is a little slower.

3. Take it out of the oven and squeeze the now soft
   garlic cloves from their skins. Discard the skins. Put

the oven tray on the stovetop, turn on the heat and pour over the stock. As it starts to bubble, scrape up all the caramelized and crusty pieces on the bottom. Pour everything into a saucepan and let it simmer on a low heat for about 20 minutes. Flick through a food magazine. Find a feature on interesting things to do with lamb for Easter.

4. Now use a stick blender or, better still, a food processor to blitz all the ingredients together. Season liberally with salt and pepper. You now have a very nice, rugged soup. You could stop here.

5. Or you can pass the soup through a fine mesh sieve. This is a slightly annoying job because you will have to scrape it through with a wooden spoon. Discard any thick, fibrous vegetal matter that gathers in the mesh. Again, you could stop here. You now have a very smooth, deep-tasting and yes, velvety soup, which will hold in the fridge for a couple of days. If it's thicker than you would like it to be, you can add a little more vegetable stock.

6. The final flourishes: warm the soup so it's just on a simmer. Add the cream and immediately whisk so it starts to foam.

7. Serve in small bowls. Dribble the surface with a tiny amount of the truffle oil and sprinkle with the chopped chives.

Of course, unless you've doubled the recipe, you are now staring at half a butternut squash, which is seriously annoying. I'm going to give you something to do with it and I'm going to give it to you in the style of one of my favourite cookbooks, *The New York Times Cooking: No-Recipe Recipes*, by Sam Sifton, who used to be that paper's restaurant critic, then oversaw the food coverage which generated this volume, before becoming a senior editor on the paper. Instead of itemizing everything, it gives rather more intuitive instructions for how to do things. If you consider yourself a bish-bash-bosh cook, and you know what I mean by that, I can heartily recommend that book. So here is a no-recipe recipe to use up your remaining butternut. I have conducted a forensic search of the digital forest on my computer and can find no references to this among my twenty-five years of reviews. I'll just have to assume it's one of mine unless a chef gets in touch to tell me otherwise.

Chop the butternut squash into 2cm cubes, slice 2 medium onions into thin rings and put it all in a mixing bowl. Add a serious glug of olive oil and then turn it all with your hands in the bowl so that everything is covered. It's easier to do this in a bowl than in the deep-sided frying pan you'll be using. Put a good knob of butter (or a tablespoon or so of olive oil if you want to keep it vegan) into a frying pan, gently heat and add half a teaspoon of chilli flakes or more if you like heat and less, if you don't. When the fat is fizzing add the squash and onions, turning everything around with a wooden spoon so the chilli flakes get mixed through, then cook gently over a low heat for 20 or so minutes, turning regularly. What started as a large volume of vegetables will quickly cook down and soften. Once that's happened turn the heat up a little and let it caramelize, while continuing to turn regularly. Do not be afraid of letting the butternut squash blacken in places or the onions caramelize. They can take it. Season liberally with salt and pepper and serve as a side dish. You may well end up buying butternut squash just to make this.

Taramasalata with radishes and boiled eggs

Inspired by the dish served by Rosie Healey at
Gloriosa, Glasgow

In the beginning there was taramasalata. It was fondant-fancy pink, courtesy of beetroot extract, and uncompromisingly sharp. Eating it made my fingers smell both fishy and smoky because of the clumsy way in which I dragged pieces of still warm pita bread through its thick creamy peaks. As a child, I liked it very much. The convention would now be for me to roll my eyes at the memory of this stuff, encountered in north-west London's Greek Cypriot restaurants; places to which I was taken occasionally by my parents mostly because my dad had a taste for lamb shoulder baked in wine until it slumped from the bone.

I won't. My recollections of this sort of mezze when I was a kid are too fond, too warm, for me to disown them. Those old-school London tavernas remain a joy, offering comfort through the familiarity and tightness of their offering. Sometimes it can be exactly what we want. In the winter of 2022, I found my way to just such a place, a fabulous old stager in west London called Tsiakkos & Charcoal. The grill in the open kitchen at the front guaranteed that the air smelt of smoke throughout, and the dining room was strung with fairy lights, possibly because Christmas was approaching, although I like to think the fairy lights might be there all year round. It had occupied its site just off the Harrow Road for decades, offering platters of dolmades and hummus and yes, taramasalata, alongside moussaka and a kleftiko over which my old dad would have swooned. My love letter of a review was met by an outpouring of affection by its regulars. They loved it for all the reasons I did: because it did that small number of things in a familiar and lovely way. They didn't want it mucked with.

More recently we have been living through the whipped cod's roe years. Perhaps chefs renamed it to distinguish what they were serving from the taverna version, although of course it was basically the same thing, just made to a mildly different recipe. Now it was only the very lightest shade of pink, because no colourings had been added. The acidity had been dialled down. But there was no point pretending. A new set of modern British bistros had alighted upon the idea of offering taramasalata among its many small plates. What really marked it out was the things with which it was accompanied or the way it was presented. Back in 2008 it was given the luxe treatment at a small, ambitious restaurant called Launceston Place in Kensington, where whipped cod's roe turned up crusted with shavings of truffle for us to play with while studying the menu. In 2017 at Salt, a fancy place in Stratford-upon-Avon, it arrived alongside a roast rump of lamb, its overt fishiness riffing on the more familiar idea of putting anchovy with lamb. In 2018 at a seafood restaurant in east London called Cornerstone it was paired with roasted celeriac and hazelnuts, to great effect. Climat in Manchester served it atop hash browns still hot from the deep fat fryer. At Sargasso in Margate, it was, as I described it then, 'piped in buxom whorls across a thick piece of oily toast'. On top of that was a lawn of peppery watercress, and perched on its summit was a still warm chive-sprinkled boiled egg, which leaked its runny yolk in all directions when you cut in. Call it taramasalata. Call it whipped cod's roe. It is clearly a friendly ingredient, which plays well with others.

I started making my own taramasalata a few years ago when I noticed that my local fishmongers, F. C. Soper in

Nunhead, south-east London, stocked the key ingredient: hefty lozenges of reddy-brown smoked cod's roe. I decided to try blitzing it with crème fraîche and a little lemon juice, and very nice it was too. I would put it on the table at the start of occasional dinner parties with a bowl of ludicrously middle-class crisps, the thick ones which can injure your mouth, but work beautifully for dredging. So this taramasalata recipe is very much mine, although there are other ways to make it. I encountered the whole dish, however, at Rosie Healey's restaurant Gloriosa in Glasgow, where the carousel of fashion had clearly turned far enough for her to list it on the menu as taramasalata. I wasn't intending to include dishes which are essentially an assembly of nice things, but I'll make an exception here because Healey's dish, which partnered the dip with crisp radishes and boiled eggs with jammy yolks, is simply the best I have encountered. Early in her career Healey worked at Rochelle Canteen, the restaurant belonging to Melanie Arnold and Margot Henderson, who in turn first ran the French House Dining Room together after Margot's husband Fergus left to run St John. Healey says she got the idea of putting crisp radishes with tarama there. Looking back at my review of a short-lived outpost of Rochelle Canteen at the ICA in London I see they did indeed serve their whipped cod's roe with radishes. The peppery crunch of the radishes goes beautifully with the softness of the tarama.

There are a few variables with the taramasalata recipe, because whole cod's roes differ a little in size and it doesn't make sense not to use the whole thing. Likewise, we are very much in the territory of personal taste when it comes to volumes of crème fraîche, lemon juice and so on. You know the mantra: taste, taste, and taste again. Meanwhile, let me take pleasure in the fact that this recipe gives me the opportunity to provide instructions on how to boil an egg.

Serves 4 or so as a dip

INGREDIENTS

250g smoked cod's roe (approximately)
175g crème fraîche (approximately)
2 tbsp lemon juice (to taste)
Cracked black pepper
A bunch of radishes, ideally still with their green leaves attached
White wine vinegar
Sea salt
Olive oil
2 large eggs

METHOD

1. Whole cod's roes come encased in a membrane. It's perfectly edible, but tends to turn into annoying strands once blitzed, so start by splitting the cod's roe lengthways, and then scraping out as much of the roe as you can from the skin. Cod's roes do differ in size but it will probably amount to around 250g.

2. Start by blitzing with two-thirds of the crème fraîche. Taste. Do you want it softer and creamier? If so, add more. If not, stop there. If you want a little acidity, start adding the lemon juice until you're happy. Add a good grind of the black pepper.

3. Wash the radishes and the leaves, pulling off any which are less than pristine. Dress the leaves with a sprinkle of white wine vinegar and sea salt. Put those on a plate alongside a pile of the tarama. Using a spoon warmed with hot water, smooth out an

indentation in the middle of the tarama and dribble in a couple of tablespoons of the olive oil.

4. And now the boiled egg method. Put the 2 eggs into a saucepan of cold water and bring it to the boil. Leave them in the now boiling water for 3 minutes. Meanwhile, fill a bowl with iced water. When the 3 minutes are up, put the boiled eggs into the iced water for 2 minutes to stop them cooking. Remove and leave them to cool, then peel and slice them in half lengthways. You should have a perfectly jammy yolk. Add to the plate of tarama and radishes.

Deep-fried spare ribs with cumin and chilli

Inspired by the dish served at Baiwei,
London (now closed)

The gaudy, red-trimmed dining room of Red Chilli in Manchester is located in a basement. On the day I descended its staircase in the autumn of 2005 everything changed for me. Up until then I'd only heard tell of the joyous whack and power of the food of China's Sichuan province; of its uncommon way with chillies and of peppercorns that literally made your lips vibrate. But I hadn't tried any of it. There were whispers of isolated restaurants, out on the furthest reaches of London's tube network, that might serve a few dishes, but I'd never made the trip. I'd made do with the various iterations of what I took to be the Cantonese repertoire, the darkly roasted duck and sweet and sour pork and ginger and spring onion prawn dishes which, courtesy of the British relationship with Hong Kong, had seemed to be our lot.

89

At the same time as Hong Kong was handed back to China and loosened its relationship with the UK, the rest of China opened up. Chinese students flocked to London, Birmingham and Manchester and all points in between. With them came the chefs ready to cook the food they recognized from home. Red Chilli, on a corner of Portland and Nicholas Street, which eventually became part of a group strung like a pearl necklace across the English north, was my first experience of the food of Sichuan. They had a standard Chinese menu, full of aromatic crispy duck and prawn toast and deep-fried seaweed. But you'd be a fool, running scared of life's possibilities, if you didn't ask for the other menu, the so-called 'spicy one'. That boasted a mellifluous language all its own. There was Hot Wok Trotter or Husband and Wife lung slices; Sichuan Mrs Spotty's beancurd or Blessed the Whole Family; Poet Dung-bo roast pork or lucky prawn cakes; silver fungus and winter melon soup.

I remember a lamb broth, bobbing with lawn-green fronds of fresh coriander and spring onions and yes, chillies, and another of eel in a dark sauce from which heat rose at the very end, and something involving wobbly pigs' innards with a deep farmyard funk redolent of andouillette, with a kind of Chinese black pudding. Because of the reputation for spicy heat, this food could all end up sounding like an exercise in machismo. In truth, it was an exercise in flavour, a bold lurch into saturated colours from something more subdued. The next year Barshu opened on a corner site in Soho and suddenly Sichuan food was all big, expansive news. Barshu hired as its consultant the writer Fuchsia Dunlop. In the late 90s Dunlop had become the first westerner to train at the Chengdu Cookery School in Sichuan, which led in 2001 to the publication of her *Book of Sichuan*

Food, republished in an updated edition in 2021. She has done more than almost anyone in the UK (and many other places besides) to demystify an extraordinarily broad and fragrant style of cooking. Just as the chefs and restaurants arrived, so did the ingredients and, courtesy of Dunlop's encouraging recipes, my cupboards filled over the years with barrel-like plastic pots of massively flavourful Sichuan chilli bean paste, with Sichuan peppercorns and sweet flour paste. With Dunlop as my guide, I learned to make a few dishes.

Reviewing new and thrilling restaurants with menus representing the food of Sichuan became a major habit of mine: there was Sichuan Folk in London's East End and Sanxia Renjia in Deptford (oh, the mapo tofu) and Seveni opposite the Imperial War Museum, an unselfconsciously nuts place, filled with smoke from in-table barbecues, pirouetting towards extractors. You reached the dining room via a fairytale wooden bridge and the ceiling was crusted with fairy lights. But by far the most beguiling was an obscure, scuffed canteen on the Bethnal Green Road called Gourmet San, word of which began to circulate online in discussion forums for people who care too much about these things, early in 2008 (closed now). I felt it was my duty to go. I was right to do so. They were big on offal. They braised trotters in Coke. Sliced beef tongue and tripe arrived at room temperature, drenched in the most powerful of chilli oils. Now cleanse your palate with a pile of chilled cucumbers in a dressing of vinegar and sesame oil with coriander and heaps of raw garlic.

We were some of the very few non-Chinese people eating there. This is not the recommendation it's always assumed to be. I've eaten in terrible Chinese restaurants full of Chinese people. Restaurants operate as third spaces, places where people of shared culture or mind like to gather, and sometimes they'll do so in spite of the food rather than because of it. Either way, for Gourmet San it became clear that was their core market. After my visit we asked if we could photograph their food to illustrate a review, as we always do, a request that has been refused only three times in my entire career; once by a (rightly) paranoid motorway services, once by a Michelin three star in Paris, and once by Gourmet San. They said almost all their clientele were Chinese and they didn't need extra customers. I did not believe then, and do not believe now, that anywhere should be exclusive in that way and certainly not down worryingly artificial lines of nationality or ethnicity. We took a shot of the outside of Gourmet San and then got a takeaway. Our photographer brought some crockery and plated it up outside on the street. Job done.

Over the years I became familiar with, and frankly obsessed by, double-cooked pork in a deep red sauce of chilli bean paste, lightly vinegary gong bao prawns with the crunch of peanuts, and Chongqing chicken, the bird deep-fried and presented in a massive bowl of dried red chillies. So when I came across this dish of small pork ribs, dusted with cumin, salt, sugar and chilli, at Baiwei in a lane just off Gerrard Street in London's Chinatown, it made complete sense. By then, a small number of restaurants serving dishes from Xinjiang in China's north, where cumin is a favoured spice, had also opened, which meant I recognized the flavours. I returned to Baiwei many times after that and always ordered it. I always went alone. I certainly wasn't going to share.

I've given the volumes for one kilo of pork ribs, but only because that makes it look like I have a restrained and dignified appetite. But these are addictive and will get eaten quickly, so you may want to double the quantities of the ribs, the master stock and seasoning. (Or triple them; I'm not your dad.) They do take a bit of work, ideally spread over two days, but it's worth it. If you can't get baby back ribs chopped up into smaller pieces, just use whole ribs. It's still hugely satisfying.

INGREDIENTS

1kg baby back pork ribs, separated (chopped into small pieces if your butcher is willing)
Vegetable oil, for frying

For the master stock
500ml chicken stock (cube is fine)
500ml water
100ml light soy
125ml Shaoxing wine (substitute with dry sherry if not available)
75g caster sugar
2 cloves of garlic, peeled but left whole
2 whole star anise
1 piece of cassia bark, also known as cinnamon bark (you will find it in the spice aisle)
4 spring onions, chopped
1 tbsp sesame oil

For the seasoning mix
2 tbsp ground cumin
1 tbsp caster sugar
½ tsp table salt
¼ tsp garlic powder
¼ tsp chilli powder
¼ tsp ground Sichuan peppercorns (optional)

Optional
4 spring onions, chopped
Sea salt
200g dried red chillies

1. Combine all the ingredients for the master stock in a saucepan, bring to the boil, then turn down the heat and simmer for 30 minutes.

2. Turn the oven on to 180°C/350°F/gas mark 4. Strain the stock into an oven pan. Add the ribs so they are submerged, and put into the oven uncovered for 90 minutes. (A quick note: in 2023 I cooked this dish for the 'guilty pleasure' round of *MasterChef* in which the critics all competed against each other. I had just 90 minutes to complete this stage and so used a pressure cooker. It took just 12 minutes from reaching pressure for the ribs to be done. If you have a pressure cooker, I very much recommend this method.)

3. Take the ribs out of the stock and put into a bowl to cool, and then into the fridge, ideally overnight, but for at least 2 hours so they are properly dry. Retain the stock. Chinese cooks re-use it for braising, often topping it up as they go, week after week, month after month, year after year. I know I'm never going to do that, so instead I use it as the base for an engrossing noodle broth, with the addition perhaps of sliced ginger and fresh spring onions.

4. When you're ready to finish the ribs, bring enough oil for deep-frying up to 180°C.

5. While that's heating make your spice mix by putting the ingredients into a small bowl and swirling until all the elements are properly merged. The cumin, sugar, salt and garlic powder are the base. You can leave it at

that or, if you want it fiery, add the chilli (as well as some ground Sichuan peppercorns).

6. Deep-fry the ribs in batches. They will take only a couple of minutes to colour and crisp, so keep watch. Put them on paper to drain. If I'm doing a lot, I like to put a rack in an oven tray and put them on there in the oven at around 170°C/325°F/gas mark 3 to keep warm.

7. When all the ribs are crisped and bronzed, toss them in a large mixing bowl with the seasoning mix. Do not worry if it feels like you've put in too much seasoning. The right amount will cling to the ribs and any excess will fall to the bottom, as it does with the Louisiana cracklins on page 42.

8. These are now ready to eat, but if you want a final flourish, fry the chopped spring onions in a wok with a little oil over a medium heat with a good fat pinch of sea salt. Throw in the dried red chillies and toss for no more than a minute. (Watch them; they scorch easily.)

9. Serve the ribs in a bowl, tossed together with the chillies. Advise your friends and family not to eat the chillies but to pick through them, because they are only there to add aromatics. Laugh at them uproariously if they ignore you and suffer the consequences. Steal more ribs for yourself while they are distracted.

Crispy duck salad

Inspired by the dish created by Mark Hix when he was at
Le Caprice and the Ivy

In the Ivy's 1990s glory days, which are sadly long gone – this
may be a cookbook, but I am still a restaurant critic – the restaurant was famous because of the famous people who went
there. Partly this was down to its location, tucked away in a
quiet corner of London's theatreland. As a result it became a
high-end canteen for the stars of the shows playing around it,
and their friends and admirers. Judi Dench went there. Ralph
Fiennes went there. Nicole Kidman went there. Hugh Grant
went there. You get the idea. I could type any famous name
without checking; the chances they didn't at some point eat at
the Ivy are negligible. Although for what it's worth, I did
check. Oh look, some of the royals have had parties there.

This has caused the restaurant interesting problems over
the years. 'Because it could be quite hard to get a table if you
were not known to us,' one senior manager once told me,
'people would assume it was some grand gastronomic experience. They'd book three months ahead, arrive for dinner,
look at the menu and be very disappointed.' The fact is the
Ivy was never about the cooking. For the most part it has
always served comfort food; luxurious, very well-made comfort food, but comfort food all the same. Think shepherd's
pie or fishcakes, sausages and mash, roast chicken and fish
and chips, with a few things like oysters and lobster to add
a light glaze of glamour. Its regulars went there because
the service was fabulous and the room exceedingly comfortable. It was also a neat wedge shape, which encouraged
people-watching. You could see and be seen. The famous

stained-glass windows, an interlocking set of diamond lozenges the colour of boiled sweets, had long given the room a cloistered air, softened by the gashes of modern art on the walls, including works by Damien Hirst and Bridget Riley.

It is a mark of my grossly privileged life that I got to eat there often over the years, partly because my parents loved it so very much. There was the time my wife and I met them there the night before my mother's mastectomy, and we celebrated life over lobster and chips. (They were paying, thank God. The Ivy was never cheap.) After both my parents had died my sister and I took a day to go around London scattering their ashes in the places they had loved most together. We stopped for lunch at the Ivy, because that was one of them, and as we raised a glass to their memory, I reached down and found a gap between the bench and the back of the banquette. While no one was looking I poured some of their mixed ashes in. They are presumably still there to this day.

It is in the nature of landmark restaurants like the Ivy that many of them eventually become commodified. Jeremy King and Chris Corbin, the skilled restaurateurs who made the modern Ivy's reputation, left in 2000 to be replaced by a succession of corporate owners. For the most part they kept it as it was until recent years, when the name and branding was spun off into a succession of far lesser cafés and brasseries which had nothing to do with the original. Many of the most senior people in the kitchen, who'd had no role in creating the menus for the cafés, have since moved on, and costs have been cut. But versions of certain dishes remain on the menu.

The crispy duck salad is one of them, along with iced berries with white chocolate sauce (see page 307). It was created by chef Mark Hix when he was overseeing both the Ivy and its sibling Le Caprice. 'When it first went on the menu at Le Caprice, it was a crispy pork salad,' he told me. 'But it didn't sell. Finally, I clocked why that was. A lot of the customers were Jewish. So I changed it to crispy duck, and suddenly it was flying out of the kitchen and went on the Ivy menu too.'

A while after I'd come up with my version of this joyous salad, I found Hix's original recipe online. It is what you'd expect of a diligent restaurant chef. Fresh duck legs have to be simmered with aromatics for 45 minutes, allowed to dry, cut up into pieces then deep-fried. The sauce for the duck has five ingredients. My version, which has been given Hix's amused approval, cuts out about two hours of work, including the cleaning of a deep fat fryer, by using duck confit, now readily available from many shops and online. It also uses a jar of shop-bought hoi sin sauce. What makes it work is the pepperiness of the leaves, which need a sharp dressing, and the sweetness of the duck. It's both adult and childlike at the same time.

Serves 4, as a starter

INGREDIENTS

2 confit duck legs
4 tbsp hoi sin sauce

For the salad
1 tbsp sesame seeds
Table salt
100g watercress or rocket, stalks trimmed (you can also add fresh
    coriander if you fancy)
6 large radishes, sliced
4 spring onions, trimmed and sliced into batons

For the salad dressing
2 tbsp olive oil
1½ tbsp sherry vinegar (white wine vinegar is a good alternative)
1 tsp sesame oil
Sea salt

METHOD

1. Gently toast the sesame seeds in a dry cast iron frying pan, over a medium heat. Keep watch. They burn easily. When most of them are lightly golden brown, remove to a bowl, add a pinch of table salt, and set aside. Wipe down the pan to remove any stray sesame seeds that are hanging about. They don't taste at all nice when burnt.

2. Separate out the duck legs and place them skin side down in the frying pan over the lowest heat. Do not add any oil. They'll produce more than enough fat of their own. Turn every 5 minutes or so, as they start to colour. After about 10 or 15 minutes, take the pan off the heat. Using a fork and a sharp knife you should be able to pull the meat away from the bone. Break it up into smaller pieces, with the skin down. Put back on to the heat. Use a spatula to continue breaking up the meat into smaller pieces. Attend to any pieces of skin that come away from the meat. They may look a bit fatty, but gently increase the heat and they will crisp up, though do keep an eye on it all so it doesn't burn.

3. Once crisped, remove the leg bones and keep them as a chef's perk. Stand by the stove, chewing off the last bits of meat while no one else is watching.

You've earned it. When the duck is broken up and crisped take the pan off the heat.

4. Put the ingredients for the salad dressing into the bottom of a bowl, including a good pinch of sea salt. Pile the leaves and sliced radishes on top, then toss and turn to coat in the dressing using your hands or, if you're a little uptight, salad servers. Portion out on to four plates or flat bowls.

5. Put the hoi sin sauce in the bottom of a mixing bowl. Add the duck and mix to coat every piece completely.

6. Top each portion of the salad with a quarter of the duck. Sprinkle on the toasted sesame seeds and decorate with the batons of spring onion.

Crispy cauliflower with salt and pepper

Inspired by the Cauliflower 'Y Ming style' served at
Y Ming, London (now closed)

The question is always asked with a certain breathlessness, as if the answer will demand the imparting of some great secret even though that answer is actually deeply banal. The question is: how do you get the best service and the best table in a restaurant? The answer is: go there a lot. Become a regular, because restaurants love their regulars. In part, of course, it's because they like the money their regulars spend and they want them to keep spending it. But they also enjoy the knowledge that, if someone keeps coming to the same restaurant, it's because they clearly like the food and the room and the service. And who wouldn't want to show someone like that a good time? You're a regular. Yes, of course you can have the best table at short notice. Plus, everybody knows what to expect from each other. One of the most exhausting parts of running a restaurant is the constantly changing cast list; the endless cascade of new customers, each with their own particular foibles. It's easy to see how beloved the known will become for both sides.

I've achieved 'regular' status a few times. I was and, to a certain extent, remain a regular at Joe Allen, which inspired the Caesar salad on page 70, though that familiarity was inherited from my parents. There was a rather nice place by the Old Vic theatre in London's Waterloo called Bar & Kitchen, now long gone, where my wife and I could pretty much walk in and get a table regardless of how busy they were. They served a great oxtail stew with fluffy dumplings and gave you glass tumblers for the sturdy red wine.

And then there was Y Ming. Many people have a restaurant which is more than just somewhere to get fed; a place where life's milestones are measured out; where birthdays are celebrated and Christmas trips marked in the diary long in advance and where the staff get to watch your kids grow up. Y Ming, a relatively small Chinese restaurant on Greek Street in London's Soho just north of Chinatown, was that for us. We were not alone. Lots of people were regulars there. It was opened by a trio of friends in 1986 but within a year, two of them had dropped out, leaving just Christine Yau, not long arrived from Hong Kong. Part of the appeal was that, compared to the huge eating houses of Chinatown on Gerrard Street which are often less dining rooms than barns, Y Ming really was compact. There were two softly carpeted ground-floor dining rooms with a third space downstairs, just off the kitchen, which I almost never ate in. The walls were jade green. There were curtains. And unlike in Chinatown, you never felt rushed. We discovered it long before our kids arrived; indeed long before I started writing about restaurants. It was our place.

Early on, Christine designated a large round table in the first of the two dining rooms as a place for solo regulars to eat together and put the world to rights. As the years passed, I would discover that close colleagues – a senior editor at the *Observer*, the publisher of one of my books – were also Y Ming devotees. One lunchtime William Tiger Sin, the gentle, wry general manager, who had been there almost as long as Christine, came across two of us eating together and beamed. He was, he said, simply delighted to see two of his favourite people at the same table, especially because he wasn't aware we knew each other. He had the veteran maître d's talent for making people feel good about themselves.

So it was comfortable and the staff were great. The third part of the jigsaw was the food. When Y Ming opened, much of Chinatown served a sometimes uninspiring menu of what Christine called 'Cantonese home cooking'. There was quite a lot of animal protein doused in black bean sauce. Christine's menu had some of the expected old stagers because they were great and we all liked them. You could get crispy duck with pancakes. You could get a sweet-corn and crab meat soup. But there was so much else, generally drawing on the northern Chinese repertoire. In time the UK would become familiar with dishes representing the fiery traditions of Sichuan and Hunan province. But some of the earliest dishes with some of that heat were to be found here at Y Ming. The dish titles, often unique to the restaurant, also had a certain mellifluous quality. There was Empress beef and Mr Edward pork,

Tibetan garlic lamb and shredded duck with winter greens. I adored their cumin-crusted spare ribs, which I ordered when I went there alone, which was often. And then there was the double-cooked pork in hot pot, a dish which is very close to my heart. You will, of course, find a recipe for that on page 170.

Y Ming closed at the very end of 2021. Christine told me that her head chef, who had been with her for over a decade, was leaving and she just didn't have it in her to train up someone new. Both she and William needed to move on to the next stages of their lives. She had long worked with various charities and outreach groups associated with the Chinese community. She would focus on that. William became the general manager of Chop Chop, a very good Chinese in the basement of the nearby Hippodrome Casino, run by the company behind Four Seasons in Chinatown, famed for its Cantonese roast meats. I later wrote about the sense of loss my family felt at the closure of Y Ming, and received many desperate messages from other regulars, who wanted to know if I could suggest an alternative Chinese place now it was gone. I simply couldn't.

There were many Y Ming dishes that I was devoted to, but none more so than their deep-fried cauliflower, despite it being possibly the simplest thing on the menu. It really isn't hyperbole to say that it made me reconsider the very possibilities of the humble cauliflower. It clearly had a lot more going for it than I had once thought. I would order the dish whenever I took someone there for the first time and watch the puzzled, wide-eyed look come across their face as they tasted it, the tips of their chopsticks hovering in the air. Yes, I would say. I know. Isn't it.

So thank you, Y Ming: for the memories, for the dinners, for the friendship. And for the crispy cauliflower.

INGREDIENTS

A medium cauliflower
6 tbsp cornflour
1½ tsp kitchen salt
1½ tsp garlic powder
Cracked black pepper
Vegetable oil, for frying

For the topping
6 spring onions, finely chopped
2 cloves of garlic, finely chopped
A thumb-size piece of ginger, peeled and finely chopped
1 or 2 finely chopped fresh red chillies (optional)
2 tsp white wine vinegar
Sea salt

METHOD

1. Bring a large pan of salted water to the boil. Break the cauliflower into florets, and then again into smaller florets. Put into the boiling water and cook for 3 minutes. Drain and lay out on a tray lined with kitchen paper to cool.

2. While the cauliflower is cooling, gently fry the spring onions, garlic, ginger, and chilli (if using) in a little vegetable oil. When the pieces of spring onion are starting to brown, drizzle everything with the white wine vinegar. The pan will sizzle. Move the sizzling ingredients around so they all get a little of the vinegar. Carry on cooking until the pan is dry again.

Sprinkle with a little salt and mix again. Turn off the heat and put the pan to one side.

3. In a bowl mix the cornflour with the salt, garlic powder and a generous pinch or two of cracked black pepper. (If the 6 tablespoons of cornflour turn out not to be enough, either because your cauliflower is especially big or because you're scaling up the recipe to make more, you need half a teaspoon each of garlic powder and salt to 2 tablespoons of cornflour.)

4. Turn the first batch of cauliflower in the cornflour mix.

5. It's time to fry. You can do this in a deep fat fryer, but I prefer to use a deep frying pan or wok with 3–4cm depth of oil in it. Put the pan over a medium to high heat. Test with a small piece of cauliflower. If it immediately fizzes and bubbles, you're good to go.

6. Fry each batch of the cornflour-coated florets until golden brown, turning them over in the oil if only one side is getting done. Remove with a slotted spoon to drain on kitchen paper. Add the next batch.

7. When they're all done, put into a serving bowl, mix with the topping, and serve. Watch the bowl empty at great speed and muse on the ratio of time spent cooking to time spent eating.

Devilled kidneys

Inspired by the version served at the Double Red Duke,
at Bampton in Oxfordshire (and a few other
versions besides)

Some dishes have entered my life, and therefore this collection, through continued exposure. I simply developed a taste for eating them and the job gave me lots of opportunity to do so. Devilled kidneys are one such. There is, after all, nothing new about kidneys swamped in a spiky, buttery sauce. The Scottish essayist and lawyer James Boswell wrote about devilling back in the eighteenth century, and the sainted Mrs Beeton includes a recipe for a devilled sauce, involving Worcestershire sauce, mustard and cayenne, in her famed *Book of Household Management*, first published in 1861. As almost every recipe Mrs Beeton published was lifted from somewhere else, it was clearly very much a thing. Certainly, by the Edwardian era, devilled kidneys had become a staple of the big country house breakfast. Apparently, the Edwardians would devil almost anything, from bones to biscuits to beef.

That said, when I started eating out professionally in 1999, there didn't seem to be a lot of them about. In a 2006 review of Canteen, a brasserie with a then modishly strong British accent, I described devilled kidneys as 'rarely seen', which, to be fair, probably only meant I hadn't seen them very often. They were doubtless still very much present on the menus of devoutly old-school British places like Rules and the Guinea Grill which I hadn't been to for a while. But new places? Not so much.

From the mid-noughties onwards, however, they were increasingly listed on menus. If anyone is to take credit for this growing prominence it has to be Fergus Henderson of

St John, which opened in 1994. Through his repertoire of roasted bone marrow, crispy bacon-wrapped pig spleen and his ways with tripe, many and various, he managed to give a taste for offal a certain glamour and sophistication. It's no accident that the art business loved St John. There was something both conceptual and literally and figuratively visceral about the place. The way he plated dishes sometimes looked like a provocation or a happening. Behold, half a pig head, staring up at you. Damien Hirst put lumps of livestock in glass boxes as a meditation on mortality. Henderson put them on the plate and told you to eat up. As a trend, and it very much was a trend, it reminded me of the feverish cults around certain music tribes in the early 80s, when I was emerging into my teens. The cool kids at my school were the floppy-haired ones in big second-hand overcoats, with a pronounced commitment to the music of Joy Division, Bauhaus and early Cure. They didn't smile much. I wanted to be like them so I grew my fringe, bought an old man's overcoat that smelt of dust and neglect, stopped smiling and did my best to get into the gloomiest of thrumming bass and guitar. It was a phase, one which soon passed, because my heart really wasn't in all that gloom and misery.

As an adult I was a much more eager convert to the trend of animal innards, and remain one. On holidays in France, I willingly ordered andouillette, that chitterling sausage which smells of unscrubbed duodenum, even though French waiters would try to dissuade me. I swooned over the offer of tripe. Once I took the chef Simon Hopkinson out on a review. As a thank-you gift, which was not expected but gratefully received, he presented me with Tupperware boxes filled with peppery tripe stew. I remember his tripe stew. I don't recall where we reviewed. I loved going to Henderson's St John and scooping hot wobbly jewels of bone marrow on to thick wedges of toasted sourdough. There is just a certain joy to dishes that carry with them the faint whiff of death. They make you feel more alive. And, as Fergus Henderson has always said, if you're going to bang an animal on the head for culinary purposes you have a responsibility to consume as much of the carcass as you can, not just the prime cuts. It is therefore unsurprising that his totemic book *Nose to Tail Eating: A Kind of British Cooking*, first published in 1999, included a recipe for devilled kidneys.

Apparently, in his thumping novel *Ulysses* James Joyce describes his protagonist Leopold Bloom as a man who 'liked grilled mutton kidneys which gave to his palate a fine tang of faintly scented urine'. I say apparently, because I have not read *Ulysses*. I've been busy. But I've always rather admired this description of Bloom. I'm not big on the taste of urine, but there is no doubt that kidneys are strongly flavoured. It's what I like about them, and why they take well to being devilled, which is to say cooked in that boisterous sauce full of cayenne and mustard. There are lots of versions about, some of which require the kidneys to be cut up into small pieces and cooked long and slow. To my mind this turns them into bullets. A lot of them avoid any sort of stock in the sauce, insisting instead that it should only be the product of melted butter, cayenne pepper and Worcestershire sauce, with its vinegar and anchovy notes.

The version served to me at the Double Red Duke, a robust food pub not far from Oxford which I reviewed in 2021 as we were coming out of the pandemic, was unashamedly generous, and hyper-glossy. It convinced me that a lot of sauce really is the way to go. Head chef Richard Sandiford, formerly of the Hawksmoor steakhouse group, presented me with the best devilled kidneys I have eaten in years. That version was the inspiration for this.

He halves his kidneys. I quarter mine, mostly because it makes snipping out any remaining connective tissue and fat much easier. I prefer a flash-fry in a fiercely hot pan, so there is still a proper blush of pink at the heart. They need to taste of themselves, which is to say kidney, or there's no point. And yes, I reduce down chicken stock because it gives the sauce body. I'm talking the real stock, the stuff sold in pouches, not the liquid from cube. That of course has its place; it just doesn't happen to be here. If you want other versions of devilled kidneys there's the Fergus Henderson recipe (which in turn draws on Caroline Conran's) or there's the one in Michel Roux's *Les Abats*, his cookbook celebrating 'the whole beast'.

This meanwhile is mine. Note the comment on the teaspoon of mustard right at the end. Wars have been fought over less.

Serves 2 generously

INGREDIENTS

3 tbsp plain flour
1 tsp cayenne pepper
1 tsp English mustard powder
Sea salt and ground black pepper
6 lambs' kidneys, suet and membrane removed, slit in half
    lengthways, then in half again, making it easier to snip out
    any suet and membrane
25g butter (plus a little more if necessary)
½ a medium banana shallot, finely chopped
1 tbsp Worcestershire sauce
200ml real chicken stock, NOT from cube
2 thick cut pieces of toast of your choice, generously buttered
1 good tsp English mustard (or Dijon, if it's what you have
    to hand)

1. Mix the flour with the cayenne pepper, English mustard powder, a good grind of black pepper and a generous pinch of sea salt.

2. Toss the kidneys in the seasoned flour to coat, and shake off any excess.

3. Get a frying pan very hot. Melt the butter, and cook the kidneys for 90 seconds on each side. Remove to a sieve over a bowl, to drain any juices.

4. Fry the chopped shallot for a couple of minutes (add a little extra butter if you think it's needed). Add the Worcestershire sauce, then the stock, and stir to scrape any crusty bits from the bottom. Turn the heat down to medium and reduce to a thick glossy sauce. Meanwhile make the toast. Butter generously while hot.

5. Add the teaspoon of mustard to the reducing sauce. Purists will insist it must be English mustard, for devilled kidneys are an English dish. I get their point. It does also add an extra dash of heat. But the fact is that Dijon does the job too. And you're cooking it for yourself, not anyone else.

6. Return the kidneys to the pan and simmer in the sauce for a couple of minutes. Serve over the toast.

*Flatbreads with brown butter and sage, or
beef dripping and chilli*

Inspired by the flatbreads served at Erst in
Ancoats, Manchester

In August of 2021, I found myself strolling past a restaurant on leafy Metzer Strasse in Berlin. It was called Leibhaftig, and offered a menu of 'Bavarian Tapas'. I posted a photograph of the sign to social media and pointed out that, while we tend to think of mangled food-trend mashups as a weird feature of Britain's try-too-hard culture, they clearly aren't. Here I was in Berlin outside a restaurant offering a Bavarian take on a Spanish tradition. I didn't have time to eat there. For the record several people replied that Leibhaftig, which translates as 'In the flesh', was rather good. Think small servings of sausages, cheese, dumplings, and combinations of all three, sometimes layered on to bread as bruschetta. So a bit of Italian amid the German-Spanish thing. What struck me was the way the now often derided small plates menu had clearly spread everywhere.

Small plates? Haven't we had enough of bloody small plates? You would be entitled to think so, given the growing objections to them. The snark and the eye-rolling have, over the years, been rehearsed in multiple online comments beneath many of my reviews. Ubiquity clearly breeds contempt. (I have more to say on this in the introduction to my recipe for duck à l'orange on page 150.) That said, there have always been some functional issues with so-called small plates, not least too many dishes arriving on tables which are too small to hold them all, in an order which is ill-defined for those who prefer a little more structure.

We may complain, but how food is served to us has never been formally agreed upon. It has always been merely a function of convention and context. I get extremely tetchy if someone I'm eating with in a Chinese restaurant insists that they get to order dishes only for themselves. Mate, you've come to the wrong party. Here, we share. That's how Chinese food works. Didn't you know? Oh, you've ordered the sweet and sour pork. That, you can keep to yourself.

Until the mid-nineteenth century the glitziest of European houses favoured what's called service à la Française for their set-piece dinners. Groups of dishes landed in waves along the table, and diners helped themselves (or, according to etiquette, helped each other). That was eventually replaced by service à la Russe, imported from the court of the Tsars, with diners being served their own individual dishes, in a form we recognize today. It was much quicker, and wasted far less food.

The point is things change. The small plates movement clearly took its lead in the UK from the growing Spanish restaurant sector. Tapas joints seemed to be having so much fun with their dinky terracotta bowls of prawns pil pil, and chorizo in cider, and patatas bravas. Other kitchens wanted a bit of that. Away with the bullying dictatorship of main courses, which demanded that everything on the plate be structured, usually around some central lump of protein. Who wants to eat only two savoury courses? Wouldn't it be more fun to just have loads of stuff?

The first time I mentioned anything like this was in May of 2004, in a review of a very enjoyable now sadly departed restaurant called Le Cercle, located in a basement just off London's Sloane Square. As I explained, 'My tongue is a fickle creature, and so is yours. Like a restless adolescent it bores easily, which is why smaller starters tend to stick in the memory better than huge, galumphing main courses.' As the name suggests, Le Cercle was French. It was a spin-off from a rather fancier place in Smithfield called Club Gascon. While I didn't quite call the food French tapas, I came embarrassingly close to doing so: there were small bowls of a snail persillade, a black pudding pie, and something involving rounds of honking andouillette. I liked it very much. I first used the term 'small plates' later that year in a review of the equally good Mayfair Indian grills restaurant Amaya: a trio of puri here, a few samosas there, maybe a couple of lamb chops. I had clearly got into a groove because the following week, in my first column of 2005, I declared that we were entering the year of small everything. It was, after all, to be the year that Jason Atherton would open the Gordon Ramsay-backed Maze on Grosvenor Square, offering up successions of small but perfectly formed delights. This, I said, was a good thing.

For the most part, however, the small plates menu was a niche affair. It only went mainstream in 2009 with the opening by experienced restaurateur Russell Norman of Polpo, modelled on a Venetian bacaró, or bar. Russell died, far too young, in November of 2023, but his impact on restaurants will be felt for a very long time to come. He popularized single-sheet paper menus, low-wattage filament lightbulbs, bare brickwork, wine in glass tumblers and, for a while, no reservations. He did an excellent job of democratizing restaurant dining, and turning people on to the bitter joys of negronis. If you have a mental image of the modern British bistro its defining qualities were down to Russell, all of which was captured in his cookbooks, particularly *Polpo* and *Brutto*, the latter celebrating the Florentine food served at the restaurant of the same name, which was his last project. The food at Polpo was certainly key: the menu of diminutive fritto misto, chopped liver crostini and cuttlefish in its own ink, crusted with gremolata, was a huge hit, spawning multiple outposts, until over-expansion led to the closure of most of them. By then its job had been done. Small plates were the thing. I came across them everywhere. At Coppi in Belfast in 2017 it was pork and fennel sausages and chicken with romesco sauce; at Jenny Kwak's Haenyeo in Brooklyn in 2020 it was a savoury custard with sea urchin and Swiss chard with miso; at Note in Dublin in 2022 it was anchovy toasts and strips of crispy pig's ear with sauce gribiche. Arguably anyone wishing to declare the small plates movement over could, however, have done so with some validity in 2015 when dear old Pret a Manger trialled a 'Good Evenings' service in a branch on London's Strand. Their small plates dinner menu included a hummus any supermarket would have shifted to the hardware section to be sold as tile grouting, and meatballs of such density they had their own gravitational field.

The fifteen minutes while I sat in a branch of Pret a Manger, waiting for my companion, sipping a tooth-jarringly sweet prosecco, very much made me reconsider my life choices. Pret quickly concluded the experiment had not been a huge success and went back to using that branch for flogging sandwiches, wraps and pretty good coffee.

There is rarely an intrinsically bad food or restaurant trend. (Apart from serving food on slates or in buckets or garden trowels and the like. That is intrinsically awful.) Some people are just really bad at executing certain trends. Then again, some people are really good at them. It became clear to me within just a couple of small plates that the team at Erst in Manchester were the latter. Erst occupies a clean-lined, blocky space in Ancoats, England's first industrial suburb, now transformed into a district of apartments, bars and

quo vadis

A LA CARTE
july 2023

THE *BITE!*

radishes, anchoïade

8

THE QV APERITIVO

bellini 12.5

SMOKED EEL SANDWICH

14.5

WHOLE BAKED GARLIC & CO

17.5

THE DREAM OF THE SMOKED EEL SANDWICH

salade niçoise

21.5

PIE *of the* DAY

22.5

rump of lamb, aubergine, pistachio & parsley sauce

39.5

"soupe du jour" 9.5

jellied pork terrine, green bean chutney 11.5

cured trout, cucumber, mustard & dill 12.5

smoked cod's roe, grilled courgettes, herbs & leaves 12.5

whole globe artichoke vinaigrette 14.5

cannelloni, summer leaves & herbs with three cheeses 23.5

"porchetta tonnata" 28.5

hake, crab broth, tomato, tarragon & rouille 36.5

rabbit, lardo, mustard, tomatoes, & basil 36.5

monkfish, green beans, parsley & anchovy sauce 39.5

 SIDES

new potatoes 6

leaf salad 6.5

green beans 6.5

potato, herb & mustard salad 6.5

QV tomato salad 7

peach, courgette, almond & basil salad 7.5

Quo Vadis, Dean Street, London W1.
2023 / chef: Jeremy Lee

Of course the food at Quo, as it's called by its regulars, is delicious.
But it also boasts a truly beautiful menu, designed by Julian Roberts
with distinctive art by John Broadley. It changes on a monthly basis.

Bocca di Lupo

Soho, London

6 GILLARDEAU OYSTERS 32-
EGG MAYONNAISE WITH CANTABRIAN ANCHOVIES 14-
                    OR PERIGORD TRUFFLES 34-
ESCAROLE, ARTICHOKE AND MIMOLETTE SALAD 14-
HARENG, POMME A L'HUILE 10-
JAMBON DE BAYONNE, CELERIAC REMOULADE 15-
ROSETTE DE LYON, LENTILLES VINAIGRETTE 12-
RILLETTE DE PORC IBAHAMA 12-
DEEP FRIED CALFS BRAIN, SAUCE GRIBICHE 12-
CHEESE ON TOAST WITH PERIGORD TRUFFLE 34-
STEAK TARTARE 12/24-

SKATE, BLACK BUTTER AND CAPERS 32-
FINE HERBE AND CHAMPAGNE ORZO 21- PERIGORD 25-
                                    TRUFFLE SUPP
RABBIT, MUSTARD SAUCE SMOKED BACON 24.50
BAVETTE, SAUCE SAINT MARCELLIN 25.50
VEAL CHOP, ROQUEFORT BUTTER 36-
FILET AU POIVRE 48-
MILK FED LAMBS KIDNEYS, LENTILS GREEN 28-
TÊTE DE VEAU SAUCE RAVIGOTE 21- PEPPERCORN
TO SHARE.
CÔTE DE BOEUF, SAUCE BEARNAISE 95-
ASSIETTE DU BOUCHON 78-

CHIPS 6- GREEN SALAD 6- BUTTERED POTATOES 6-
CREAMED SPINACH W/ FOIE GRAS 8.50
            HARICOT VERT 6-

PEAR AND ALMOND TART 9-50
CRÈME CARAMEL 7- ARMAGNAC PRUNE 3-
POT DE CRÈME, AUX GRIOTTINES 9-50
PETIT POT AU CHOCOLAT 8-
REGALIS AND TOMME DE SAVOIE 12-
MONT BLANC 18-

Bouchon Racine, Cowcross Street, London EC1.
2024 / chef: Henry Harris

The menu at Bouchon Racine, the 2023 rebirth of Harris's original Racine in Knightsbridge, is rewritten on the blackboard every day, and then carried around the dining room from table to table as necessary. Its legibility depends on who was handed the chalk that morning.

restaurants. The kitchen there is led by a former plumber called Patrick Withington, who at twenty-seven gave up one trade to learn another, via a bakery called Trove in Levenshulme. The menu at Erst really was just a list of small dishes designed to go along with drinks. It totalled only nine. We ordered all of them. There was a lamb's heart salad, with grilled green beans and a green chilli sauce. There was a rough-cut steak tartare topped with a dollop of tonnato sauce, a mayo blitzed with tuna, anchovies and capers, as seen in that great Italian old stager vitello tonnato. There were fat, round potatoes, first boiled, then squeezed to bursting from their skins and deep-fried until they formed a mess of golden, crisp crevices and fronds.

But it was these flatbreads, so bubbled and blistered and springy, which really made me swoon. Withington used them as a platform for huge flavours but with the lightest of touches, as if they were pizzas that couldn't quite be bothered to get fully dressed. That first time I ate there, the flatbread was offered two ways. We could have it with freshly chopped tomato pulp, grassy olive oil and a knuckle-crack of garlic, as a gentle take on pan con tomate. Or it came brushed thickly with a herby, garlicky butter. On the side was a quenelle of whipped lardo, the smooth back fat of the pig, for anyone who wanted to baste it further. I described this as dripping toast that had been given a glamorous Hollywood makeover.

The fact is you can put anything on these breads: dollops of the salsa verde from page 22, perhaps with extra salted anchovies; gossamer slices of the best Spanish ham with the chilli relish from page 20. I offer two possibilities here from the Erst playbook, one meat and one vegetarian. The key thing is to slather it all on as quickly as possible. And then tear at it like the ravenous animal you are.

As for the dough, no, its preparation is not quick. Although it's described as a flatbread, it's actually a fully leavened recipe and those do take time; this one especially so. Start the day before.

Makes 8 flatbreads

INGREDIENTS

2g yeast
360ml warm water
500g oo flour
60g rye flour
14g salt
35ml olive oil

METHOD

1. Put the yeast into the warm water for 10 minutes.

2. Meanwhile, mix the flours with the salt in a large bowl.

3. When the 10 minutes are up, pour the water and olive oil into the flours and mix to incorporate. If you have a mixer with a bread paddle, put it on to mix for 5 minutes, or mix gently by hand.

4. Put the dough in a lightly oiled oven tray. Leave at room temperature. Every half hour fold one end into the middle and then the other end over it. Repeat with the sides. Do this four times, across 2 hours.

5. When the 2 hours are up, put the dough into the fridge overnight, covered.

6. The next morning, separate the dough out into 8 equal sized balls, and place back in the fridge until at least an hour before you're ready to cook them. Use a little extra oo flour if it helps you separate out the dough.

7. Take the dough from the fridge at least an hour before you want to cook. When it's time, use your thumbs to ease each ball of dough into a disc at least double the size of the original, so it looks like a slightly thick mini pizza.

8. If you don't happen to have a scorching hot, live-fire grill at home, as they do at Erst, you can bake these quickly in the oven on its highest setting. Lightly oil an oven tray and put it into the oven as it heats up. Once it's smokingly hot, slap a couple of the breads at a time on to the tray and shove it in the top of the oven for 5 minutes, then turn them over for 2 or 3 minutes. They will come out mildly inflated and brown and crisp.

9. However, the best way to cook them at home is using a dry, ridged, cast iron skillet. Put it over a high heat until smoking hot. Turn on the extractor fan. Wait for the smoke alarm to go off. Apologize to everyone in the house. Slap the bread into the pan and cook on one side for 5 minutes until it's starting to blacken in places, then turn on to the other for a couple more minutes. Give it one more minute on the original side then dress with one of the following toppings (or one of your own choice). Cut into four and serve immediately.

Brown butter, sage and Parmesan

Enough for 2 flatbreads

INGREDIENTS

100g unsalted butter
10 fresh sage leaves, shredded
2 tbsp grated Parmesan (use animal rennet free Parmesan to
   keep it vegetarian)
Sea salt and ground black pepper
White wine vinegar

METHOD

1. Melt the butter over a medium heat. It will start to
   fizz and foam, as moisture cooks off. Carry on
   cooking. Watch the colour darken from straw yellow
   to light brown. When you see brown speckles at the
   bottom of the pan, take it off the heat and chuck in
   the shredded sage leaves.

2. Let it fizz for 10 seconds or so, then pour everything
   out of the pan and into a bowl. Stir in the Parmesan,
   season generously with salt and pepper to taste, and
   add a splash of white wine vinegar. Stir to combine.
   As it cools it will of course start to solidify. Do not
   worry. When you spread it liberally on the hot bread,
   and liberally is the way to do this, it will melt again.

3. Add an extra grating of Parmesan and a grind of
   black pepper if you wish.

Beef dripping and chilli

This will make far too much but it's impossible to make in tiny volumes

INGREDIENTS

100g beef dripping
1 tbsp Dijon mustard
1 tsp chilli flakes
½ tsp sea salt
A good grind of black pepper
10 cornichons and a bunch of fresh chives, roughly chopped, to
   garnish, and dressed in the pickling liquor from the
   cornichons

METHOD

1. Heat the beef dripping in a pan over a medium heat until it's completely melted. Transfer to a bowl big enough to whip it in. Let it cool for about half an hour, until it starts to go cloudy, which is a sign that it's resolidifying.

2. When it reaches that point, use an electric hand mixer to whip the dripping. It will turn white and creamy. Mix in the mustard, chilli flakes, salt and pepper, and whip again. Adjust the seasoning. It will stay soft at room temperature.

3. Smear the seasoned beef fat on to the hot flatbread liberally. Top with the vinegared mix of chives and cornichon.

Intercourse: No, I am not Marco

One day in the early autumn of 2006 I took a train from London Paddington to Swansea and from there a connection to Carmarthen in the depths of west Wales, where I picked up a taxi. About twenty minutes later I arrived at a sturdy whitewashed pub called Y Polyn, tucked into the junction of two country roads. I went inside and announced to the man behind the bar that I had a table for one booked that evening in the name of Mr James. He nodded slowly, and said, 'Yes sir, but we both know that's not your name.'

I have never really been anonymous. I am fully aware of the argument in favour of anonymity for restaurant critics. It means that you are, or should be, treated just like any other customer. They don't know who you are and what you're doing there, and will not therefore be tempted to try to show you an especially good or even just a better time than anyone else. Your experience would be clear-eyed and unadorned; it would be unsullied by attempts to pelt you with freebies and hose you down with the Cristal.

The anonymous restaurant critic is the very Platonic ideal of the trade's practitioner.

In which case, I should never really have been allowed anywhere near the job. Certainly, a bit of notoriety came with the family name. By the time I was born in 1966 my late mother, Claire, was already well known as a newspaper columnist and writer, and would become only more so as the years and the television work piled up. She was on television as an agony aunt in the 80s and 90s when, for the most part, there were just four channels. If you even just burped on TV back then millions saw it, and she did a lot more than that, turning up first as pundit, and later as the host of her own shows. I well recall the bow wave that would form as the family processed along the streets of London's West End, perhaps to the theatre or dinner out, Claire to the fore; the way people would keep their faces still, their gaze fixed ahead, until just after they'd passed her and would then gesticulate furiously to each other about who they had just seen. For her the public's faces were for the most part placid; for us, walking a few footsteps behind, it was a sudden chaos of jabbing fingers and whispered blather. This, as a child, was what fame looked like.

Some of that would eventually head my way, at first by association. When I was sixteen years old, I was suspended from school for smoking dope, and because Claire was famous it made the newspapers. Even if my face wasn't out there, my name was. A couple of years later, when I was a student, I was asked if I would appear on a TV show called *Whose Baby?*, in which a celebrity panel tried to guess which famous parent the young person in front of them belonged to, by asking pointed questions. It sounded like a fun day out for an inveterate show-off, and there was a bit of dosh involved too, so I did it. I hadn't clocked that it was the sort of late-afternoon TV a lot of students at Leeds University where I was studying would watch. It felt like everyone on campus saw it go out. In any case, by then I was a classic student hack, working my way up through the editorial ranks of the large student newspaper I would eventually win the cross-campus ballot to edit. Already, whether I liked it or not, more people knew me than I knew, which is the most basic definition of fame.

To be clear, I did like it. At any point, as my career in journalism developed, I could have declined the offers of work first on radio and then on television to go alongside my job as a print journalist. But I didn't, partly because the disciplines interested me, partly because it was flattering and partly, of course, because it was a way of earning extra money, and financial independence is the most obvious kind of independence. I presented documentaries for Channel 4. I became the food reporter on BBC1's *The One Show*. Eventually I became one of the critics on *MasterChef*, a perfect job for someone who was partial to a bit of infamy. The audience is so huge that, although I only film with them for perhaps five or six days a year, it has made me very visible. That said, the level of recognition is limited. A lot of the time people will squint at me and say, 'Aren't you famous?' The answer is in the question: if you don't know who I am then obviously not. Or there are those who, because they recognize me as a big man, with big hair, who has something to do with food, insist that I am the chef Marco Pierre White. Google us. We look nothing like each other. But that's the name they reach for. Some of these people can be extremely insistent, despite being told repeatedly that, no, I'm not Marco. I've even had to get out my debit card to prove it. Such is my vast level of fame; I like to think he suffers the same problem in reverse. In the smartphone age the familiar way to acknowledge that you've come across someone you recognize and whose work you appreciate is to ask for a selfie. I am always flattered to be asked and generally happy to oblige, though with one condition. I check they know who I am, and I don't just mean 'that bloke off *MasterChef*'. Do they actually know my name? In this I believe I am doing them a favour. After all, why would they want a picture of themselves with a stranger? About half the time they don't know my name, which is just fine.

In 1999, when I became the *Observer*'s restaurant critic, I hadn't done much television work so none of this was an issue. For the column it really didn't matter anyway, because by then I had that thing so highly prized among newspaper journalists: a picture by-line. My mug had been staring down from beside the headline on news reports, features and celebrity profiles for a good few years. In those days there were relatively few companies doing PR for restaurants compared to now. For the most part all they really cared about were the eight or so people who reviewed for the nationals. I quickly learned that part of their job was to supply their clients with photographs of the critics. Within a few weeks a picture of me, usually a blow-up of my by-line pic, was on the wall of professional kitchens across London, alongside those of my colleagues. A few weeks after that, some of them had been graffitied with rifle crosshairs. They were watching for me.

And that's the point. In the restaurant reviewing game, you don't need to be your actual, fame-hungry celebrity to lose your anonymity. Indeed, maintaining any anonymity at all is very difficult. Famously, the *New York Times* restaurant critics, in common with most in the US, have long made their anonymity a cornerstone of their practice. Absolutely no picture by-lines for them. Plus, the job was well enough paid that they didn't have to countenance the shoddy idea of additional careers in TV or radio. But long before the advent of the Internet in general and social media in particular, the New York restaurant world would quickly work out and share the vital intelligence on who the *Times* critic was. Jolly stories circulated about Frank Bruni, the *New York Times* critic from 2004 to 2009, using disguises, a rumour he refused to confirm or deny when I put it to him at the time, but which he later confirmed after he quit. Still, numerous New York chefs and restaurateurs told me they knew what he looked like anyway. Before I met him in person, I knew what the current incumbent, Pete Wells, looked like. There were pictures out there. In 2013, over eight years before he stepped down as critic for *New York Magazine*, Adam Platt abandoned what he called the 'time-honoured kabuki dance that takes place between chefs and restaurateurs and the people whose job it is to cover them', by allowing his face to be slapped on the magazine's cover. Not least because he knew he was no longer anonymous. As the American food TV host Andrew Zimmerman put it in a tweet: 'Big Reveal . . . for the 3 People in NYC who don't know what he looks like.'

The big question is this: does it really matter? Honestly, no. It is common to compare restaurants with theatre, and not simply because they both can entail a certain amount of performance. Both are dependent on preparation in advance. The producers of a play can't change the script, or the lighting, the set or the cast or the music just because someone in particular happens to be in the audience. Likewise, restaurants can't change their recipes or their ingredients, their front of house staff or their glassware, just because I turn up to eat. Or to put it another way, bad restaurants can't suddenly become good because of who is sitting at table seven.

We can, however, make sure they don't know we're coming. Yes, I book under a pseudonym. On the night I arrived by myself at Y Polyn, I had booked under the name of the protagonist of a soon-to-be-published novel of mine, *The Oyster House Siege*. Nathan James was a petty crook dragged into a robbery gone wrong, leading to a hostage situation in a restaurant kitchen, in which everyone starts cooking. At other times I would use Basset, the surname of a fictional restaurant critic from another novel of mine called *The Apologist*, about a man who decides to apologize for everything he's ever done wrong and who becomes so good at it he's appointed Chief Apologist to the United Nations, tasked with travelling the world apologizing for the sins of slavery, colonialism and the rest of it. I was tickled by the idea of my fictional critic, Marc Basset, emerging out into the real world by booking tables.

Most of the time, however, it's much more prosaic than that: I book under the name of my dining companion. In the age of online booking platforms, I also have a few 'alternative' email addresses. It's hardly the stuff of James Bond, but it works.

And now, here I am through the door. Surely, they can try to show me an extra special time? Yes, they can but I am wise to it. They can try sending me things I didn't order, 'because the chef would like you to try it'. I always send them back with a polite request only to be given the things I requested. I've seen portion sizes increased. At one restaurant it was sardine persillade: fillets spread with garlic and chopped green herbs and grilled. I was seated near the pass, so saw numerous portions go out and each time, it was two fillets. Until it arrived with me, when it was three. Did they really think I wouldn't notice? It was a clumsy and unattractive move that went into the review. Then there's the attempts at preferential service. There have been occasions when I have received my order before the people at the next table, who were already seated before I arrived. I've pointed it out. The general manager of one rather sprauncy urban brasserie in London once told me, after I'd reviewed, that if they have a critic in, they up the level of service at the half dozen tables surrounding them. I concluded that if they could pull that off, they probably deserved a good review. Finally, there is the bill. When most people send a bill back to be corrected it's because there's something on there they didn't have: a couple of extra cocktails they didn't order, or a dish they did order but which never turned up. In my case, if I ever send a bill back to be corrected, and it happens quite a lot, it's because it's missing things I did order, presumably in an attempt to make the experience look less expensive than it actually was.

This makes me look rather po-faced and self-important, doesn't it. After all, I'm not reporting on race crime or social injustice or political incompetence (although over the years I have covered all those things). I am reporting from the front line of the mighty struggle for dinner. From time to time, I've been asked if, when I show up, restaurants lose it. The truth is that if they're any good at what they do, if they have confidence in their restaurant, then no. Or at least not in my presence. Perhaps they go into the kitchen and swear about the utter tosser who has just sat down to eat. Behind the kitchen door or in the back bar or out the back by the bins they can call me whatever they like. I probably deserve a lot of it. Meanwhile I'll just get on with my job, such as it is.

Which is exactly what I did at Y Polyn on that dark night in 2006. I acknowledged that no, my surname wasn't James, but I did still have a booking for one and perhaps he could show me to my table. He grinned, nodded and seated me. The food pub was a project by a couple of chaps who had once edited and reviewed for the *AA Restaurant Guide*. Now they had crossed the road to join the hospitality business they had once surveyed. I had their deep, lustrous rust-coloured fish soup, topped in the traditional style with a thick Gruyère-laden toasted crouton, and garlicky rouille. I followed that with pieces of medium rare saltmarsh lamb and a treacle tart to finish. It was that endlessly attractive thing: the best ingredients, shown off to their best advantage by sensitive and tasteful cookery. No, they hadn't known I was coming. No, they hadn't expected a restaurant critic. But they knew exactly what they were doing when I got there. And that was all that mattered.

Meat

All the roast chickens

Inspired by the birds at L'Ami Louis, La Petite
Maison and Zuni Café

Restaurants struggle with the domestic. You almost certainly
make better roast potatoes than any restaurant does. I know
I do. Now, of course, you want my method. Here you go:
peel the potatoes and cut them into mid-sized pieces but
make sure a few are cut small. This will be important later.
Boil the potatoes until almost totally cooked. Drain and chill
in the fridge in one layer for at least an hour, but ideally for
two. Put about 1½cm of vegetable oil into an oven tray and
shove it into a hot oven for 15 minutes until smoking. Add
the potatoes, turning them in the sizzling oil, then roast for

about 45 minutes to an hour until golden and crisp, turning them again every 10 or 15 minutes. Along the way steal all the small ones, which will be ready far quicker and which are your reward for going to all this bloody trouble for everyone else. Drain them briefly on kitchen paper, season with sea salt and serve immediately.

In restaurants, roast potatoes are too often under-roasted, or stodgy from having been made too far in advance. They're under-seasoned, too big and just not crisp enough. They are the word 'disappointment' fashioned out of carbohydrate. The problem is that they really need to be made to order but they take too long to make on service. Similar issues apply with things like apple crumble and, of course, the great British Sunday lunch, which is not a moment for poise and finesse, but for generosity and gravy. Lots of gravy. It makes sense, I think, that the best Sunday lunch I have ever had in a restaurant was in a place called the Lamplighter Dining Rooms in the Lake District. It wasn't the most elegant or classy of spaces. It was like eating in your nan's front room, sometime around 1983. What mattered was the food. You had to tell them what roast you wanted and for how many people, at least forty-eight hours before getting there. Basically, it's like calling your parents and telling them you'll be home this weekend for lunch. And yes of course I want the cauliflower cheese. It's completely domestic. It's the only way to get it right.

Then there's roast chicken. Over the past quarter century I have been subjected to far too many desperate and dismal versions of what should be a basic test of any kitchen's abilities. You know the deal: flaccid skin, dry meat, no flavour, no hope. I long ago concluded it was not something that was worth ordering. Occasionally, though, I would hear about a roast chicken that simply had to be tried and a few of them justified the buzz. In 2018, for example, I found myself in San Francisco with the chance to go to the famed Zuni Café, the restaurant made famous by the late Judy Rodgers, in turn a graduate from Chez Panisse just across the bay. Her roast chicken, cooked in a wood-fired oven, was talked about by friends of mine in hushed tones. The recipe in the *Zuni Café Cookbook* fills over four pages and involves pre-salting the bird for 24 hours before stuffing fresh herbs under the skin with nimble fingers, then taking it to a retrospective of Bergman movies and discussing with it the significance of the figure of death in his oeuvre. If you follow the recipe to the letter you do get to spend a lot of time with that chicken, so you might as well incorporate it into your life. And the result? Very nice indeed, if a little short on lubrication. Much of the excitement comes from the accompanying salad full of crisp croutons fried in chicken fat.

These trophy roast chicken dishes tend to big up the bird they're using. At La Petite Maison in London's Mayfair, for example, it's a black leg chicken, roasted with big fat slabs of baguette which soak up the garlicky juices (and a lobe of foie gras which nobody needs; it's just structured fat). It was a revelation when it first went on the menu in 2007 at £35 for two; fifteen years later it costs £130 and rising. And then there's the equally spendy chicken at L'Ami Louis in Paris, which first opened in 1924. The late A. A. Gill once wrote a piece for *Vanity Fair* describing L'Ami Louis as the worst restaurant in the world. He objected, I think, to the way in which it bought into all the clichés of the French bistro, including the knowingly battered interior, sold at enormous expense. Come for classic dishes which laugh in the face of innovation and huge wines from big names at stupid prices. It's where Orson Welles ate. It's where François Mitterrand brought Bill Clinton. But then Paris has always been superb at nurturing its clichés and at the right time I love a bit of that. I have been only once, for my fortieth birthday. We had the poulet de Bresse avec pommes allumette. Yes, the chicken and chips, which was every bit as expensive as that at La Petite Maison. But oh, what a chicken, and oh, what chips. The bird had deep, dark, crisp skin and flavourful meat. The chips were matchstick thin and came in a rustling heap a foot high. It didn't matter what you did to them: eat them, stick them in your ears, throw them in your neighbour's lap. They never seemed to be finished. I was a very happy birthday boy.

My table at L'Ami Louis was booked for me by Simon Hopkinson, the founding chef at Terence Conran's Bibendum in 1987, itself a tribute to classic bourgeois bistro cookery. The title recipe in *Roast Chicken and Other Stories*, the hugely loved cookbook he wrote with Lindsey Bareham, is partly based on that served at L'Ami Louis, which is the excuse he gives for the huge, shameless volumes of butter employed. While he loves great produce, he does not fetishize the quality of the bird. What matters is the cooking. As he writes, 'A good cook can produce a good dish from any old scrawbag of a chook. A poor cook will produce a poor dish even from a Bresse chicken.' The Paris-based American food writer Patricia Wells describes the recipe in her 1989 book *Bistro Cooking* as literally 'L'Ami Louis's Roast Chicken' and favours poultry fat – presumably duck fat – over butter, but has a great tip involving the giblets, if you can get them.

My method merges those of both Hopkinson and Wells, with a touch of La Petite Maison. It involves a fast roast at high temperature and shouldn't take much more than seventy-five minutes. It's damn good. Trust me.

INGREDIENTS

1 chicken, with giblets, roughly 1.5–2kg (but smaller is fine)
Sea salt and ground black pepper
100g salted butter at room temperature
1 lemon
Sprigs of fresh thyme if you have them, but no worries if not
A day-old baguette

METHOD

1. Take the chicken from the fridge a couple of hours before it's time to cook, so it can lose some of its chill. Remove the giblets from the cavity and set to one side.

2. When ready to cook, heat the oven to 220°C/425°F/ gas mark 7.

3. While the oven is heating, season the bird liberally with salt and pepper, then slather on the butter in a thick overcoat, across the breast and over the legs. Your chicken should end up looking like it's wearing a yellow duvet of butter. Take a photograph and send it to your friends or they won't believe what you've done.

4. Put the chicken into an oven tin big enough so there's a little space around the bird.

5. Slice the lemon in two and squeeze over the juice of both halves.

6. Season the cavity with salt and pepper.

7. Take the giblets out of their plastic bag and insert them into the cavity with half the squeezed lemon

and the thyme if you have it. If your chicken didn't come with giblets, don't worry. It will still be delicious.

8. Put into the preheated oven. Every 15 minutes or so, baste with the juices.

9. After 45 minutes turn the chicken on to its breast, season its back and return to the oven for about 10 minutes.

10. During this time cut 4–6 long, thick diagonal rounds from the baguette, depending on how much space you have in the tin.

11. After 10 minutes, when the back has a little colour, return the chicken to the breast-up position. Surround it with the pieces of baguette. Return it to the oven. After another 5 or so minutes, take it out and turn over the buttery, juices-sodden croutons, as they most surely now are. Return to the oven for another 10 minutes. The bird's juices should run clear when it's pricked between breast and leg, and the legs should move easily when tugged. If either of these is not the case, return it to the oven for another 10 minutes.

12. Take the bird out and let it rest for at least 15 minutes, under foil.

13. Before carving, lift the whole bird up vertically over the tin, so that all the juices from the giblets which will have steamed inside can add to what's in the pan. Remove the giblets and discard.

14. Make sure everyone gets a crouton when you serve up the chicken. Spoon over the pan juices.

Malaysian chicken curry

Inspired by the dish served at Bugis Street
Brasserie, Kensington

Sometimes, to get to the good food, I first have to eat the bad food. In this case the bad food was symbolized by an egg so over-boiled, a thick green rim had developed around the yolk. It's caused by a reaction between the sulphur in the yolk and the hydrogen in the whites to produce hydrogen sulphide. This is more information than anybody needs. Just know that a green-rimmed yolk is not something anybody wants to see on a badly made Caesar salad. Or anywhere for that matter. I ended up with that egg because, in May 2019, I received an email from a chef at a Holiday Inn on London's Cromwell Road and wanted to do the right thing.

They had recently opened their new restaurant, he said. Would I come and review it? The arguments for not doing so were splendid. Given its proximity to Heathrow, it was clearly an airport hotel. What was the likelihood of finding a good meal in one of those? I certainly never had. Surely that was where appetite went to die? The opposing arguments were equally splendid. Wasn't dismissing out of hand the offering at such a hotel just pure, unalloyed snobbery? Not that I necessarily disapprove of snobbery. After all, isn't one person's snobbery just another person's informed discernment? Still, the dining rooms of airport hotels are places people go to eat, less out of choice than expediency. They have a flight to catch early the next morning. They need dinner. Why shouldn't those people get good food? Why shouldn't those kitchens be capable of cooking well? This head chef was so confident in his offering he had emailed a restaurant critic. Surely it would be churlish not to accept?

So I went, with hope in my heart and credit on my card. It was, of course, all kinds of awful. There was a Caesar dressing that tasted of emulsifier and despair. Salt and pepper squid shed its breadcrumb shell the moment it was nudged with a fork, like a snake with heat exhaustion. On a menu that attempted to explore the entire world, but got completely lost en route, there was a beef rendang which, I said, was 'a mud-coloured slippery splatter of a stew, with a blunt hint of tired spice'. I wrote my review by opening the barrel and shooting all the fish.

But good things really do come from bad. I noted, as a way of making a point about this being an airport hotel, that the beautifully dressed Singapore Airlines crew were boarding a bus as I arrived, presumably on their way to their next flight. In the comments section, a reader pointed out that, while the Singapore Airlines crew might sleep at the Holiday Inn, they were often to be found eating at the Bugis Street Brasserie, then located inside the Millennium Gloucester Hotel, just across the road from the back door. (It has since moved down the road to the Bailey's Hotel, owned by the same management.) It was, he said, famed for its menu of dishes from Singapore and Malaysia. Maybe I should revisit that corner of town and this time go to the right restaurant.

Happily, I did. The Bugis Street Brasserie is named after a renowned area at the heart of Singapore. In the days before the city state became known for a morally authoritarian government that prohibited even the selling of chewing gum, Bugis had a delicious reputation for loucheness. Bugis Street was a welcoming space for people of all sexualities and genders and for those who merely wanted to walk among them. That is long gone, but the sense of Singapore as an Asian culinary crossroads is very much intact on the menu. I ate smoky pieces of chicken satay, hot off the grill, with a peanut sauce layered with aromatics and spice. There was a laksa of profound depths and thrills, and a classic nasi goreng of spiced rice mined with chicken and prawns and topped with a golden-yolked fried egg.

And then there was the Malaysian chicken curry. Oh, that chicken curry. It looked vaguely terrifying: chicken thighs, on the bone, bobbed in a deep, brooding rust-coloured liquor, which lay in turn beneath a heavy layer of transparent oil, as if it was contained by a glass tabletop. In the long-cooked mixture of aromatics and coconut milk, spices and chilli, it tasted very much like the place where the Indian subcontinent and Thailand had met and decided to become close, intimate friends. It was also one of the most thoroughly comforting dishes I had ever eaten. I'd tried other versions, particularly at C&R Café, a tiny Malaysian restaurant tucked away down an alley just off London's Chinatown. It too was delightful, but the broth was much thinner. I preferred the substantial, sustaining version at Bugis.

I went searching for recipes. Curiously, all the ones I found online were for skinless chicken fillet. And yet every time I had eaten it in a restaurant the chicken had been served with bone and skin intact, and rightly so. Personally, I rather like the slippery texture of long-stewed chicken skin. I understand many disagree but even if you end up removing them, both add something to the richness and depth of flavour during the cooking. Any recipe that I came up with would, like that at the Bugis Street Brasserie, have to involve bone-in thighs and drumsticks. Just put a bowl in the middle of the table for the bits you want to discard.

Serves 2 greedy people, or 4 with a bit of self-control

INGREDIENTS

vegetable oil for cooking
800g bone-in, skin-on chicken thighs and drumsticks (roughly 4
    thighs and 2 drumsticks)
Kitchen salt
400ml coconut milk
1 lemongrass stalk, bashed about a little
1 cinnamon stick
2 star anise
1 tbsp fresh lime juice
1 tsp caster sugar
250g peeled potatoes, sliced into chunks

For the spice paste
6 dried red chillies
5 small shallots, peeled and chopped
4cm piece of ginger, peeled and chopped
3cm piece of galangal, peeled and chopped (or more ginger if
    you can't get galangal)
3 cloves of garlic, chopped
1 lemongrass stalk, white part only, chopped
4 macadamia nuts or 8 cashews
1 tsp belacan shrimp paste (substitute with 2 tbsp fish sauce if
    unavailable)
1½ tsp ground turmeric

METHOD

1. Put the dried chillies into a bowl with enough hot
   water to cover for about 15 minutes, until soft.
   Remove the chillies. Reserve the chilli soaking water.
   Roughly chop the chillies and put them into a food
   processor with all the remaining ingredients for the

paste – apart from the turmeric – and a large pinch of salt. Blend until smooth. If it seems too rough or isn't blending, add a little of the water in which the chillies were soaked, a tablespoon at a time. Pour the paste into a bowl and mix in the turmeric. It will save turning your food processor yellow.

2. Put 3 tablespoons of oil into a saucepan or, better still, a large wok, and place over a high heat. Season the chicken pieces with kitchen salt. Add to the pan skin side down, in batches if necessary. Cook until the skin has started to crisp and turn golden. Take the chicken out of the oil and set to one side.

3. Pour away the old oil, and add 4 tablespoons of fresh. Heat the pan on high, then reduce to medium and add the paste. Stir it often as the water cooks off. Wear an apron, to avoid getting splattered. After 10 minutes or so, you will see the oil rise to the surface.

4. Add the chicken pieces and cook on high, stirring so they become caked in the ever-thickening paste. This should take about another 10 minutes.

5. Add the coconut milk, lemongrass, cinnamon stick, star anise, a fat pinch of salt and 125ml of water, and turn the heat down low. Cook gently for about 45 minutes until the sauce thickens, stirring every now and then.

6. Season with a tablespoon of lime juice, a teaspoon of sugar and more salt to taste.

7. While the curry is cooking, boil the potatoes until just done. Drain and add to the pot. Allow to simmer for at least 5 minutes before serving.

8. The curry can be served immediately, or held for a day or two in the fridge, allowing the flavours to meld and deepen. Just warm gently when you are ready to eat.

9. Serve with rice.

Chicken in a mustard sauce

Inspired by the rabbit in a mustard sauce served
by Henry Harris at Racine

The people who write about food in Britain, be it served in restaurants or for recipes and features, can be a fractious lot. Some enthuse about a particular chef; others think they're not all that. Some swear by a certain maker of Stilton; others insist their direct competitor is far superior. Occasionally, though, everyone agrees. In the thirteen years from 2002 that chef Henry Harris's restaurant Racine was open, I didn't come across anyone who had a bad word to say about it. Racine, on the Brompton Road in London's Knightsbridge, was everybody's fantasy version of a bourgeois French country restaurant made real. Harris had grown up in a family which paid keen attention to the joys of the table and, with his brother Matthew, was part of the original brigade at Bibendum, led by Simon Hopkinson, in a kitchen celebrating the classics. He was deep-steeped in this food. At Racine, Harris did it all: fish soup the colour of copper coins and leeks vinaigrette, calves' brains in black butter with capers and duck confit with lentils, steak tartare and of course his rabbit in a mustard sauce with smoked bacon. It was all so damn comforting.

Harris closed Racine in 2015, but this repertoire stayed with him, and was for a while allowed to see the light of day at a group of London pubs for which he was the executive chef. Then in late 2022 he and Dave Strauss, another industry veteran famed for his gifts front of house, decided to reprise Racine above the Three Compasses pub in Farringdon. At an age when most cooks have decided the job is just too physically daunting, he went back to the stove. And of course, the opening menu included his rabbit in a mustard sauce. The sauce is old-school: glossy, deep and profound. The compounds which give mustard its heat are deactivated through cooking, so what you get is flavour rather than fire. I made up this version years ago and use it with chicken thighs, not least because rabbit isn't always that easy to get hold of. If you do decide to go with rabbit, it has to be farmed. Wild is far too tough for grilling and is only really good for braising and terrines. The original dish includes rashers of crisped smoked bacon perched on the top. In mine the bacon is part of the sauce. The key to it is to roast the chicken thighs, until the skin is really crisp.

INGREDIENTS

1 large onion, sliced into rings
6–8 bone-in, skin-on chicken thighs
200g smoked bacon lardons
2 tbsp olive oil
Sea salt and ground black pepper
A couple of knobs of butter
Half a dozen fat cloves of garlic (optional)
400ml chicken stock from cube
100ml double cream
Dijon mustard

1. Heat the oven to 220°C/425°F/gas mark 7. You're going to roast these chicken thighs hot and fast.

2. Put the sliced onion across the bottom of an oven pan. Place the chicken thighs on top, skin side up. Chuck the lardons over and around them. Dribble on a couple of tablespoons of olive oil, season liberally with salt and pepper and add 2 good knobs of butter. Throw in the cloves of garlic. They aren't important to the recipe. I just can't resist the opportunity to roast garlic with chicken thighs. They go soft and mellow and squidgy and can be eaten whole.

3. Roast the chicken thighs in the oven for around 45 minutes, and certainly until the skin is crisp. Baste them every 15 minutes or so. About halfway through the cooking give them 10 minutes skin side down so the backs also crisp up. Then turn back skin side up for another 10 minutes so the skin is really crisp.

4. While the chicken is roasting, warm a serving dish which is big enough and has high enough sides to restrain the sauce.

5. When the thighs are done, take them out of the pan, shaking off any caramelized rings of onion or lardons. Put the chicken in the serving dish to rest. It will not get cold and will benefit hugely from the 15 minutes or so rest it will take to make the sauce.

6. The pan will have lots of fabulous juices in it. Put it on a medium heat, and pour in the stock from cube, scraping up everything from the bottom of the pan. Let it bubble away and reduce a little for 5 minutes.

7. Pour in the double cream and whisk to incorporate into the stock. Let it simmer and thicken further (but don't let it boil).

8. Whisk in a good tablespoon of Dijon mustard. Taste. (Always taste.) If you think it can take more, add a teaspoon at a time. Dijon mustard is a very good emulsifier and it will bring the whole thing together.

9. Once it has thickened enough to lightly coat the back of a wooden spoon, pour everything in the tray over the chicken thighs.

10. Serve with rice, or crusty bread and a sharp green salad. Pretend you're a rustic French farmer.

Life lessons: learning to cook fesenjan

At Persian Cottage, Middlesbrough

Mohsen Geravandian doesn't so much cook ingredients, as interrogate them. He leans his compact body into the rim of a covered pot to sniff, and shifts his head from side to side to detect any changes in the situation from one location to another. He stirs another pot with a graceful arm and shoulder motion, and lifts his chin as he studies the surface of a bubbling liquor for signs that there have been the necessary developments. 'The smell of food will tell you when it's done,' he says. And: 'The stirring of the food makes it beautiful. It is all about the attention.' No, he says, he has not written down a recipe for the dish he is preparing for me, here in the tidy kitchen of Persian Cottage, his Iranian restaurant in Middlesbrough. If I want to learn how to make the mighty ground walnut and pomegranate molasses chicken stew that is fesenjan, I will have to pay attention. I will have to ask the right questions.

Deciding to review Persian Cottage in 2019 felt like a punt on my part. We were due to record an episode of *The Kitchen Cabinet* in Middlesbrough, a north Yorkshire town around an hour's drive to the south of Newcastle. Middlesbrough has one major claim to food fame: the mighty parmo. The word is short for chicken Parmesan, even though these days it is generally made with Cheddar. It refers to a large chicken or pork schnitzel which is breaded and fried, then topped with béchamel sauce and cheese, and grilled until golden and bubbling. It was created by a former US Navy chef called Nicos Harris, who had been treated in Middlesbrough for injuries sustained during the Second World War. He decided to stay on in the town and eventually opened a restaurant where, in 1958, he started serving the chicken Parmesan. Over the years the current version has become a fixture of fast food and café menus in the town and is now, depending on your point of view, either a distinctive regional dish, or the very last word in drunk food. Perhaps it is simply both. It is certainly delicious.

Middlesbrough has rarely been disturbed by national newspaper restaurant critics. For me to go there and review a restaurant serving parmos would be lazy in the extreme. In any case, we would be both talking about and tasting them during the recording of the show. I needed to find something else. A deep dive into the often unreliable online review sites and local blogs led me to Persian Cottage. I booked a table for the eight of us, on the grounds that you rarely eat badly in a Middle Eastern grill house. It was a very good call. We loved the smoky chicken kebabs, stained yellow by their turmeric-boosted marinade, and the spiced minced lamb kebabs and of course the buttery wonder that is the Persian way with rice, each fluffy long grain seemingly resting upon, rather than sticking to its neighbour. And then there was the sweet and sour fesenjan. It's as dark as night from the pomegranate molasses, and dense and slightly oily from the huge volume of ground walnuts with which it is made. It really was unlike anything else I had ever tried.

The story of the man behind the restaurant which served it to us is equally extraordinary. Today Mohsen is a highly respected businessman, providing employment to members of his family and the wider Iranian community. He drives a shiny Volvo. His restaurant has won awards and plaudits. In 2000, however, he was just another asylum seeker, stowing away in the back of a truck crossing the Channel from Calais. He set foot on UK soil for the first time by clambering out of the back of that truck. It was the last leg of a journey which had taken him across Turkey, Greece and Europe, often on foot, in search of safety and freedom. 'I had to leave Iran,' he tells me, over a thimble-sized glass of hot sweet Persian tea, before we start cooking. 'I got drunk at a friend's wedding. The police caught me and put me in prison for three months. By the time I came out I was a marked man.'

Leaving was a massive wrench. He was close to his family, he says. His late father was a respected chef and restaurateur in the southern Iranian town of Ahvaz, close to the shores of the Persian Gulf, and Mohsen was the one of his nine children who had wanted to be a cook. 'As a kid I used to sit on the table next to him in the kitchen and try to do what he was doing,' he told me. But now he really had to go. After a period in an asylum-seeker centre in Essex he went to stay with friends in London, where he found work as a cook in various Persian restaurants. Later he opened a falafel stall and another serving shawarma in Camden Market. Then he got a call from one of his brothers who had flown into the UK with his wife, also to seek asylum. 'He sent me a photograph of the address where he had been sent by the UK government, because he had no idea where he was. It was in Middlesbrough.' After coming and going from the town for a few months, Mohsen decided to make his life there with his extended family. In 2015 he opened his restaurant in this former shisha bar, polishing the wood floors until they shone, hanging the wood-panelled walls with Persian art, and working hard to remove the less than desirable tenants in the flat upstairs. 'It was hard at first,' he says. 'People kept telling me to serve parmos and chips but I didn't want to do that.' Bit by bit the local Persian community found him.

I ask him if he learnt the fesenjan he now serves from his father. 'No,' he says. 'He didn't make it. My mother used to make a version but it was very different. She made hers with a lot of tomato. I learnt mine from the Persian chef I trained with in London.' There are, he says, many ways to make it. 'There are as many recipes as there are people making it.' A little research tells me it can also be made with lamb and duck, or topped with meatballs rather than whole cuts. There is also a Sephardic Jewish version of fesenjan, a recipe for which appears in Claudia Roden's *Book of Jewish Food*, but it reads like a half-forgotten echo of the original northern Iranian dish. It measures out the walnuts and pomegranate molasses in a few tablespoons, whereas Mohsen practically measures his out in kilos and litres.

In the kitchen he gets two big pots on the go. In one a

couple of onions, sliced into fine rings, are cooking down. Eventually they will be spiced with turmeric and black pepper and a little sunset-yellow saffron water. The other pot is home to a huge drift of ground walnuts. These are being toasted in the dry pan over a low heat, and must be turned and turned again so that the ones which end up at the bottom are never given enough time to burn. Skinless chicken legs are added to the onions and browned. Mohsen adds salted water to them so that they can braise. I ask if it could be stock. Mohsen agrees it could be, and that some people do use it, but he never has. Eventually some of the chicken broth will be added to those walnuts, to make first a porridge and then, courtesy of the oil-black molasses, a dark stew in which the chicken will bob, until a sheen of pure walnut oil floats to the surface. A little sugar is added to offset the sourness. Alongside the stew he prepares the rice, greasing the bottom of a pan with vegetable oil, and slicking it with more of the water infused with saffron. Pre-cooked rice goes into the pan. Holes are poked in the surface and melted butter is poured in. The pan is sealed with foil and it goes on the heat. This will eventually produce the much-prized tahdig, the crisp layer at the bottom of the rice pan which famously people fight over. When it's ready he does not attempt to turn the large pot out, so the crisp surface is the top of a rice mound. Instead, he scoops out the rice until he gets to the bottom. Then he lifts the tahdig or crisped layer out and puts it on a separate plate. It is daffodil yellow and evenly cooked.

The fesenjan is now ready too. It is time to eat. It is a quiet weekday lunchtime so we can sit in the dining room, at a table laid with flatbreads and dishes of salad and olives dusted with sumac. The first time I ate this dish back in 2019 I found the stew almost overwhelming. A little went a long way. Sitting here with Mohsen I realize I had been doing it wrong. We each of us have a plate of the rice, by turns yellow and white, into which we upend pats of butter. Quickly they melt in the heat. Then we bring the stew to the rice, where the walnut and pomegranate sauce serves more as a condiment than broth. It is rich, yes, but also soothing and intensely comforting. For texture, there are cracker-like shards of the tahdig to crunch through.

And so to the recipe. I have adapted it a little for home rather than restaurant cooking because the volumes will be smaller. I use stock from cube for braising the chicken, but it is very much based on the version taught to me by Mohsen at Persian Cottage.

INGREDIENTS

600g walnuts, blitzed in a processor to a rugged crumb
2 medium onions, sliced into thin rings
Vegetable oil
1 tbsp ground turmeric
1 tsp cracked black pepper
4 whole chicken legs (drumstick attached to thigh), bone-in, skin-off
Salt
1 litre chicken stock from cube
5–10 strands of saffron, in 200ml warm water
450ml pomegranate molasses
3 tbsp caster sugar

METHOD

1. Put the ground walnuts into a large, ideally non-stick pan or casserole dish and toast over a low heat. Do not add any oil. Make sure to stir every few minutes, bringing up the ground walnuts at the

bottom so there's no risk of them burning. You are looking for them to darken in colour and release their fragrant oils. It's a job that requires patience. It will take about 30 minutes for the walnuts to have toasted fully.

2. While the walnuts are toasting, gently fry the onions in 3 tablespoons of vegetable oil, in a pan big enough eventually to take the chicken legs. When the onions have become translucent, soft and are starting to brown, add the turmeric and cracked black pepper and stir to season the onions.

3. Season the skinless chicken legs with salt, then add them to the pan with the onions and brown on all sides. When they are browned, pour on the chicken stock to cover, along with 100ml of the saffron water. Turn down the heat and simmer for half an hour.

4. You now need to put the liquor in which the chicken legs have been braising into the toasted walnuts. I found the simplest way to do this is to take out the legs and most of the onions (using a slotted spoon) and put them into a separate bowl to wait their turn. Then pour the stock into the walnuts. Put the walnut pan on the heat, stir, and add the pomegranate molasses. Stir again to bring the pomegranate molasses up from the bottom so the mix darkens. Bring the pan to a gently bubbling simmer and cook covered for an hour, stirring occasionally. By the end of the hour, you should see a sheen on the surface because the walnuts will have released a lot of their oils.

5. Add the chicken and onions to the walnut mix, stir in the sugar and cook on a low heat for 90 minutes. Serve with rice.

Or you could have a go at . . .

My slightly risky, mildly problematic version of a tahdig

It's clumsy because frankly, knowing the state of the crispy bottom of the rice when you cannot see it is an art rather than a craft. You need Mohsen's highly trained nostrils to know exactly when it's there. That said, on the couple of occasions I've scorched it a little, the crunchy layer has still been delicious. A true tahdig is made with sella basmati, which is basmati rice that has been parboiled before polishing. Apparently, that's what results in the loose individual grains. I do it with straight basmati, and still get pleasing results. As to the things I add, I just made that up a few years ago. Your Iranian friends might not approve. Then again, they might appreciate the fact you made the effort.

INGREDIENTS

250g basmati rice
Sea salt and ground black pepper
1 large onion, or 2 medium onions, sliced into rings
Vegetable oil and a knob of salted butter, for cooking
60g sultanas (optional)
60g pine nuts
4 tbsp chopped fresh flat-leaf parsley
Saffron water from the above recipe (optional)
75g melted butter

1. Rinse the rice in cold water. My friend Tim Anderson, the Japanese food expert, admitted to me a while ago that he doesn't bother doing this any more. He says he can't quite see the point. It's your call. Either way, put the rice into a saucepan with 375ml of salted water. Cover the pan and cook on a low to medium heat for 12 to 15 minutes, until all the water has been absorbed. Leave the lid on for a couple of minutes after it's finished cooking, then fluff it up with a fork. Better still, buy a rice cooker. They really are superb pieces of kit. With basmati, you will be instructed to use 1½ cups of water to 1 cup of rice. It does the job every time.

2. Sauté the sliced onions in vegetable oil and a knob of butter, until most of them have caramelized. Season with salt and pepper. While that's happening soak the sultanas in warm water for 10 minutes and drain.

3. Toast the pine nuts quickly in a pan. Watch out. They burn easily.

4. Now mix the onions into the rice (including the fats in which they have been cooked), along with the pine nuts, sultanas and chopped flat-leaf parsley.

5. Get a high-sided frying pan and cover the bottom and sides with a light sheen of vegetable oil. Now add a few tablespoons of the saffron water and swirl it around.

6. Put the rice mixture into the pan. Smooth off the surface and make four deep indentations with your

finger. Pour the melted butter into the holes and dribble any remaining butter across the surface. Do the same with any remaining saffron water. Cover with a square of greaseproof paper larger than the frying pan, then fix in place with a saucepan lid which, being reasonably close to the size of the pan, will fit.

7. Cook over a low to medium heat for around 20 to 25 minutes, but keep lifting the edge of the greaseproof paper and having a good sniff. The cooked rice smell should give way to something closer to cooked popcorn when the base has crisped. Remove the greaseproof paper.

8. You now have two ways to go. You can be brave and turn it out by placing a large plate over the top of the rice and, with an oven glove over the base of the pan, flip it. Or you can just scoop the rice out into a bowl and then lift out the crisped base. Either way it will be delicious and the perfect accompaniment to the fesenjan, or any other stew for that matter.

Duck à l'orange

Inspired by the dish served at Oslo Court, London

There was a time in the mid-1990s when about half the restaurant dishes served in London seemed to be plated in towers. There were plinths of crushed potato, laid with pink slices of lamb, crowned by fronds of seasonal greens. There were seafood towers and aubergine towers, meringue towers and weird wigwams of sausage draped in onion gravy. Dinner was like a fourteen-year-old boy: endlessly priapic. By the time I picked up the knife and fork professionally in 1999, we were already laughing and pointing at the whole tower plating thing, and rightly so. First, it was tricky for waiters to get those under-engineered arrangements to the table with the towers intact. Things stacked on top of each other do tend to fall over, what with gravity and all. And second, the elements of the dish would tend to cool very quickly when not in contact with a warmed plate.

Restaurant fashions have come and gone and come again throughout my quarter of a century: open kitchens, closed kitchens, tableside theatre, sharing plates, family style, fermenting, smoking, pickling, tasting menus, nose-to-tail, farm-to-fork (where else would your ingredients come from, other than a farm? Tesco?), that odd period when ingredients would seemingly only be placed on one side of the plate. It is in the nature of fashion that as each period passes, we tend to look back upon the one just gone as a portrait of the self when desperately young and unsophisticated. Oh, look how silly we were then and look how smart we are now. But actually it's just a function of a short attention span. We get bored with stuff. Which means that, while some of what went before is weird, or plainly doesn't function, we risk forgetting the good things.

For a long while it was fashionable to mock the classical repertoire served in a certain type of British and American restaurant during the 1960s and 70s. Think of them as the Robert Carrier years. His cookbook *Great Dishes of the World*, first published in 1968 and updated repeatedly thereafter, was the bible for this sort of cooking. We had surely outgrown coquilles St Jacques, steak Diane and crème caramel? But give it time. Eventually we wise up and realize there's nothing wrong with the dishes of the past. They've just been around a while. Indeed, many of them are utterly delightful.

Happily, some restaurants float on through time, never paying the blindest bit of attention to fashion. As long as their customers like what they do then there's no need to fix what isn't broken. Oslo Court, located on the ground floor of a mansion block in London's St John's Wood, has never regarded either that classical repertoire or that way of doing things as broken. There are salmon pink napkins and table-cloths. There is melba toast on the table, and butter served in curls. Starters include crudités and globe artichokes, crab à la Rochelle and avocado with prawns. For mains there's sole Véronique and lobster Thermidor. Until Covid when it was retired there was also a dessert trolley, stacked with profiter-oles and strawberry tarts, cheesecake and trifle. I have long said that when it is dinner time in London, it is forever 1977 at Oslo Court.

It began life as a drinking club during the Second World War, mostly frequented by Norwegian freedom fighters shel-tering in London. It's believed that's where the current name of the restaurant, and the mansion block it sits in, comes from. There were a number of incarnations after that before it was taken over in the early 70s by a Yugoslav-Welsh couple who turned it into a restaurant. Oslo Court eventually landed a few years later in the care of Galician-born Tony Sanchez, who had trained as a chef in Geneva and knew the ways of cream and brandy. He and his family have taken care of it ever since. I interviewed Tony in 2002. 'There is no passing trade here,' he told me, proudly. 'People come to us through word of mouth or simply because they have always come here.' A lot of those people are from the local Jewish com-munity. 'For me and my brother it was marvellous to find the Jewish community,' Tony said. 'In London in the 70s it seemed nobody liked to eat. They only want to drink. I'm not hungry, they say. Bring me a drink. Then we come here, the bar bills go down but they want the food. They love their food.' There are no pork mains, but there are latkes. (To be fair, it is tailored only to the most casually observant Jews. The distinctly non-kosher menu is full of shellfish, and meat and dairy are more than on nodding terms.) 'Most people who come here know what they are going to have before they even arrive,' Tony said. 'They don't want to look at the menu, even.'

They know for example that among the mains there will be crispy duckling. The version at Oslo Court has always been a crisp-skinned delight, the fattiness of which is cut through by the offer of an orange sauce. There's a reason duck à l'orange is a classic. It works. Forget what's fashionable. On occasions, when I've tried it elsewhere, the sauce has been over-thickened with cornflour, and so sugary as to remind me of boiled sweets. If you do it properly, that sauce should have a bit of body, but also a proper meatiness. Duck à l'orange is a savoury dish, not a dessert.

Cards on the green baize canasta table here: preparing it is a bit of a faff, not least because simply roasting a duck is far more of a faff than roasting a chicken. My duck roasting method comes from my immediate next-door neighbour, Marc. You rarely get to choose your neighbours, but we got very lucky with each other. He has a flair for meat cookery, and his was the best roast duck I have ever tried. The skin was crisp and yet the meat was not at all dry, which is too often the case. If this doesn't work for you, it's not my fault. It's his. Beware: there is a surprisingly modest amount of meat on a duck. I have given the instructions for one duck, which can serve four but only just and only with a lot of sides. Consider roasting two.

INGREDIENTS

1 x 2–3kg duck with giblets
Sea salt and ground black pepper

For the sauce
The giblets from the duck
1 onion, roughly chopped
1 carrot, roughly chopped
A few sprigs of fresh thyme
A few glugs of olive oil
500ml beef stock
2 oranges
The peel of one of those oranges
1 tbsp plain flour
25g caster sugar
1 tbsp white wine vinegar
20ml Cointreau or other orange liqueur

METHOD

1. Remove the giblets from the duck's cavity and set
   aside. Prick the skin of the duck all over with a fork.
   Then, holding the bird carefully over the sink, pour a
   whole kettle's worth of just-boiled water over the
   skin. This will help to tighten it up.

2. Leave the duck to dry on a rack for a few hours. You
   want the skin as dry as possible. If you have a defrost
   function on your oven, give it an hour of that. Marc
   isn't beyond turning a hair dryer on his for 10
   minutes or so. I admire his commitment.

3. While the duck is drying, heat the oven to
   220°C/425°F/gas mark 7. Put the giblets, chopped
   onion, carrot and thyme into an oven tray. Pour on a

couple of glugs of olive oil, season liberally with salt and pepper and roast for 30 minutes or so, until the giblets are properly browned. (If your duck didn't come with giblets, just roast the vegetables until browned. It will still be fine.)

4. When they are done, put the tray on a medium flame on the stovetop, pour in the beef stock and scrape around the bottom of the tray to get up any of the caramelized bits. Now pour the entire contents of the oven tray, giblets, veg and all, into a saucepan. Simmer on a low heat for at least half an hour. This will be the base for your sauce.

5. Crank the oven up to 230°C/450°F/gas mark 8.

6. Pull any excess lumps of fat out of the duck's cavity and set aside. Season the bird very liberally with salt and pepper, then put on more salt than you think is at all reasonable and place on a rack in an oven tray.

7. Roast on high for the first 15 minutes, then turn down to 170°C/325°F/gas mark 3 for the next hour. Turn it back up to 230°C/450°F/gas mark 8 for the last 10 minutes. If you are concerned about the size of your bird, calculate a cooking time based on 20 minutes per 500g plus 10 minutes, but still top and tail that cooking time with a blast of high heat as described.

8. During the roasting you may need to pour off duck fat. Along with the excess fat from inside the bird, you can use this to roast potatoes. (See my method at the start of the section on all the roast chickens, on page 122.)

9. While the duck is roasting, rinse the oranges under hot water and give them a gentle scrub to get rid of any wax on the skins, then use a veg peeler to take off the entire peel from one of the oranges in thin strips. Use a small knife to scrape off as much of the pith as possible. Remember, I'm not watching and don't care if you do a poor job of this. Slice all the peel into a fine julienne. Blanch in boiling water for 2 minutes, then put straight into cold water for a couple of minutes. Drain and set aside.

10. When the duck has finished roasting, set it aside to rest under foil. Pour off any remaining fat (go on; add it to the roasties), leaving a couple of tablespoons. Put the tray on a medium heat so the fat remains hot. Sprinkle on the flour and stir with a wooden spoon as they cook together.

11. After about a minute pour in a little of the liquid from the stock pan to scrape up the fat and flour mixture. Let that cook for a couple of minutes, then add the rest of what's in the stock pan. Don't worry about straining it. Just add the whole lot. Put it all on a low simmer.

12. While that's simmering, put the sugar into a saucepan with 50ml of water. Cook on a low heat at first until it's dissolved, then turn the heat up and boil. Watch it form a caramel. Keep an eye on it. When it turns golden brown, take it off the heat, wait 30 seconds, then add the vinegar and stir. This is a gastrique.

13. Strain the entire contents of the oven pan into the saucepan with the gastrique and put on a simmer. Add the Cointreau and put it on a low boil for 10 minutes or so to reduce.

14. The next bit is up to you. Juice the 2 oranges. Start off by adding half the juice to the pan. Is that orangey enough for you? If so, stop there. If not, add more to taste.

15. Finally add the julienned peel. Your sauce is complete.

16. Carve the rested duck and serve with the sauce. Make sure everyone gets some of the julienned peel.

Sweet soy-braised pork shoulder, served ssam style

Inspired by the dish served at Kushi-ya, Nottingham

Certain reviews still make me blush, not because I was wrong about the food, or the service or the room. I hold by what I said about all that stuff. It's the other things that make me cringe: the language used to frame it, the witty asides, the terribly clever analysis which a few years later don't look quite so witty or clever. In October of 2002, for example, I went to Whitstable on the north Kent coast to write about a tiny place called Wheelers, a postbox of a café on the high street with an outrageous salmon pink frontage. It's a seafood bar which was opened in the mid-nineteenth century by one Richard 'Leggy' Wheeler. I imagine he was quite tall by the standards of the day, hence the nickname. It would become the flagship for a chain of rather fancy seafood restaurants across London. They were pretty successful, until they weren't. The Wheelers in Whitstable is, as they themselves say, the last one standing, just as it was the first.

It has long been well known for its seafood counter selling

Whitstable oysters, crab, big fat prawns and mussels, lobster and the like. You can buy what's on offer to take home or grab one of the half-dozen seats and eat them there. What I didn't know, until someone pointed it out to me, was that through a doorway at the back of the shop was a tiny dining room seating another dozen people. Back then the chef was a man called Mark Stubbs, who had worked for Gordon Ramsay in London but clearly now fancied something a little more humble. It was then so humble it wasn't licensed to sell booze. If you wanted wine, you had to get it from the off-licence across the road. The food was rugged but good: king prawns with baked figs, a tart of leeks and smoked haddock with warm mustardy lentils, a fillet of snapper with a saffron, chive and prawn risotto. I was delighted with myself. I had made a discovery.

Except I hadn't. In the review I referred to it as a hidden gem, which was far from the truth because, its physical location aside, the place wasn't hidden at all. It was always fully booked, and twice over for lunch at weekends. There was a waiting list. Everyone in Whitstable knew about the back room at Wheelers, along with a lot of other people from elsewhere. The fact that I, the fancy restaurant critic down from London, hadn't heard of it didn't mean it was unfound. It just meant it was new to me. I was behaving like one of those unenlightened explorers from the early twentieth century who grandly announced they'd found some lost tribe deep in a jungle, when they weren't lost at all because they knew exactly where they were all the time.

Yes, I can bring restaurants to a wider audience, but that's a very different thing to making a discovery. On one occasion I had to be in Preston in Lancashire for lunch. I didn't want to waste an opportunity to review in a city where I had only eaten once before. But it was a Tuesday and almost everything obviously reviewable – that new place doing tasting menus, the venerable bistro near the station – was closed. Until Thursday. I brought up a Google map of Preston on my computer, input the search term 'restaurant' and then clicked on every single red knife and fork logo on the map that didn't seem to belong to a Burger King, Turtle Bay or Nando's. Eventually, just beyond the university, I found a place called Roasta. It was a tiny Cantonese café, which offered huge plates of duck wings, duck necks and gizzards deep-fried with salt and pepper and roast belly pork with crackling like honeycomb. It was tremendous. I give myself full marks for putting my back into locating somewhere to review, but by no stretch of the imagination did I find Roasta. The place was doing a roaring trade.

By 2022 when I visited the Japanese-inspired Kushi-ya in Nottingham I made sure not to congratulate myself on having found a hidden gem. Yes, it was located down the sort of scuffed alley off the city's high street where I could imagine furtive lovers went for a post-pub grope on a Friday night. Yes, you could easily not find it without clear instructions. But again, everyone in Nottingham seemed to know about it. And rightly so. Two young beardy chefs, Simon Carlin and Tom Clay, had developed their menu as a side hustle, while holding up their day jobs in restaurants around Nottingham. Now they had found an attic space, complete with gnarly beams, in which to investigate various nooks and crannies of their Japanese interests. There were wild mushrooms in a nutty brown butter ponzu sauce, with a confit egg yolk in the centre. There were skewers of glazed and barbecued duck hearts. There was a cross between a spring roll and prawn toast, in which the sesame-seed-crusted fried bread formed a cylinder around squeakily fresh prawns. Best of all, there was a piece of pork shoulder long braised in a sweet soy broth then glazed and grilled. It was offered up with lettuce leaves to use as wraps in the Korean 'ssam' style, alongside various sauces and a little bowl of tempura 'scraps', a witty reference to the extra bits of fried fish batter you can ask for in your local chippie. Their kitchen uses a barbecue to finish the meat, but you can do it just as well under a hot grill. And instead of scraps I've suggested using finely broken-up pork crackling, made from the skin that will come with the pork shoulder anyway.

I chose Kushi-ya to be my restaurant of the year in 2022. In large part it was because of this dish. I didn't bring a hidden gem out into the light. I didn't find anything. But I did make a personal discovery.

Feeds 4 greedy people as the main event

INGREDIENTS

1.5kg piece of pork shoulder (ask your butcher to take the skin off for you and score it; make sure to take it home – you'll need it)
A little vegetable oil
Table salt

For the braising liquor
500ml good chicken stock (the real stuff, from bones)
200ml light soy
1 chicken stock cube diluted in 800ml hot water
100ml mirin
2 tbsp dark soy
1 tbsp Chinkiang vinegar (substitute with balsamic vinegar)
100g caster sugar
1 star anise
2 cloves of garlic, roughly sliced
1 thumb-size piece of ginger, roughly sliced

METHOD

1. Heat the oven to 150°C/300°F/gas mark 2.

2. Scrape as much of the fat off the back of the pig skin as possible, then lay it out flat so the skin dries completely. For best results leave the skin to dry out in the fridge overnight.

3. Heat a couple of tablespoons of vegetable oil in a sizable casserole pot with enough room both for the pork and for a volume of liquid. Season the pork with a little table salt, then sear in the pot on all sides until browned. Remove from the pot and set aside.

4. Put all the ingredients for the braising liquor into the pot and bring to a simmer on a medium heat. When it's simmering, add the pork so that it's almost entirely submerged. Cover the surface with a piece of greaseproof paper. Put the lid on the pot and place it in the oven.

5. It should take 2½ hours, but start checking after 2 hours. Use two forks, to check that the meat will pull away from itself. You want it to separate but not completely fall apart. When done, take it out of the oven and leave it to cool in the liquor, while you prepare the crackling.

6. Turn the oven up as high as it will go, which is probably 240°C/475°F/gas mark 9. When the oven is at full temperature, season the pig skin with a little table salt, then put it on a wire rack over an oven pan, at the top of the oven. Keep an eye on it.

The skin should turn into crackling within about 20 minutes, though it may take longer depending on your oven. You want all of it to go crisp. (Top tip. If it's winter, when you take it out, hold the pan outside for a couple of minutes. The shock of the cold will help it to crisp.) When it's cooled, break it up into small fragments and put it into a bowl for later.

7. Meanwhile take the pork out of the liquor. Break it up into pieces, and arrange in a single layer in an oven dish.

8. Strain 750ml of the braising liquor into a saucepan, bring to the boil and reduce by three-quarters until it forms a glaze. If it's not sweet enough, add a spoonful more of sugar. When it's a glaze, pour all over the pork resting in the oven dish.

9. Turn the grill on to its top setting, and put the pork as high up in the oven underneath the element as possible. The sauce that's dropped to the bottom of the oven dish should start to bubble. Turn the pieces of pork in the bubbling glaze, until they've taken on colour and are fully glazed in the sauce. This can take 10 to 15 minutes depending on the heat of your grill.

10. Take the oven dish of now glazed and grilled pork out of the oven and let it rest for 10 minutes.

11. Serve with Iceberg or Cos lettuce leaves, various relishes, and the pork crackling. Invite everyone to make wraps with the leaves, filling them with pork, crackling and sauces of their choice. The red chilli

relish from page 20 and the coriander relish from page 21 work especially well.

A note on scaling up this recipe: if you want to do double or even triple the amount of pork, perhaps because you want to serve the dish for a large group, avoid scaling up the volume of liquor or you will end up with litres of the stuff. The best approach is to find a pot in which the same volume of liquor in this recipe will still cover the pork, and let it braise for a little longer. If you do decide to, say, double the amount of liquid, still only take off 750ml and reduce that down, rather than double the amount.

Tandoori lamb chops

Inspired by the lamb chops served at Tayyabs in Whitechapel, London

I read about Tayyabs, a Pakistani grill house in London's Whitechapel, long before I ate there. Mostly, I read about their lamb chops, an apparent wonder of crisped fat, and char, and vigorous spicing. They were described in precise, nerdy detail by multiple contributors to an online restaurant discussion forum called eGullet, where people who would elsewhere come across as belly-obsessed weirdos could mither and fret over the smallest details of their lunch. Oh, how they loved to debate those lamb chops, and the things that made them special.

In the early 2000s eGullet was my favourite waste of time, although I could easily pass it off as vital research for my job. In both the best and the worst way of the web it became a community of like-minded souls, who would argue, discuss, and sometimes fall out with each other over which establishment was best and which was not. And then for the most part, they would agree to disagree. Heston Blumenthal's Fat Duck in Bray was endlessly inventive and very much worth the cost, or perhaps it wasn't. Pierre Koffmann's Tante Claire was an unimpeachable temple to French classicism, or perhaps it was just a bit behind the times. Sean Hill's Merchant House in Ludlow was worth the trip, Rules still deserved your money despite being the oldest restaurant in London, and has anyone tried this new place off Carnaby Street called La Trouvaille? Well of course someone has. And then we all had.

I was not the only journalist who hung out there. Marina O'Loughlin was a member of eGullet before she became restaurant critic for London's *Metro*, and long before he was paid to do so Tim Hayward, who went on to become the restaurant critic for the *Financial Times*, would post finely turned paragraphs for free. The late Anthony Bourdain made the occasional appearance too. We were a gang.

Certain restaurants would be the subject of feverish discussion, only later to disappear as the herd moved on. But Tayyabs was a constant; a place that any self-respecting restaurant obsessive had to have visited. It started life in 1972 when an immigrant from Pakistan called Mohammed Tayyab gave up working in the garment factories of east London to open a café. Eventually he started making the dishes his mother had taught him before he left for London, which came from Pakistan's meaty traditions of grills, and long-simmered stews with breads (rather than the more rice-based dishes with the vegetable-led traditions of India, which increase the further south you go). His cooking became a community focus for the many others who had come to the area from northern Punjab and wanted a taste of home. Bit by bit the business expanded from its first site on Fieldgate Street into the adjoining addresses. There was the original café, a restaurant, a shop selling Indian sweets and eventually, at the far end, a place called New Tayyabs which occupied what had been the Queen's Head pub. The original café would close at 5 pm each afternoon, and the entire staff would move down the street to the new address for the evening service.

By the time I first went there in 2003, as part of an eGullet group outing, all the premises had been knocked together to create a slightly snazzier space of interlocking rooms leading to the large tandoor-dominated kitchen. That said, it was still a hectic experience. The waiters in those days had one mission: to get you in and out as quickly as possible. If you wanted to draw out dinner a little you had to work at it stubbornly. Tayyabs, being a Muslim-owned business, does not have a licence, but they have never objected to you bringing your own booze. They can supply a corkscrew where necessary, or an opener for the tall bottles of Cobra beer that inevitably litter tables.

The lamb chops, which were £4.20 for four sizable specimens when I first went, were everything I had hoped they would be: crisped but tender; boldly spiced without being thunderous. They came on a cast iron skillet, heated to smoking so that the onions underneath, dressed with just lemon juice, salt and pepper, fair sizzled. You heard the lamb chops coming before you saw them. Over the years I have ordered a lot of tandoori lamb chops in Pakistani grill houses across the UK. Many have been a huge, tough, dull disappointment. Some have been okay. None have ever matched those at Tayyabs.

Twenty years after my first visit I went there for lunch to try and establish why that might be. Mohammed died in 2014 and the business is now run by his three sons Aleem, Saleem and Wasim. The latter served for a while as hands-on head chef, having learnt the recipes from his father, and he still oversees the kitchen. The chops, Wasim told me over a few dishes, are first coated in a spiced yoghurt marinade before being left to chill for 24 hours. It means that their preparation is a constant rolling process. 'When I was a kid, my job was to get the yoghurt ready, then Dad would come in and he would spoon out the spices into the mix. He had a very particular set of spoons for the job.'

Was Mohammed the only one who did it? 'Yes, only him. He knew the mix off by heart. Bit by bit I learnt the mix by watching him and eventually I was allowed to do it.' To this day, only the three brothers know what goes in the yoghurt. 'And it's almost always me because I'm here almost every day,' Wasim says. This is no small undertaking. Tayyabs gets through about 150kg of lamb chops a day, around a metric ton a week. Before being dipped in the yoghurt they are beaten out, which tenderizes them but also creates more surface area. Wasim lists the marinade ingredients. I ask if he has ever written it down. Wasim shakes his head. 'Never. We've never shared the recipe with anyone.' The recipe is a piece of oral history, which has been passed through the family for fifty years. Although my beat is now food, for years I was a general reporter covering everything from politics to crime to social policy. I used to revel in the idea of the scoop. Today, it feels like I've got one of those: the ingredients for the mighty Tayyabs lamb chop marinade. Except I now need to work out exact amounts and how to scale everything down from the ten kilos of yoghurt with which they start.

Wasim takes me into the semi-open kitchen where, against the back wall, a gas tandoor is roaring the orange and yellow of the brightest sun. There's an open grill across the top, laden with searing chops, ready to fulfil the first lunch orders. Cast iron skillets are also being superheated across the top of another tandoor. All is heat and noise and fire. Wasim lifts a couple of chops off the grill and we stand there eating them with our hands, ripping away the meat from the bone, the hot, crisped fats running. I try to pretend I'm not burning my fingertips.

Looking around the kitchen, I am struck by the contrast between the restaurant kitchen and the domestic. Restaurant kitchens have certain pieces of kit perfectly engineered for singular jobs, like these vertical gas tandoor ovens, which can reach temperatures you might struggle to achieve at home. And then there is the interesting question of the virtues of cooking at volume. Some dishes are simply better made in large amounts and through endless repetition. Just as there's little point making a small cassoulet or a tiny pot of curry goat, I suspect part of what makes these lamb chops work is the sheer volume that is made here, in a kitchen constantly working to get their star dish right.

So I'm going to say here and now that if you want the Tayyabs lamb chops, go to Tayyabs. While you're there, try the deep, dark dry meat curry and the seekh kebabs and the nutty, fragrant daal, and the flaky, ghee-slicked breads. Try it all. But definitely have the lamb chops.

That said, after a lot of trial and error, I am happy and smugly proud to say that this version really is terrific and will reward the effort and the takeover of a shelf of your fridge for much of a day. Tayyabs uses best-end lamb chops which have the benefit of the bone, and a long ribbon of fat. It makes them easier to hold with your hands, and provides for more crusty bits. I've also done it with loin lamb chops, which are thicker and meatier, but have less of the bone, and with cutlets from French-trimmed lamb racks which are tidier. It's your choice. I make no apologies for proposing a sizable serving. Indeed, while I've mostly given the volumes for the marinade in teaspoons and tablespoons, I've also included grams so you can scale it up if you wish. People can eat these in volume. One friend, who knows Tayyabs well, asked me if there was anything in the recipe which surprised me. The answer was yes: the inclusion of ready-made mint sauce. Then again, as it's basically a combination of mint, vinegar and sugar, its benefit to a marinade is obvious. For what it's worth, I went for Colman's. One thing: I've left out a single ingredient from the Tayyabs marinade list and compensated for it elsewhere. It means that I haven't given up the entire famed Tayyabs lamb chop recipe.

Some secrets are worth keeping.

INGREDIENTS

500ml natural full fat yoghurt
1 tbsp (15g) smoked paprika
1 tbsp (15g) chilli powder
1 tbsp (15g) kitchen salt
1 tbsp (15g) garlic paste
1 tbsp (15g) ginger paste
1 tbsp chopped dried fenugreek
1 tsp (5g) chilli flakes
1 tsp (5g) ground cumin
1 tsp (5g) ground coriander
60g ready-made mint sauce
50ml lemon juice
25ml vegetable oil
20 lamb chops

1. Put the yoghurt into a large mixing bowl and add all the seasonings and spices, plus the mint sauce, lemon juice and oil. Stir to combine.

2. Beat out the lamb chops between two pieces of greaseproof paper until they are 25% to 50% wider than when you started.

3. One by one dredge the lamb chops through the yoghurt, then take them out and lay them flat in a dish. Just to be clear, the chops are dipped and removed; they are not just submerged in the yoghurt and left.

4. Cover the dish tightly with cling film and put into the fridge for at least 6 hours, but ideally for 24 hours. You may want to wrap the dish in a couple of extra layers of cling film, otherwise your fridge will smell of nothing else. Note: do not be tempted to leave the chops for longer than 24 hours, as they can tend to discolour rather unappetizingly.

5. Now they need to be grilled. I've tried two methods: my domestic oven grill on fan, after it's been given a good 15 minutes to heat up, and over coals on my stone-built barbecue. I'm delighted to say both are effective. Let them go until the ribbons of fat are becoming charred and blackened, then turn them over and cook the other side. Let them rest for 10 minutes before serving. With a lot of kitchen roll.

Triple-cooked pork in hot pot

Inspired by the double-cooked pork in hot pot served at
Y Ming, London (now closed)

Writing is an act of extraordinary arrogance. All writers are, through the mere act of shaping sentences for public consumption, insisting that what they have to say is worthy of other people's time.

Listen to me.

Listen to me now.

I am telling you things that you will find interesting.

Of course, you can try to mitigate the arrogance by using the language of modesty. That could work for some. Sadly, I'm not very good at modesty; I wish I were better at it.

Being a critic in whatever medium is arrogance, squared. It is not merely the shaping of an idea. It is the assertion of taste; the insistence that, through experience, you are better placed than the majority to pass judgement on somebody else's work.

Over the years people have questioned me on this. Aren't opinions on restaurants all just subjective? Aren't my reviews just one person's view? I could argue that there are certain things that are objectively right and wrong. A split crème brûlée like sweet scrambled egg is wrong. Crisp, golden rustling chips are right. Flaccid, soggy chips are wrong. But that's missing the point. My job is not merely to reach a judgement, but to argue it in such a compelling, authoritatively readable way that you believe me; that what I say makes sense. There's also the other test: go to a restaurant I have reviewed for yourself and see if you agree. If you do, hurrah. If you don't that's fine too. Now you know that if I say somewhere is good, you'll probably think otherwise and vice versa. Readers have to build a relationship with the critics they read. They have to read them over time to get a sense of who they are, and what their weird foibles might be. For example, I dislike having my wine poured for me. I don't enjoy the lack of control, often for practical reasons. Other people love it. The fools.

Part of the job is owning your opinions. Because if you've been positive about a restaurant or a chef or a dish, you are likely to see that opinion quoted back at you for a very long time to come. Are you comfortable with that? You better be. When I started, which was in the very earliest days of the web, it wasn't something I had to think about much. Occasionally a quote from one of my reviews would turn up in a press release for a new venture launched by people involved with a previous business about which I'd written. I might see my words on a piece of promotional material in a restaurant's window. Sometimes, if it was especially positive, they might slap up the whole review. I've noted a marked tendency to put framed copies of the very positive ones on the walls of the men's toilets, above the urinals. I've often been given the chance to re-read my work while having a pee. I think the choice of location shows an admirable and appropriate degree of respect for the critic's work.

As everything moved online, being presented with my own words became more and more common. This has its downsides. Restaurant reviews are snapshots of a moment in time and while they can stand as an assessment for a reasonable period, they can't stand forever. Menus are rewritten. Chefs move on. Sometimes restaurants change ownership. And yet, a quote from a ten- or fifteen-year-old review can hang around digitally. From time to time, I've remonstrated; suggested that perhaps it's a little misleading to quote that review from 2007 given it's now 2022. Happily, this is rare, as is people making up quotes from me, though that does happen occasionally.

Put that aside. Generally, seeing my stuff quoted with my name attached is BLOODY MARVELLOUS. It means somebody actually read something I wrote and agreed with it, even if they did have skin in the game. Whatever. Those are my words and that is my name. Yes, I know. It's pitiful, isn't it.

There was one moment like that which has meant more to me than any other. To introduce the recipe for salt and pepper cauliflower on page 100 I wrote in detail about Y Ming, the very special, now sadly closed Chinese restaurant on London's Greek Street, where my wife and I were regulars long before I became a restaurant critic. There was one dish on the menu with which I was especially besotted: it was the double-cooked pork in hot pot. It came in a beautiful ceramic bowl with a lid. When you lifted the lid, you got a waft of soy and caramel and the lightest of funks from the long-cooked preserved vegetables at the bottom. On top, half submerged in a sweet soy-based broth, were thick slices of slow-cooked pork belly with the softest ribbons of wobbly fat the colour of antique ivory. It was deeply comforting. It was satisfying. What's more, the menu description explained that this dish was 'praised by food writers' including both Jonathan Meades and Matthew Fort, then two of the biggest names in British restaurant reviewing, for *The Times* and the *Guardian* respectively. I read both writers avidly. I loved not just their opinions but their subtle, supple prose. It turned out they were who I wanted to be when I grew up. I just didn't know it yet.

Inevitably, in 2002 I reviewed Y Ming. And of course, I wrote about the double-cooked pork in hot pot. A few months later I went back for dinner. My name had been added to that of the other food writers who had praised it. My name remained on the menu until the restaurant closed almost two decades later at the end of 2021. Yes, of course, it's a sign of my massive vanity that this gave me a huge amount of unalloyed pleasure. But I'd be lying if I said otherwise. Occasionally people would tell me that they'd been to Y Ming. Sometimes it was on my specific recommendation. They would tell me that one of the dishes was endorsed by me and that of course they ordered it. I would ask: how was it? They would say: terrific. Or something like that, because it really was.

So naturally, here it is. I'm not going to be casual about it. This one requires effort. It has a few stages, to which I've added one, making it triple- not just double-cooked. It requires several pans and a bit of patience but I think it's worth it. Two versions of the restaurant's recipe were sent to me, by both Y Ming's redoubtable owner Christine Yau, and her general manager William Tiger Sin. I hope they won't be too put out if I say both versions required a bit of decoding. They were written in the sort of shorthand that restaurants which have been open for a very long time tend to use. I would therefore like to record my huge debt of gratitude to my friend the cook and writer Jeremy Pang of School of Wok, *The Kitchen Cabinet* and so much else. He helped me come up with a version of the recipe for the home cook. For a start he explained how to prepare Tianjin preserved vegetables, a distinctive product made up mostly of chopped cabbage which has been highly salted and mixed with a generous amount of garlic. It arrives compressed into a plastic bag in turn inserted into a distinctive, squat, brown-glazed ceramic pot. Tianjin preserved vegetables are available at most Asian supermarkets and are very much the key to this dish.

INGREDIENTS

2 spring onions
3 thick slices of ginger
500g square piece of pork belly
100g Tianjin preserved vegetables
Vegetable oil
1 clove of garlic
3 tsp Shaoxing wine
1 tsp soy
1 tsp caster sugar

To finish the hot pot
75ml light soy
1 tbsp dark soy
50ml Shaoxing wine
1 tbsp Chinkiang vinegar (substitute with white wine vinegar)
75g caster sugar
100ml water or chicken stock (not from cube, which would add salt; the real stuff)
8–10 whole shitake mushrooms, 60–70g (substitute with chestnut mushrooms if shitake are not available)
2 thick slices of ginger

METHOD

1. This pork will first be boiled, then fried, then steamed. Hence the triple cooking. Start by bringing a pan of water, big enough to take the pork belly comfortably, to the boil. Bash the whites of the spring onions and put them into the pan with the slices of ginger and the pork belly. Turn down the heat and

simmer for half an hour. Strain and leave to cool completely. When it's cooled, cut into slices the thickness of a standard smartphone. (Thank you to the *London Evening Standard* restaurant critic Jimi Famurewa for that measure of thickness.)

2. While the pork is cooking and then cooling you should get on with the preserved vegetables. Put them into a bowl and steam them for 15 minutes. A note on steamers. The steam function of a rice cooker is good for this because it's a relatively short steam. You will, however, need a larger pan-top steamer to finish the dish. In my experience rice cookers don't enjoy being used for long steams, often turning themselves off.

3. Once the 15 minutes are up, put the steamed preserved vegetables into a sieve and rinse them in cold water over a bowl to remove as much of the salt as possible. You want to do this until the water in the bowl beneath is pretty much running clear. Massage the pieces of cabbage to help remove that salt.

4. Put a little oil into a frying pan over a medium heat. Add the rinsed, preserved vegetables and the chopped garlic clove. Cook, turning in the pan, until they're almost dry. Add the Shaoxing wine, soy and sugar. Cook again, until it's again pretty much dry. Reserve.

5. Clean out the frying pan. Put it over a medium heat and add a couple of tablespoons of vegetable oil. When it's hot, add the thick slices of pork belly and fry on each side until just coloured. Reserve.

6. It's time to build the hot pot. Make the braising liquor by mixing the two soys, the Shaoxing wine, vinegar, sugar and water in a measuring jug. Into a pudding bowl large enough for all the ingredients, put a layer of the preserved vegetables. Put in a layer of whole mushrooms. Now arrange the slices of pork belly vertically so the rind is at the top. Put any remaining preserved vegetables around the sides, along with any remaining mushrooms. Tuck in the slices of ginger. Pour over the liquor.

7. Cover tightly with silver foil, and steam in the pan-top steamer for 2 to 2½ hours, until the pork is completely tender. Keep an eye on the water simmering in the pan so it doesn't dry out. Add more water if necessary. Serve with rice.

Life lessons: learning to make kibbeh bissanyeh

With Amoul Oakes

People open restaurants for different reasons. Some do it simply because they like feeding people. Others do it in a foolhardy attempt to make money. Amoul Oakes opened hers as an act of memory: as a statement of who she is and where she came from. Amoul's Hideaway in London's Little Venice, which closed in 2017, was a tribute to her native Lebanon, expressed one beautiful dish at a time. It was a re-imagining of a 1950s and 60s childhood in a town called Marjeyoun, close to the Israeli border, where her fez-wearing father Habib was the mayor; where life was dominated by a kitchen ruled by her mother and her five aunts; where recipes were never written down and everything was directed by sounds and smells.

Amoul came to London in 1985 with her advertising executive husband Leslie. She first opened a deli in 2003, inspired, she says, by a dismal newspaper review of a Lebanese restaurant in the capital. 'The review didn't understand Lebanese food at all,' she says. 'It was a terrible piece of writing.' I ask the name of the journalist responsible. Happily, it turns out to be someone I dislike intensely. That deli led in 2010 to the restaurant. Amoul was in the kitchen with a couple of helpers. Her daughter Zeina took a break from documentary film-making, to run front of house. I love the idea of someone taking revenge on a lousy piece of writing by opening a restaurant serving the good stuff. 'I didn't open it to make millions,' Amoul says. 'I just wanted to introduce people to real Lebanese food.' Today, I am in the kitchen of the Maida Vale flat she shares with Leslie and their newly acquired, bouncingly excitable boxer dog puppy. Amoul is going to show me how to make the stand-out dish from my dinner at the restaurant back in 2015, the kibbeh bissanyeh.

Back then, after I had placed my order with one of her sons, Amoul came to the table to check our choices. She had such a warm, natural authority, I found myself seeking her approval. I wanted to know if I'd missed out anything vital. Yes, she said, the kibbeh bissanyeh. I should also have that. I did as I was told. If you're aware of the word 'kibbeh', you'll probably know it as a deep-fried and encouragingly brown, crisp dumpling stuffed with ground lamb. It's made with a casing of bulgar wheat and ground meat – lamb or beef – shaped into a delightful oval, with pointed ends. The forming and shaping of kibbeh is a matter of huge personal pride among Lebanese cooks, who will quietly compete to make the most exquisitely shaped and uniform examples. Read a few recipes and it quickly becomes clear that, like Rachmaninov's Piano Concerto No. 3 in D minor and plate-spinning, it's something which takes serious practice. I don't think I would manage to learn to make them adequately in the time it's taken me to write this book. So let's not waste time on the unobtainable (though if you want to have a crack at them there are plenty of recipes online, including one by the Mexican-American actress Salma Hayek).

Then there is the version baked in the oven, which is the meaning of the word 'bissanyeh', to use Amoul's spelling. (It is also spelt 'bil sanieh'.) It's less well known, but much easier to achieve. In my review, I described it as 'the mothership of meat loafs; the meat loaf all other meat loafs hope to be one day, if they pass the right exam'. I liked it very much. I liked the crisp surface, and the soft centre, and the crisp bottom, and the big hit of spice and meatiness.

By the time I arrive at her home today Amoul has already cooked down the minced lamb for the filling, with the chopped onions, pine nuts and that boldly citrus spice sumac. The pan is to one side cooling. Her casing will, however, be made with beef. 'My sister prefers lamb,' Amoul says. 'But my grandchildren don't like it so much so I use beef.' I do adore how these quirks and changes come into family recipes. Amoul says, 'I believe that recipes are a guideline. I always look at recipes and then do it my way.' That said, in 2008 she did publish her own cookbook. It includes a good guide on how to make today's dish but it's both useful and a privilege to get a personal lesson.

While the bulgar wheat soaks, Amoul shows me the beef. 'It must be very lean. This is brisket.' To describe it as minced is to understate what has happened. It is practically a paste, the result of being shoved through the mincer three times.

'In the old days it would be done with a pestle and mortar,' Amoul says. The modern mincer saves a lot of arm effort. The bulgar wheat is drained and the excess water squeezed out by hand, before it's added to the beef. In go salt, pepper and cinnamon. 'My mother always used cinnamon,' Amoul says. 'She believed it was the Venus of spices.' The mix is blitzed with two chopped onions and lots of marjoram. It's blitzed and blitzed again. The result is something pale, pasty and almost dough-like, which disguises the fact it is 50% ground beef.

Now we build the dish. A deep oven tray is generously greased with vegetable oil. It turns out vegetable oil will play a big part in this version of kibbeh. Amoul presses in a thick layer of the meat-bulgar paste, until it is flat and even. On to that goes the minced lamb, followed by another thick layer of the paste. It is a paste-meat-paste sandwich. And now the fun stuff. She uses a sharp knife to poke a hole about the diameter of her index finger, or a wooden spoon's handle, in the centre of the tray right down to the bottom. Next, she wets the knife and goes around the edge of the tray releasing the mix from the sides. She scores the surface deeply with four cuts from the central hole to each corner, before scoring the top layer in all directions to make lozenge shapes roughly 2cm x 4cm, so that it looks much like a tray of baklava. It is precise and beautiful.

If you follow recipes regularly, most stages of the preparation feel logical: the onion goes inside the chicken before roasting; the sugar is folded into the whipped egg whites. Every now and then, something takes you by surprise. That's what happens here. So far, this dish has been extremely lean and unfatty. No longer. Amoul takes a bottle of vegetable oil and starts by pouring it into the central hole until it is full. She continues until the entire kibbeh is under a reflective lake of oil at least half a centimetre deep. The recipe in her book merely tells you to 'drizzle evenly'. This isn't a drizzle. It's a monsoon.

Next to us the oven has been heating on its very highest setting. Amoul puts the tray on a rack in the middle. I say: 'You're frying it in the oven.' Yes, she says. Exactly that. A little over 30 minutes later what emerges is as crisp and brown as the dumpling version. Amoul lets it cool for 10 minutes then pours off the excess oil, before leaving it to cool further. 'Would you like some baba ghanoush with it?' she asks me. Yes, I would like that very much. Three aubergines are set to char on the hob's naked flame. A large tub of tahini is dragged from the fridge. Lemons are juiced. Just 15 minutes later we have a smoky rough aubergine purée, to go with still warm slices of the kibbeh bissanyeh, which can now be cut straight from the tray. We eat it with dollops of garlicky goat's milk yoghurt with cucumber.

I eat lunch with Amoul and her family, looking out over the garden, with the sounds of a London day floating past. I asked her why she closed the restaurant. 'I didn't want to stop,' she says. 'But I had to be there every day and, in the end, it was too much.' But that doesn't stop her cooking her favourite dishes. 'I find it therapeutic,' she says. 'I usually have music on in the background. It takes me back.' That's the beautiful thing about the most domestic of dishes. For those with a connection to them they are time machines, transporting them to another moment and another place. For the rest of us, they are a sweet insight into another kind of life.

Serves 6

Recipe adapted from the version in *Amoul: Some Family Recipes* by Amoul Oakes, self-published in 2008

INGREDIENTS

For the stuffing
1 tbsp pine nuts
1 large onion, finely diced
500g minced lamb shoulder
Sea salt and ground black pepper
1 tbsp sumac (or substitute with a tablespoon of lemon juice)

For the casing or, as it's known, the kibbeh
500g fine bulgar wheat
1 onion, peeled and quartered
½ tsp ground cinnamon
½ tsp salt
½ tsp white pepper
½ tsp dried marjoram
500g very lean beef (brisket trimmed of fat works well. Ask your
    butcher to mince it finely three times until it's practically a
    paste. If your butcher needs convincing, plead with them. Say
    I made you ask)
Vegetable oil, for frying and drenching

METHOD

You can refer to the description in the text above for a nar-
rative version of this. Otherwise start here:

1. Put the bulgar in water to soak for an hour.

2. Heat a tablespoon or two of vegetable oil in a frying
   pan over a low heat. Add the pine nuts and fry so
   they just start to colour. Watch they do not burn.
   Add the diced onion and fry gently until soft.

3. Add the minced lamb, and fry gently, breaking up any
   clumps with a wooden spoon. Season with a little salt

and pepper, add the sumac or lemon juice, stir, and continue to cook for 10 minutes or so until the pan is dry and the meat crumbly. Leave to cool.

4. Turn the oven on to 240°C/475°F/gas mark 9.

5. Put the onion and all the seasonings for the kibbeh into a food processor and blitz until fine. Add to the minced beef.

6. Drain the bulgar wheat, then squeeze out as much of the water as you can with your hands. Add that to the minced beef and onion mixture. Mix to combine, then put the mixture through the food processor in batches, until you have a bowl of something pale white and paste-like.

7. It's time to build the dish. Generously oil an oven tray measuring roughly 25cm × 25cm. Take half the kibbeh mixture and press it into an even layer across the bottom of the tray. Top with the minced lamb in an even layer. Then top that with an even layer of the remaining kibbeh mixture.

8. Use a knife, or the handle of a clean wooden spoon, to make a hole dead centre of the pan, right down to the bottom. Now wet a knife and go around the edge of the mixture, gently releasing it from the sides of the tray.

9. Next use the knife to cut a diagonal to each corner through the top layer of mixed beef and bulgar, starting from the hole in the middle. Cut a pattern of lozenges roughly 2cm × 4cm through the top layer, so it ends up looking like a tray of baklava.

10. Finally pour vegetable oil into the hole until it overflows and covers the entire surface to a depth of ½cm. This looks like an unnatural thing to do, but honestly, it's fine.

11. Bake in the middle of the oven for 30 minutes, by which time the surface will be clearly browned and crisp. If, at any time, the edges appear to risk burning before the centre has started to crisp, turn the oven down a little.

12. Let the dish stand for 10 minutes to cool, then carefully pour off as much of the excess oil as you can while holding the kibbeh in place. No, I didn't say everything would be easy.

13. Let it cool for a further 30 minutes. Serve with baba ghanoush and yoghurt with cucumber.

Intercourse:
What's the bloody point of me?

What do I know? Really. Just what the hell do I know?

Or, to put it another way, what qualifies me to be a restaurant critic? It's not like there's an exam you can pass. There's no Higher National Diploma in plate-sniffing, no internationally recognized kite mark that proves the holder is a certified expert in navigating sharing plate menus, judging soufflés and spilling old-school sauces down their shirt. Though if there were I might enjoy working my way through that syllabus. In this regard, the job of newspaper restaurant critic is little different to any other job in journalism. You don't even need a qualification in journalism to be a journalist. I don't have one. Having spent the first year after finishing my degree editing a weekly tabloid student newspaper, I concluded that another year being taught what I had already been paid to do was not a good use of my time. It didn't mean that I thought I knew everything. I still had to read up on essential law for journalists so I didn't get myself or my employer sued. I also had to manufacture a speedy kind of longhand to make up for my lack of shorthand. But I had the basics.

The fact is that paid journalists writing for newspapers, either in print or online, qualify for their jobs one piece at a time. Is what you've just had published accurate? Is it readable? That said, a bit of knowledge of something is always handy. In Britain undergraduate degrees in journalism are relatively new. It used to be either in-work training or a postgraduate qualification. Over the years I have regularly been asked by aspiring journalists whether they should do one of the new undergraduate courses. I have always advised them against it. Media organizations have newsrooms full of people who know about journalism. What we need is people who know about something else. So study something that interests you now. Learn about the nuts and bolts of journalism later. When a war breaks out in the Balkans it can be helpful if, say, you have a member of staff who has studied Serbian history. The science correspondent would not have the time to be a research scientist, but a degree in physics or biology might be helpful. The legal correspondent doesn't need to have been a practising barrister or solicitor, but they might find a law degree useful.

A lot of the time you simply learn your beat on the job. Journalism is full of smart people who chose not to go on to further study, people who are superb at finding stuff out and serving it up in an elegant, engaging, approachable way. In my years as a general reporter and feature writer I developed knowledge of and contacts in some disparate areas, simply because I wrote about them so often. Eventually I was commissioned to write even more about them. I was great on art fraud disputes, Holocaust historiography, the landscape of race crime and UK drugs policy. I knew a lot of police officers. Weirdly, I wrote four large pieces about fights over the legacy of the British actor and comedian Peter Sellers. *Cosmopolitan* employed me to write an occasional column on sex from the male point of view. That required me to interview my friends, as I'd been with the same woman, now my wife of over thirty years, since I was twenty, so I was short on first-hand experience. But that was okay. I was a good reporter.

In 1999 when Sheryl Garratt, then editor of the *Observer Magazine*, invited me to take on the restaurant column, my apparent qualifications for the job were extremely limited. I'd written a couple of 'weekend away' columns, which were travel pieces within the United Kingdom that tended to include something about the dining options. In July of 1997 I had also deputized on the restaurant column, a review of a moderately nice modern brasserie called Belair House in Dulwich, not far from where I live. With a less than literary flourish I described the langoustine ravioli as 'a solid bit of work' but said the sauce 'lacked any real fishy pungency as if the dear creatures had been too early separated from the heads and shells that would have lent the stock a real kick'. Looking back, I see the five house wines were £12 a bottle and that I made astonished noises about the silliness of £50 bottles, 'the sort of thing you need to have on hand for weddings, funerals and bar mitzvahs'. Bless.

That was what Sheryl had to go on and yet she still gave me the job. This is not generally the way with reviewers. The new lead film or theatre critic is generally appointed from among those who have previously been doing the job, either elsewhere or as what's called a 'second string'. They are expected to have watched a lot of film or theatre. Restaurant critics? Not so much. While not everyone goes to the cinema or theatre, everyone has to eat. The late A. A. Gill of the *Sunday Times* had once worked as a chef, but that is rare among our number. I can think of a few who transferred from advertising, once the domain of the long expenses lunch. We tend to be generalists, given the job not because we are assumed to know our sauce Béarnaise from our sauce Ravigote, or at least not at first, but because it is believed that we can write a readable column. From time to time someone will say, 'Oh, I'd love your job, getting paid to eat all that lovely food.' I tell them rather pompously that I do the eating for free; it's the writing I'm paid for.

And yet knowing things really does help. When I made my pitch for the job it was based on a lifelong love of restaurants, what doting parents call a healthy appetite, and almost no real knowledge at all. By the time of my appointment, I was slowly learning to cook. Various recipe books that my wife had asked for one birthday had essentially become mine, as I worked my way through the essentials of meat roasting times and trudged the foothills of French sauces. But compared to what I know now, I was a blank page. Those reviews in my very first year were as mixed a bunch as any year that would follow. There was a delightful French bistro in Brighton called La Fourchette, where the chef terrified our friends by sweeping up their baby and taking her to the kitchen. There was the first outpost of what today has become a major chain called Thai Square. There was a pub in west London called the Cow, owned by Tom Conran, designer son of the late Sir Terence. Tom wrote me a stiff letter afterwards because I had mentioned a triptych by Francis Bacon that was hanging on the wall of the dining room, mostly because I could not imagine an artist whose work was less of an aid to the digestion than the ironically named Bacon. While utterly engrossing, they tend to look like an impressionistic account of the inner workings of an abattoir. Conran said I had put it at risk from criminals who might wish to steal it. I responded that if he was really that concerned about the security of his art collection, perhaps he shouldn't hang it on the wall of his restaurant where literally anybody could view it. These stories are fun. But what I find more intriguing is that I seem to have got away without making some massive culinary howler: misidentifying ingredients, or the antecedents of dishes, or raising a critical eyebrow over something which had been perfectly executed but was simply new to me. I assume it was because, if I didn't recognize a word on a menu or an element of a dish, I did some research.

Now I have longevity. With that does come knowledge and experience. I have tracked certain chefs through their careers, have seen the way their food has developed. In 2006, I spent time with a young, clean-shaven Portuguese chef called Nuno Mendes, who was following in the footsteps of Heston Blumenthal of the Fat Duck by exploring the wilder shores of what was known then as molecular gastronomy. He was cooking in an old East End boozer retitled Bacchus, where they offered what he and his business partner called 'fine dining in trainers'. It was the place for scallops with green apple 'air', cauliflower 'cous cous' and pine nuts – there were a lot of inverted commas on that menu – or a pear cake with blue cheese ice cream. It didn't survive because, while it was great value, not enough people could get their head around eating that sort of ambitious cooking, in that sort of bare-bones room. Mendes prospered though. Over the years I tracked him through high-end tasting menus at Viajante, and his crab donut phase for the A-listers at the Chiltern Firehouse in 2013, to his investigations of his Portuguese heritage first at Taberna do Mercado in 2015 and later in 2022 at Lisboeta. The Abade de Priscos, an egg yolk and pork fat custard with a port wine caramel, that he served at both of those latter places was an extremely long way from anything he served at Bacchus. It was rich and rustic, and rooted in an ancient culinary tradition that made the best of what was to hand – why use butter when you have lard? – rather than pushing at the boundaries of anything. I described it as 'the smoothest, richest set sweet custard you will ever taste, like two-denier silk stockings being pulled across your tongue'. That doesn't mean, however, that I've included a recipe. Some dishes are best left alone. Meanwhile the once clean-cut chef who serves it has become a bit of a star and grown a fabulous grey beard. We have grown old together. Likewise, in 2002 I tipped seven chefs for future greatness including Angela Hartnett, who was then working for Gordon Ramsay. By the 2020s, she had a three-strong group of Italian restaurants, and we would be occasional colleagues on *The Kitchen Cabinet.*

The point is I know chefs. And general managers. And restaurateurs. And designers. I know about ingredients and their suppliers, have visited a large number of them at source. I have learned, as we all have, that the food of China and India and Thailand is not just one homogenous thing, but a patchwork of many traditions and styles. I have come to understand that 'authentic', the greatest red herring in gastronomy, is not the same as 'nice', and that too many kitchens haven't the first clue how to make a good Caesar salad (see page 70). So yes, in answer to my own question I now know rather a lot, which is surely as it should be after twenty-five years?

But none of that justifies me doing the job. There are lots of people who know lots of things about food and restaurants, many of whom don't earn a penny piece from that knowledge. Which raises another question: in the Internet age, when there is a seemingly inexhaustible supply of people writing online for free about restaurants and food, is there any need or justification for salaried people like me? If you want to know whether a restaurant is any good you surely don't need me? You can go online and, courtesy of Tripadvisor, Google, Yelp and the rest, read any number of reviews written by people who have been to those restaurants. There are lots of restaurant blogs, written by people for whom eating out is their hobby. I know, because I consult a lot of them. Surely the age of the paid 'expert' has passed?

I could answer this by raging about the unreliability of online review sites; the way you cannot tell whether the writer has a vested interest to be either gushingly positive or grindingly negative. I could point out that way too many bloggers take comps from the restaurants and are either less than explicit about the fact or don't own up to it at all. By contrast I could big up the value of having someone both paid to gather expertise, and with a sufficient budget to pay for all the restaurant experiences they write about. You simply cannot rely upon a review of a meal if it was gifted.

All of this is true, but none of it justifies the job I and a few others are lucky enough to do. That is a far more mercenary affair. The simple justification is the volume of people who choose to read us for as long as we make the effort to be readable. That doesn't mean banging on about what we did on our holidays, or the hilarious if annoying thing our spouses got up to last week, or some tedious anecdote about getting our car nicked before dedicating a couple of paragraphs to the restaurant. It means coming up with something well-structured and authoritative, which wears its knowledge lightly and turns a nice, chewy, enjoyable phrase now and then. If it makes you laugh, all to the good. It should definitely make you hungry, and maybe a little jealous. It means recognizing what a privilege it is to have this job and giving a damn about it.

The newspaper business, indeed all journalism, is built on the size of its audience. In the old print-only days of newspapers, revenues came from the number of copies sold, the number of people who read each copy and therefore the amount that could be charged for advertising space. In the online age, when ad sales can be the key source of revenue, their value is still calculated in the same way. If a lot of people read a particular writer there is money to be made from the advertising that appears alongside it. I have often been asked whether bloggers writing for free pose a challenge to my livelihood. The answer is grandiose but no less true for that: only if those bloggers write better than I do. The vast majority do not. Local and regional bloggers can be useful for snuffling out places I might not otherwise have heard about but oh god, the prose. Too often it's a stumbling, rambling witterfest of shapeless babble. And don't get me started on the violence inflicted upon the poor defenceless English language by the people who post those reviews to Tripadvisor.

Some of them, however, are very good writers indeed and if that's the case, an interesting thing happens. They tend not to remain unpaid for very long. Newspaper and magazine editors find them, and commission them. At which point they do indeed become my competition. But the challenge remains the same: to give the readers a better reason to read me than them. As long as people still want to read well-written prose about restaurants there will still be jobs for paid writers with sizable appetites.

I hope.

Seafood

Sardinian seafood fregola

Inspired by the dish cooked by Francesco Mazzei at
St Alban, L'Anima and Sartoria

I missed the first chance I had to eat Francesco Mazzei's
engrossing, enfolding Sardinian seafood fregola. Perhaps if I
had spotted it in 2006 on the menu at a relatively short-lived
restaurant called St Alban, just off what was then London's
Lower Regent Street, I would have liked the place more.
Instead, my review was rather glum. I whined about chargrilled quails being fiddly to eat, grumbled about an overly
strident sauce with the delicate rabbit, and dismissed the
room, with its padded banquettes in primary shades, as looking like a lounge for British Airways Executive Club card

holders. It was a pointed sneer, a grim masterclass in reverse snobbery.

St Alban should have been a roaring success. It had been opened by two of London's most gifted restaurateurs, Jeremy King and Chris Corbin, who in 1990 had relaunched the Ivy and then, after selling up, gone on to gift the capital the swooned-over Wolseley and later Brasserie Zedel. But St Alban never quite worked. It was a rare misstep for two men who appeared to get almost everything right.

Mazzei, who is originally from Calabria, was the opening chef but left after a couple of years to open L'Anima, a clean-lined, glass-walled restaurant in the City with snow-fields of white tablecloth and a menu of dishes from the foot of Italy's boot. I raved about the greaseless fritto misto there, about tiny clams and plump mussels opened on a charcoal grill in a dense liquor that I wanted to lap at like a cat. Most of all I raved about the seafood fregola. The latter are tiny oven-toasted balls of semolina dough, not unlike what's known as Israeli cous cous. Here, they came simmered until soft, in a fish stock enriched with a tomatoey dice of stewed squid so fine you couldn't quite tell where the fregola ended and the squid began. After that it was loaded with all the good things: fat prawns, clams, mussels, handfuls of fresh green herbs and just a hint of chilli. L'Anima was the epitome of crisp, sharp-edged sophistication. And yet its star dish, at least as far as I was concerned, represented all that was good about food rooted in the domestic.

Eventually L'Anima closed and Mazzei moved west into the plushly furnished, lightly tasselled Sartoria, in Mayfair. Naturally, I followed him. Naturally, I ordered the fregola. Naturally, I raved about it again. Later Jeremy King pointed out that the chef I now so clearly adored had been at the stoves of the restaurant I didn't love quite so much all those years ago. He sent me the opening menu from St Alban. There it was: the seafood fregola. Many chefs have dishes like this: guaranteed crowd pleasers which remain a part of their repertoire throughout their career, give or take a few changes along the way. Mazzei came up with this one after a visit to the Gallura region of Sardinia, during a research trip with Chris Corbin, not long before St Alban opened. 'I came across a small restaurant and there was this old lady cooking fregola with clams and bottarga,' he later told me. 'Her version was white.'

His brings in the stewed squid, and looks like a cross between a risotto and a paella. 'This makes sense,' Mazzei says. 'If you look at the map there is a clear line between Sardinia and Spain.' The first time I saw Mazzei's fregola recipe, published on a food website, it read like a list of 'mise en place', the various parts of a dish prepped in advance making it possible to get orders out of the professional kitchen within a few minutes. Key to it is the stewed squid, which is made in volume in a restaurant kitchen in advance. A few heavy spoonfuls of the squid mix would work wonders if stirred through a bowl of pasta or a risotto. His recipe specified 3g of chives, 3g of dill, 5g of basil be stirred through the finished fregola. The cook charged with making the dish will have, lined up in front of them, aluminium pots full of enough finely chopped herbs prepared in advance to get through both lunch and dinner. They will know to take just under a teaspoon for each serving.

That sort of precision is vital for a Mayfair restaurant charging nearly £30 a serving. It won't work for our purposes. And in any case, it's a dish that needs to be scaled up to serve four or more. That's what my version does. I specify various types of seafood for this. You can of course use whatever fish you have available. Using live clams and mussels in their shells will add a depth to a fish stock made from cube, if that's what you're using.

Serves 4

For the stewed squid
2 tbsp olive oil
1 clove of garlic, finely chopped
1 sprig of fresh thyme
100g shallots, finely sliced
400g squid, cleaned and finely diced as small as possible
100ml dry white wine
2 tbsp tomato purée
Fine salt

For the fregola
4 tbsp olive oil
2 cloves of garlic, finely chopped
2 tbsp finely chopped shallots
1 red chilli, finely chopped
1 sprig of thyme
220g fregola
600ml fish stock
2 seabass fillets, cut into pieces
250g clams in their shells, rinsed through a couple of changes of
    cold water
300g mussels in their shells, debearded and rinsed
120ml tomato sauce (a good jarred ready-made tomato sauce for
    pasta will do)
120g cherry tomatoes, halved
250g peeled prawns
A small bunch of fresh green herbs, finely chopped, including
    basil, tarragon and chives (you could also include chervil and
    flat-leaf parsley)
Sea salt and ground black pepper
½ a lemon

1. For the stewed squid, heat a frying pan until medium hot, add the olive oil, then add the chopped garlic, thyme and shallots and cook gently for a couple of minutes until the shallots are soft. Watch that the garlic doesn't scorch.

2. Add the diced squid and as soon as it starts giving off its juices add the white wine. Once the alcohol has evaporated, add the tomato purée and simmer for 4 or 5 minutes until the squid is tender. Season to taste with salt and remove the pan from the heat. This mix can be made in advance (and in volume) and if put straight into the fridge will keep for 3 days.

3. For the fregola, heat a sizable sauté or paella pan until medium hot, add half the olive oil, then add the garlic, shallots, chilli, thyme and cook gently for 1 minute.

4. Meanwhile, warm the fish stock in a pan.

5. Add the fregola to the sauté or paella pan and turn in the hot oil for a couple of minutes (as you would rice at the start of a risotto). Add the stock, bring to a simmer, then stir through the stewed squid and cook for about 10 minutes, adding extra stock or water if necessary to keep the fregola covered. Stir every now and then. Enjoy the meditative process. Stirring dishes like this is one of the joys of cooking.

6. While the fregola is gently simmering, heat a separate frying pan until hot, add the remaining oil and fry the pieces of seabass fillet on each side until golden, then remove from the pan and set aside. (You could use

red mullet fillets, scallops and the like if they're available.)

7. After 10 minutes, add the unopened clams and the mussels to the fregola and cook for 2–3 minutes, or until they open. Discard any that do not open.

8. Add the tomato sauce, cherry tomatoes and prawns. Once the prawns are cooked, stir the chopped green herbs through the fregola. Season with a good grind of black pepper.

9. To serve, ladle into four warmed flat bowls. Top with the pieces of seabass (or other fish). Dribble a little good olive oil over the top if you have it to hand, and add a squirt of the lemon. Mazzei uses Amalfi lemons when in season but you're not Mazzei: a standard lemon will do just fine.

Clams with black beans and chilli

Inspired by the dish served at Träkol, Gateshead

Eating in a restaurant can be like dating. It's not always obvious which dish will come home with you from a night out. In 2018 at Träkol, a noisy bistro housed in a set of shipping containers on the Gateshead side of the Tyne, I was served a long-braised, then crisped, salty pig cheek, topped with an amber tangle of XO-sauced slaw. It was a big burst of umami; of crunch and soft and salt and fat. So basically, it was all the good things. I would have been very happy eating that again and again. There was a perfectly cooked whole turbot, bearing the squared-off griddle marks of the kitchen's live-fire grill. There were slices of salt-baked tomato, with pink slices of lamb heart piled on toast, with added salty anchovy. There was a huge Middle White pork chop, served just lightly pink at its heart, alongside half a pig's head, with crackling like glass. For the record, there were six of us that night, our numbers boosted by my colleagues from Radio 4's *Kitchen Cabinet* with whom I had just recorded a show over on the Newcastle side of the Tyne. Towards the end of dinner one of those companions sat back from the table and said, 'I think this may be my new favourite restaurant in the whole country.' It didn't feel like hyperbole.

These weren't the things with which I went home. Instead, it was a dish of fingernail-sized surf clams with black beans and chilli which stayed with me. This, I acknowledge, is a little odd. Seafood, indeed almost anything, cooked with fermented black beans is a classic of the Cantonese repertoire, and god knows I've spent enough time hanging out in those sorts of Chinese restaurants over the years. So why pick it out from this non-Chinese menu? Perhaps it simply stood out at Träkol, because it was such an outlier amid the clatter and noise of everything else. Either way, within days I was back home buying palourdes clams and seeking out recipes. I already had a highly developed clam habit. They are very satisfying to cook. Yes, they need a thorough washing first, but the liquor they release as they open turns them into a self-seasoning wonder. You can do them with crisped lardons and a glug of white wine. You can add a little cream to that. You can cook off a little shop-bought green curry paste, then deglaze with light coconut milk and a splash of fish sauce before throwing them in the pot, to create a completely ersatz but very enjoyable Thai (ish) clam dish. Whatever you do with them, there's something joyously communal and mucky-handed about eating clams in the shell. There is no tidy way in which to consume them. It's a hands-on job, full of slurpage, and the sharp clatter as the empty shells hit the discard bowl.

At Träkol, they came dressed in crispy chilli oil, which is one way to do it. The recipe for clams with black beans and chillies that I eventually came up with is a culinary non-sequitur in that, for the burst of chilli heat, I add Sichuan chilli bean sauce along with the chopped fresh red chillies, a clear interloper in a Cantonese dish. Then again, as I've said, I have no interest in authenticity. I only claim that it tastes nice, and that it gives you a way to vary the heat depending on taste. Sichuan chilli bean paste is a deep red condiment-cum-sauce ingredient: a ripe, fragrant flavour bomb, made with fermented broad beans, chillies and salt. It is very much worth having a jar of the stuff in the cupboard. It often comes in a pleasingly barrel-shaped pot, in commemoration of the barrels in which it was originally fermented.

Serves 4 with rice, and perhaps another dish

INGREDIENTS

1kg live clams
2 tbsp fermented black beans, rinsed and drained
2 tbsp vegetable oil
3 cloves of garlic, sliced
4 slices of ginger
2 spring onions, cut into 4cm pieces
1 tbsp Sichuan chilli bean paste
2 tbsp Shaoxing wine
1 tsp sugar
1 tsp sesame oil
1 tsp soy
2 fresh red chillies, chopped
3 tbsp chopped coriander (optional)

1. As ever with clams, pick out any that are cracked. Drop the rest on to the bottom of the dry sink to dislodge any silt. Put through a couple of changes of cold water.

2. Crush the rinsed black beans in a bowl with the back of a spoon to break them up.

3. Heat the vegetable oil in a wok over a high heat for a minute. Add the garlic, black beans, ginger and spring onions and toss for about 30 seconds. Now add the Sichuan chilli bean paste. Mix it in with the other ingredients and let it sizzle in the oil for about a minute to release its fragrance.

4. Add the clams, and pour the Shaoxing wine in around the side of the wok. Give all the ingredients in the wok a good mix. Turn the heat down to medium and cover with a saucepan lid.

5. Lift the lid now and then to check that the clams are opening. The time this takes may vary a little depending on the clams, but will rarely be more than 10 minutes and probably 5. Bosh them around a little with a wooden spoon to check they are opening. Shake the wok to keep it all moving.

6. When all the clams are open, add the sugar and the sesame oil and mix. Check the broth. If it's not salty enough, add the soy to taste.

7. Sprinkle with the chopped chillies and coriander (if using), and serve.

Sardines à l'huile

Inspired by the herrings with potatoes served at Chez
Georges in Paris (and an idea from Henry Harris at
Bouchon Racine, in London)

Restaurants must nail a bunch of things to be a success. Many
of them are obvious: nice food, staff who aren't psychotic, the
kind of room you want to sit in to eat the nice food, rather
than somewhere that feels like death's foyer. Others are less
obvious. Gifted chefs rarely get to run kitchens just because
they know how to cook. Being a culinary genius is never
enough, whatever TV cooking shows might suggest. They
also have to know how to write a menu full of those dishes
people will want to eat in significant number, how to order
the right volume of ingredients to service that demand, how
to calculate gross profit and so on. It also helps to have a
talent for working out how to repurpose ingredients bought
in for one dish which didn't sell, into another which will, while
making it look like that was your plan all along. The economics of restaurant kitchens are never just about what you do
serve; they're also about what you don't. Anything wasted
isn't just a shame. It's money off the bottom line.

A key part of this is portion control. Restaurants have to
give the impression of generosity, even if what's on your
plate is merely a function of the menu price, itself a function
of the ingredient price. (Rule of thumb: ingredient costs
should be 30% of the final price on the menu.) Restaurants
can go bust very quickly if they screw up portion control.
And when they seem to abandon portion control altogether
it can feel utterly subversive. In the summer of 2016, I went
into dribbling rhapsodies over a tiny place in London's Hoxton

called Petit Pois Bistro. As its name suggests, it did a small range of French classics very well. The moules marinière were plump and came in a deep liquor that demanded to be mopped up by slab after slab of their warm sourdough. There was a thick disc of black pudding, pin-pricked with jewels of fat under a perfect poached egg, followed by impeccable steak frites with frothy Béarnaise sauce. It was all very nice. But that wasn't what really sent me off on one. It was the chocolate mousse. It was deep without being cloying, and offered up a huge, satisfying chocolatey hit. This was a chocolate mousse to eat with a friend.

What sealed the deal for me was the way in which it was served. It wasn't portioned out. They simply brought to the table one of those large, beige, patterned and glazed mixing bowls your parents had when you were a kid, and you may still have now; the sort you have to hold in the crook of your arm if you really want to get purchase on its contents with a wooden spoon. It was full to the brim with chocolate mousse, the surface hidden under a thick, unsullied snowfall of cocoa powder. Then they told us to help ourselves. I hesitated for a moment. This was how it was done at home, not in restaurants. This was how your friends fed you. If a restaurant did that, did it mean the restaurant was my friend? Clearly, they loved and trusted me. It was a stunningly simple and compelling act of generosity. I took a fair portion and when I'd finished that, another small scoop, but only because I could and I felt it necessary to engage fully with the moment. This was a seriously rich chocolate mousse and there was such a thing as enough, even for me. I didn't need the second scoop. Then again who ever *needs* chocolate mousse?

As a journalist I am paid to overthink things, so I did a bit of that. The whole sweet psychodrama of deciding for yourself how much you wanted to eat was a giddy complex dance of shame and appetite. Of course you could scoop away at the bowl until you could see the glaze, but what would this restaurant which clearly trusted you think of your behaviour and life choices if you did that? Surely you wanted to reward their trust and sense of decency with an equal display of good manners and self-control? It struck me that some people might find the whole damn thing just too complex and demanding. Who wants to sit in a restaurant worrying about what the staff will think of us if we go back in for seconds? Happily, I am not one of those people.

Which brings me to the wonderful Chez Georges, which has been trading on Rue du Mail in Paris since 1964. When people ask me for Paris restaurant recommendations, Chez Georges is always first on the list, because it is everything you want a Parisian bistro to be. It hasn't been gussied up, as has happened to Allard and Benoit (both lovely in their own way, but just a little glossy for my taste). The frontage of Chez Georges is a bit cracked and knackered. The half net curtains in the windows were probably lovely when they were first hung, whichever side of the millennium that was. There is a bit of grime in the cracks of the long narrow room's tiled floor. The walls are nicotine yellow; there are arched mirrors and little red-shaded lamps attached to the spaces in between them. Push through the doors and the arc of thick velvet curtain behind them to keep out the street cold and you will get noise and bustle. You will be chivvied along by black-clad, white-aproned waitresses with a low centre of gravity and sturdy arms for carrying. If they attempted to change or, god forbid, update any of this, there would be outrage and fury. As ever, Paris really does cleave to its clichés, and nurtures them carefully.

And the food? It is what you want it to be: snails in garlic butter, champignons à la Grecque, steak au poivre and uncompromisingly stinky andouillette with chips. They'll bring you crisp radishes to crunch through while you're trying to decide, and hunks of baguette with salty butter from Brittany.

Then there's the soused herring with potato salad. The potatoes arrive in a large glass bowl, flecked with the brilliant green of fresh herbs. They are a little bland and rightly so, for the herring has got the saltiness covered. The fish comes in a large square tureen and you are invited to help yourself. Lift off the lid and take out the light brown fillets with the flash of silver from the hint of skin, with their tangle of marinated fresh onion. Drain off a little oil. They will eventually take the tureen away but they'll check with you first before doing so. Have you had enough? Jolly good. Remember, you've still got a main course coming. You need to leave room for the ris de veau aux morilles and the baba au vieux rhum Saint-Etienne.

The Chez Georges soused herring is a restaurant dish made domestic courtesy of the way in which it is served. It therefore makes sense for me now to take it back to the kitchen at home. My original plan was to work out how to souse my own herring, but Henry Harris at Bouchon Racine (who inspired the chicken in a mustard sauce recipe on page 138) made it clear that would be tricky. Fresh herring are surprisingly hard to come by in the UK, because they tend to be made into rollmops or kippers. Henry serves a version of the Chez Georges herring dish, but he starts with cured and cold-smoked herring fillets imported from France in significant volume. I suggested to him that I try doing it with sardine fillets instead, given they are very much a related pelagic fish, and Henry told me he'd already done a version like that. So I thank him for all the guidance. The point is that they are served at the table out of the dish in which they were marinated in the vegetable oil, with the onions and aromatics. And note: it is vegetable oil not olive oil for, like the original herring, this has its origins in northern European waters.

Serves 6 as a starter

INGREDIENTS

20g sea salt
70ml white wine or sherry vinegar
500g sardine fillets (ask your fishmonger to do the filleting,
    generally starting with a kilo of sardines)
3 large onions, halved, then thinly sliced into rings
2 medium carrots, peeled and sliced into thin discs (if you want
    the authentic pretty petal look, once you've peeled them, use the
    corner of a metal peeler to cut four equidistant vertical grooves.
    Then, when you slice them, you will have the desired shape.
    Unless you think life is too short for this sort of malarkey)
A few sprigs of fresh thyme
15 whole black peppercorns
Vegetable oil
1kg waxy new potatoes (Ratte, Anya or Charlotte will do very
    nicely)
Fresh chives and flat-leaf parsley
Also lemon juice or vinegar, sea salt and black pepper

METHOD

1. Make a 2% brine solution by adding 20g of sea salt to
   one litre of water. Add 70ml of vinegar. Mix to
   dissolve the salt. Put the sardines in enough of the
   brine in a Tupperware box to cover, put the lid on
   and leave in the fridge for 24 hours.

2. When the time is up, drain the fillets. Get a nice
   ceramic dish which will make you feel like you're

running a cute bistro in the 2nd arrondissement. Put in a layer of sardines. Top that with a generous layer of the sliced onions and some of the carrot slices, a sprig or two of thyme and a few black peppercorns. Then add another layer of sardines, cover with the other ingredients and keep layering until you've used up all the sardines. Top up with vegetable oil to cover and put back in the fridge until dinner the next day.

3. Cook the new potatoes in their skins until done. If you were a conscientious chef, you would now peel the potatoes but you're not, so don't feel you have to. When they have cooled enough to handle, slice them into discs. Put them into a large serving bowl and sprinkle on the chopped chives and flat-leaf parsley and a small amount of salt. Serve still just warm, with the sardines. With which your guests will serve themselves.

4. I find that these sardines need a really good squirt of lemon juice or white wine vinegar, and a serious sprinkle of sea salt and cracked black pepper.

Indeed, in the day or two after I'd made them, I realized that my favourite way to eat them was actually not with the potatoes, but with well-toasted slabs of sourdough. Slice the sardine fillets into three or so pieces and put into a bowl with a generous amount of the onion, carrot and fresh thyme. Dress well with vinegar or lemon juice and salt. Toast the bread and while it's still warm dribble with spoonfuls of the vegetable oil in which the sardine fillets were marinated. Then layer on the pieces of fish, onion and carrot. Sprinkle with a few thyme leaves. Add a grind of pepper and cut the toast into thick fingers. These make terrific if slightly messy canapés.

Vegetables

Globe artichokes stuffed with spiced rice

Inspired by the enginar çiçeği served by the late Esra
Muslu at her restaurant Zahter, London (with a small
diversion into the globe artichoke vinaigrette served at
both Oslo Court and Colbert)

In 2003 I interviewed my late mother, Claire, for a large feature
to mark the publication of her memoirs. While she achieved
great success and fame as an advice columnist, broadcaster
and writer, her beginnings had been meagre and her childhood
abusive, although she had spared us kids the gory details by
simply not talking about it. She had broken off all contact with
her own parents when she was a teenager, and as a result we
had never met them. We had no competing source of

information. Now Claire had written it all down and I finally got to meet the story on the page. There were many revelations during the conversations I had with her after reading the book, almost all of them irrelevant to a cookbook like this. But there was one detail that stuck with me. She talked about being evacuated during the Second World War to the English countryside and how the people who had taken her in did so grudgingly and meanly. Food was hard to come by and the dull ache of hunger a reality. She and a few of the other displaced London kids took to nicking crops from the local farmers' fields. 'There was good eating to be had from a newly picked swede,' she told me casually, one day.

I have always been struck, and hugely moved, by the contrast between that working-class child literally scraping away in the mud for the food she needed, and the groaning table I took for granted as a greedy kid in the cherry-blossomed north-west London suburbs. In adulthood, Claire became someone who, rather than fight for scraps, could luxuriate in the joys of dinner, and oh how she did so. I know now that my privileged childhood diet was defined by the relatively exotic and the luxurious. The globe artichokes we sometimes ate in the 1970s with a thick, mustardy vinaigrette sum that up for me. The fact is that a globe artichoke is not simply something you get to eat. It is a culture to which you must be introduced, or at least in the Britain of the 1970s and 80s it was. You had to learn how to eat one, because the huge sea green thistle, its leaves shyly closed, does not immediately tell you what the hell to do. Pliny the Elder, the Roman author of the *Naturalis Historia*, an encyclopedic account of the natural world around him, was not a fan. 'We turn into a corrupt feast the earth's monstrosities, those which even the animals instinctively avoid,' he wrote of his fellow Roman countrymen's taste for them. I can only assume poor old Pliny had never been served a good one.

There is something sweetly meditative about the process of pulling off each leaf, dipping it into the vinaigrette, then dragging its root over your teeth to get at the edible bit. You work your way inwards, the pile of discarded leaves in front of you growing ever larger, until you reach the centre. Now you must navigate the business of pulling off the 'choke', the very centre of the thistle, with its hairy filaments. But with a bit of effort, you will reach the prize of the heart, to be doused in yet more vinaigrette. For years the classic globe artichoke vinaigrette was absent from restaurant menus, perhaps because it was regarded as simply too old-fashioned. But eventually the good things, however old-fashioned, get re-discovered simply because they are good. In more recent years I have eaten it at Colbert, the Sloane Square outpost of the group which grew out of the Wolseley. It is also regularly on the menu at Oslo Court in London's St John's Wood. (For more on that wonderful place see the recipe for duck à l'orange on page 150.) It is relatively simple to prepare. Just follow the first stage of the recipe below. Serve it with a very generous volume of the vinaigrette from page 26. And never underestimate just how much of that vinaigrette you'll get through. If you're eating it properly.

The opening in late 2021 of chef Esra Muslu's modern Turkish restaurant Zahter, just off London's Carnaby Street, introduced me to another, much more intricate way with the globe artichoke. For enginar çiçeği – literally stuffed artichoke – the choke is removed after the thistle has been boiled, leaving a void down to the heart, which is filled with a spiced, lemony rice. More of the rice is shoved into the gaps between the leaves and then it's all topped with a sweet-sour chimichurri, toasted almonds and jewel-like pomegranate seeds. It becomes a substantial item. Yes, you drag your teeth over the base of each leaf as with the vinaigrette version, but now you also get the fragrant rice. After I'd tried it the first time, Muslu explained that her food draws on the vegetable-led traditions of southern Turkey, rather than the meatier traditions represented by the smoky ocakbaşi restaurants that crowd in around north London's Green Lanes, where a lot of the capital's Turkish community lives. That said, if you look for other recipes online, you'll see that they usually include minced lamb in the stuffing. This non-meat version is very much Muslu's.

After eating it a couple of times, I came up with my own version. Because it was such a complex dish, I sent that recipe to Esra. She very kindly complimented me on what I'd come up with but told me it wasn't quite right, and then invited me into her kitchen to see how it should be done. Hers was unlike almost any other restaurant kitchen I'd ever set foot in, and I've visited many. Because the dishes were so particular, she had drawn much of her brigade from the ranks of women in London's Turkish community, many of whom had never before worked in a professional kitchen. But they were the ones who understood the spices and the methods that underpinned these dishes and so those were the ones she needed. It is common to describe the staff of a restaurant as being like a family, but this was far more like that than most. Late in the morning of that day, work stopped and a prep table in the centre of the kitchen was spread with bowls of yoghurt and honey, soft buns, olives, salads and so much more, and together we ate a pre-service brunch. It was a domestic moment, amid the commercial kitchen, presided over by Esra, who was clearly deeply loved and respected by her staff.

In August of 2023, to the shock of London's restaurant community, it was announced that Esra had died, after a horribly short illness. She was only forty-four years old, but in that time had achieved a huge amount, including multiple restaurants in both Istanbul and London. My review of Zahter, published in January of 2022, began with dessert because she served the very best baklava I had ever eaten: it was light and fragrant and somehow both soft and crisp. I'm not going to attempt a recipe for that. I know my limits. But perhaps this recipe for her fabulous artichoke can stand as my memorial to her.

I'm not going to pretend. Unlike globe artichoke vinaigrette, which is straightforward, this takes effort. I can see exactly how it works for a restaurant, with the various elements lending themselves to prior preparation, so the dish can be brought together on service. Perhaps think of this one as a dinner party dish. It's fine cold. It's even better if the key elements are served still just warm.

Serves 4

INGREDIENTS

4 large globe artichokes
½ a lemon for the boiling pot
Sea salt
50g sliced almonds, toasted
The seeds of ½ a pomegranate

For the rice
2 medium onions, chopped
140ml olive oil
200g baldo rice (at a pinch, substitute with arborio if not
    available)
1½ tsp ground cinnamon
1½ tsp ground allspice
½ tsp ground black pepper
1 tbsp caster sugar
1½ tsp table salt
6 spring onions, roughly chopped
100g fresh dill, roughly chopped

For the chimichurri
35g fresh flat-leaf parsley, stalks removed
35g fresh dill
½ a red onion
2 fresh red chillies, deseeded
Juice of 2 lemons, and their zest
60ml white wine vinegar
1 tbsp caster sugar
230ml olive oil
Sea salt and ground black pepper to taste

METHOD

1. Artichokes usually have their stalks still intact. With a sharp knife slice those off so the base of the artichoke is flat. If you're simply serving them whole with vinaigrette, put them into a big pan of boiling water. Squeeze in the juice of half a lemon and then throw in the squeezed-out lemon half. (The juice stops them going too brown.) Add a good pinch of salt. Put a lid on the pot and boil for at least 20 minutes. Check whether they are done by sticking the tip of a sharp knife into the base. It should slip in easily. It can take up to 40 minutes or perhaps even more, depending on the size and age of the artichokes, for them to be done. Drain and leave to cool on their side so water between the leaves comes out, turning a couple of times so that gravity gets to do its thing. Serve each one on a plate, with a big bowl on the table for the discarded leaves, and volumes of the vinaigrette from page 26.

2. If you're making the stuffed artichoke, cut off the stalk as above, then cut off the top third of the thistle. These leaves can be tough to cut through. I

find a solid serrated bread knife does the job. Trim round the edges with scissors to even them up. Follow the cooking instructions above. Once cooked, because you now have a nice flat cut surface, you can leave them to cool upside down, to remove the maximum amount of moisture.

3. When they have cooled enough to handle, pull out the centre leaves, which should be white with a purple tinge. Eventually you will see the hairy 'choke' beneath. Pull that out too. Use a spoon to scrape it off the heart. This is fiddly. It's annoying. It takes time. It's also worth it. Eventually, you will have cleaned out the whole choke and be left with a void in the centre of the artichoke. Well done.

4. Now make the rice. In a saucepan gently cook the chopped onions in the olive oil over a very low heat, until they are exceedingly soft. This can take 30 minutes. Meanwhile soak the rice in double the volume of room temperature water. Drain the rice and rinse.

5. When drained, add the rice to the onion and olive oil mixture and stir together. Now add the cinnamon, allspice, black pepper, sugar and salt and stir to mix through. Add the same volume of boiling water to rice, so 200ml. Stir the mixture together, put a lid on the pan and leave to cook unmolested on a very low heat until all the water has been absorbed, probably 30 minutes. Take off the heat and leave to cool with the lid on. When cool add a little more salt if you think it needs it. Mix in the chopped spring onions and the dill.

6. While it's cooling, make the chimichurri by pulsing together the ingredients in a food processor. Do not run it for too long. You want it roughly chopped, not puréed. (You can, of course, finely chop the ingredients by hand.) Add more salt, sugar or acidity to taste.

7. It's time to dress the artichokes. First season each one liberally with sea salt, not just in the hollow in the centre, but between the outer rows of leaves. Now dress them lightly with the chimichurri, again both in the centre and between the leaves. Finally, stuff loosely with the rice mixture.

8. To serve, top each artichoke with a good thick layer of the remaining chimichurri. Then sprinkle on a generous amount of the almonds and the pomegranate seeds.

In memory of Esra Muslu
1978–2023

Dry-fried green beans with ground mushrooms (or minced pork) and chilli

Inspired by the dish served at the Four Seasons Chinese restaurant, located at 12 Gerrard Street, London (and many other places besides)

The listing above for the address of Four Seasons, not easily confused with the fancy hotel chain of the same name, is very specific. This is because there are two Four Seasons on Gerrard Street in London's Chinatown. The other one is next door, at number 11. I have no idea what goes on in there. Never been. Never will. I am number 12 until I die. I started going years ago, having read a piece by Simon Hopkinson who said they serve the best Cantonese roast duck in London. He knows a few things about duck, that man. While I cannot claim to have tried all the versions, a task I would be available for if time allowed, it is certainly the best Cantonese roast duck I have ever tried. The skin is dark and lacquered and pleasingly salty. It is crisp in places and has just the right ballast of fat. You can order it off the bone, but don't do that. Ask for it on the bone. That gives you something to hold on to. The meat is tender and well rendered.

Four Seasons is a simple, bustling space of white walls and yellow tablecloths. At some point a few years ago it became the place I went to alone at lunchtime, if time allowed, on the day we were recording an episode of *The Kitchen Cabinet*. We record the show from 7pm in front of a live audience, and because of the travel it doesn't always leave time for dinner (if you don't count our famed train picnics on the way back; I love a pack of supermarket charcuterie and a torn baguette as much as the next greedy-guts, but let's not mistake that for dinner). Better to eat properly at lunchtime. Plus, lunch alone, with your thoughts, is always a good idea before the carnival of an as-live radio record in front of 200 or more people. I have always liked the fact that the staff at Four Seasons never seemed to pay me the slightest bit of attention, despite the fact I was and remain a serious regular. I have always just been another bloke eating alone with a copy of the *New Yorker* magazine for company. In early 2020, as Covid was raging through Wuhan, Chinese restaurants in the UK experienced a sudden drop in custom. People were boycotting them as if they might be a source of contagion. As an act of solidarity with the Chinese restaurant community, I reviewed Four Seasons. I drew attention to my habit. In the end, of course, the empty seats in Chinatown proved a harbinger for what was to come with lockdown and the closure of all restaurants, along with pretty much everything else.

When the lockdowns ended, I went back to Four Seasons. My order remained the same: a portion of Cantonese roast duck and the dry-fried green beans with minced pork. A while ago I had become a carb dodger. It isn't that I don't like carbohydrates. I love them. Give me bread and pasta and rice and potatoes. Give me all of them. If a review requires me to eat carbs, I will do so and with serious enthusiasm. But as a man whose job requires eating and who has a sluggish metabolism, every little helps in the battle against too much me. I took to having these vegetables with my duck instead of rice. I love the way the beans crinkle in the heat of the wok, and how their flavour intensifies. I love the addition of the small amount of pork, which plays the supporting role of condiment rather than main event.

I have been cooking my own version at home for years. I could, I suppose, have looked up an actual recipe written by someone deep-steeped in the Chinese culinary tradition. But the truth is that I like mine. It's straightforward and satisfying. The inclusion of minced pork should, of course, bar its inclusion in this section of non-meat dishes. But first, you'll always find it listed amid the vegetable dishes on Chinese restaurant menus. And second, I've included a version using blitzed mushrooms which is entirely vegan. My instructions start with that.

Serves 4 with other dishes

INGREDIENTS

400g chestnut mushrooms (it will look like a lot but it will cook
    down to under a quarter of that weight) or 150g minced pork
Vegetable oil, for frying
4 spring onions, finely chopped
2 cloves of garlic, finely chopped
A thumb-size piece of ginger, peeled and finely chopped
1 or 2 fresh red chillies according to taste, finely chopped
    (optional)
1 tbsp light soy
1 generous tbsp hoi sin sauce
400g green beans, topped and tailed, and cut in half

METHOD

1. If using the mushrooms, blitz them to what looks
   like a crumb in a food processor. Put 2 tablespoons
   of vegetable oil into a high-sided pan or better still, a
   metal wok. Add the ground mushrooms and cook
   them over a gentle heat until all the moisture has
   been driven off. This can take 15 to 20 minutes. Keep
   moving them around so they don't stick to the pan.
   When finished, remove the mushrooms from the pan
   and reserve.

2. Heat 2 tablespoons of vegetable oil in the pan or
   wok over a medium heat, then add the spring onions,
   garlic, ginger, and the red chillies if using. Stir-fry for
   a few minutes until the spring onions have clearly
   wilted and softened.

3. Return the cooked mushrooms to the pan and mix in with the other ingredients.

4. If using the minced pork, add that to the wilted spring onions, garlic, ginger and chillies now and stir to break up any clumps. Gently brown the pork thoroughly for 5 to 10 minutes until it's dry and almost crumbly.

5. Now we have either the ground mushrooms or the minced pork in the pan. Whichever one you're using, the rest of the method is the same: add the soy and the hoi sin and mix everything around until it's fully coated. Keep cooking and moving it around in the wok until dry and a little crusty.

6. All of this can be done in advance. You can stop now if you like until you're ready to finish the dish.

7. When it's time to do so, put the wok over a high heat, and when everything is sizzling add the green beans. Give them time against the surface of the wok. Toss with the other ingredients.

8. After a couple of minutes put a lid over the pan and turn the heat down to medium.

9. If you like your beans crunchy, 5 minutes will do it. If you want them softer, leave them to cook for longer. When you're happy with the texture, take the lid off and stir-fry on high for a couple more minutes. You can add an extra splash of soy at this point if you think it needs a little extra seasoning.

10. Serve with rice. Or a whole Cantonese roast duck if you happen to have one to hand.

Grilled leeks with pistachio 'romesco'

Inspired by the dish served by chef Andrew Clarke at
Acme Fire Cult, Dalston

The first time I met Andrew Clarke it was not to discuss the
impressive things he can do with a fatty piece of animal and
a live-fire grill. It was not to discuss his way with shellfish,
steamed open over hot coals. It was to talk about the often
gruelling business of being a chef. In the autumn of 2016
Clarke, an impressive-looking man in possession of many
vibrant tattoos and a long plaitable beard that a Viking would
envy, had posted an image of himself to Instagram, holding
a mug, a bottle of spirits on the table in front of him. The
implication was that the contents of one was now inside the
other. The caption to the moody black and white picture
drove the point home. 'This was me ten months ago,' it said.
'Inside I was suffering from a pain so extreme that I could
barely cope.' It went on to detail his slump into depression,
his journey out of it, and followed that with a call to arms. He
wanted to encourage colleagues to talk about what they had
gone through.

The restaurants I have spent so many years reviewing can
be curious places of split personality. On the one side of the
door is a dining room specifically designed to encourage
relaxation; on the other side of the door can be an environ-
ment specifically engineered for maximum stress. They are
rooms full of fire and knives and tension. The relaxed people
at the table are too often benefiting from the massive stress
of the people at the stoves. Clarke and I talked in detail that
day about the disfigured nature of cheffing. 'Kitchen life
encourages drink and drug abuse,' he told me. 'If you do well

on service you reward yourself. And if you do badly you console yourself.' It's also a profession which can too often pay scant attention to working practices and reasonable hours. Around that time the union Unite conducted a survey of professional chefs in the UK. Almost half regularly worked between forty-eight and sixty hours a week. Seventy-eight per cent said they'd had an accident or a near miss through fatigue. More than a quarter were drinking to get through their shift, a figure which doubled to 56% when it came to taking painkillers. A startling 51% said they suffered from depression due to overwork. Bullying and abuse were simply seen as part and parcel of a career in the kitchen. I remember well the concerned father who emailed me about his son who had quit a career in Michelin-starred kitchens because of the behaviour of head chefs, 'which in any other field would mean summary dismissal and probably charges of assault'.

Part of the problem is that for a long while, various bits of the media bought into this. Gordon Ramsay built an entire television career on various formats, including *Hell's Kitchen* and *Kitchen Nightmares*, which seemed to demand that at some point he would shout and humiliate someone. If there were tears, all to the good. As he was a gifted chef who had achieved three Michelin stars at his flagship restaurant, among so much else, it was assumed that this was what it took. I am ashamed to admit that for a few years at the start of my time writing about restaurants, I assumed this to be the case too. As research for various features, I spent time during service in top-flight kitchens; saw the flare and spit of anger. When I questioned it, I was told it was just a part of the job. Oh. Okay. I had also read and revelled in the late Anthony Bourdain's memoir *Kitchen Confidential*, which portrayed New York chefs as some confederacy of raucous, often drug-addled pirates. It was a hell of a read and projected a certain filthy glamour on to what previously had been seen as the most unglamorous of jobs.

Clarke was there to tell me that drugs and depression and bullying and abuse did not need to be a part of working in hospitality. Along with fellow chef Doug Sanham he had founded Pilot Light (pilotlightcampaign.com), a social impact initiative designed to make the industry a better, healthier place for the people who work in it. He started a conversation; one which received extra impetus when the pandemic shut down kitchens and gave a lot of chefs the space in which to review their life choices. The vow of silence about senior chefs treating people appallingly was broken. Cooks started talking to journalists about behaviour they no longer regarded as acceptable. The issues have not gone away completely or even, depressingly, at all. But at least they are being discussed.

Happily, Andrew Clarke has continued to work in the restaurant business, because he's a terrific chef. In 2022, with fellow chef Daniel Watkins, he opened the boldly named Acme Fire Cult, in a semi-industrial space in Dalston, north London. It is the restaurant I referred to in the very helpful 'Advice to Readers' right at the start of this book. If you took my advice and made my version of their Bombay Mix, to stave off hunger while reading, you'll know what a good idea it is. It turned out that what I suggested – buy ready-made Bombay Mix and add nuts – is exactly what they do.

As I said when I reviewed the restaurant, Clarke would make a good cult leader. He really does have the beard for the job. The name Acme Fire Cult seemed to pick up on what was then the increasingly popular vogue for live-fire cooking. Except in one key regard. A lot of places that used flaming logs and charcoal were meat-centred. That had been the case with restaurants in which Clarke had worked previously. Acme Fire Cult was led by an interest in vegetables.

Or, as Clarke put it, they wanted to get away from the image that grilling was all about 'dude food'.

I ate some brilliant things that night, courtesy of the grill: smoked new potatoes in a tahini mayo with nutty chilli oil, charred cauliflower florets in an Indian-spiced butter sauce, a simple platter of the best grilled vegetables, dribbled with a luscious salsa verde. But the one that stayed with me, which made the biggest impression upon me, was the grilled leeks with pistachio romesco. It was just so clever: an impressively green plate of slow-grilled leeks, served at room temperature, dolloped with a fighty, mildly fiery, highly textured sauce the colour of a bowling green.

This recipe is not Andrew Clarke's pistachio romesco. He told me that he uses Iranian pistachios as 'they have the best flavour and the greenest colour', which you will find hard to obtain. He also said that the secret ingredient is a green leek oil, made using a piece of kit called a Thermomix, which you won't have at home unless you are a complete domestic cooking nerd. If you're interested, you need to bring one part of shredded leek tops, to three parts extra virgin olive oil, up to 60°C in the Thermomix, blitz it for a minute, then strain the now bright green oil through a muslin overnight. These are the sorts of things great restaurant chefs say and do. I have made adaptations for my kitchen and, I hope, for yours.

While we're on the subject it's worth acknowledging that this is in no way a romesco sauce that the Spanish would recognize. You can practically hear the Catalans rolling their eyes at the mere use of the word to describe this dish. A romesco is made with blitzed almonds and/or hazelnuts, and variants of dried chillies and roasted tomatoes, and should be a deep red. This is bright green, so I've put the word 'romesco' in quotation marks. Then again, as it's a rugged sauce involving ground nuts, olive oil, roast garlic and capsicums of one kind or another, I really don't think the title is too much of a stretch. Although I'm giving you the recipe for a whole dish involving grilled leeks, the sauce will go well with practically anything.

Serves 4 as a starter

INGREDIENTS

3 sizable leeks
1 medium head of garlic
2 large green bell peppers
1 or 2 fresh green chilli peppers, depending on how much heat
    you like
100ml good olive oil
25g fresh chives, finely chopped
100g shelled pistachios
1 tsp ground cumin
30ml white wine vinegar
Sea salt and ground black pepper
2 tbsp dry white breadcrumbs (I use panko, but stale ground
    bread will work perfectly)

METHOD

1. Slice off the root of the leeks and take off the top where the leaves start to divide. Slice what remains into three equal parts and then halve each of those vertically. Simmer in boiling water for 5 minutes, then leave to drain for at least an hour, and ideally for 2. Leeks are engineered to hold water and you need to get as much of that out as possible. Go watch an episode of that thing you're not really enjoying on

Netflix. Do not worry if they fall apart a little. It's part of the charm.

2. After the credits have rolled, heat the oven to 180°C/350°F/gas mark 4. Break the head of garlic in half, put both halves into an oven tray, dress with a little olive oil and bake for around 25 minutes, until the cloves are soft. Take out of the oven and leave to cool. When cool, squeeze the roasted garlic from its skins into a bowl. Discard the skins. I know you know to discard the skins, but you can't be too careful.

3. Cut all the peppers into quarters and remove the stems, seeds and white membrane. You now need to roast and blacken them. If you have a gas hob, put silver foil directly on to the hob around the burner to save making a terrible mess that has to be cleaned up afterwards, and place the peppers over a large flame. Turn them with tongs now and then so all parts get blackened. I find putting a wire cooling rack over the top of the hob makes it a little easier. Once the skin is completely blackened, which will take 10 or 15 minutes, put them into an oven dish and cover tightly with foil, so they steam as they cool. If you don't have a gas hob, you will need to put them under the grill to blacken them.

4. Once the peppers have cooled, use your thumbs to rub off the skins. It's a mucky job and you may need to wash your hands a couple of times. You will get most of the skin off on the first pass. Scrape with the blade of a sharp knife to get the rest off. I then put

them into the still hot oven for 10 minutes to dry out a little. It's an optional stage.

5. Put the olive oil in a saucepan with the chopped chives, and warm gently over a low heat. Simmer for about 5 minutes, then take the pan off the heat, cover and leave to cool.

6. It's time to make the sauce. First blitz the pistachios in a processor. You want a fine rubble rather than a dust. This sauce needs texture. When done, take them out and put to one side.

7. Now put the roasted peppers, roasted garlic, cumin, vinegar, 1 teaspoon of salt and 3 tablespoons of the chives in oil into the processor. (You will have some of the chive oil left. You will need it later.) Blitz until reasonably smooth, then put into a bowl.

8. Add the pistachio rubble and the breadcrumbs and give it a good stir. Add more salt and/or vinegar if you think it needs it.

9. To complete the dish, heat a dry cast iron skillet until it's starting to smoke, or a well-seasoned cast iron frying pan. (A non-stick pan will also do the job.) Add the leeks and let them brown and caramelize. Turn them every now and then. You want them grilled but also soft. It should take 15 to 20 minutes. Andrew Clarke has a big live-fire grill. If you have one of those, by all means use it. Alternatively try grilling them in a toastie machine if you have one, with the lid down so both sides of the leeks are grilled at once. It does a very nice job, although you will need to do them in batches.

10. I like to plate this on one dish from which everyone can serve themselves. Put a big dollop of the romesco in the middle of the plate and smooth it out into a disc. Layer a third of the grilled leeks on top, then dribble with a little of the remaining chive oil. Add another layer of romesco and another layer of leeks, and a further dribble of chive oil. Add a third and final layer. Sprinkle with a little extra sea salt and ground black pepper. This is best served at room temperature.

Kale laing, or kale braised in coconut milk with ginger, garlic and chilli

Inspired by the version served at Chef 'Budgie' Montoya's restaurant Sarap (now closed)

I have never been to India or China. I have not travelled across Mexico, Thailand or Lebanon. I do not have a phone full of photographs and a quiver full of traveller's anecdotes. It could therefore be argued, convincingly, that I have no right claiming knowledge of the food of all or any of these countries. I get the point. Friends of mine who have travelled extensively in these and many other countries do, I'm sure, possess a depth of knowledge that I do not. However, my home is in a city which attracts people from all over the world, and with them comes their food. It is one of the reasons I love living in London. Historically, it has always been a place to which people come. My own great-grandparents came here from somewhere less than Jew-friendly on the Polish-Ukraine border and they, and their cohort, brought with them their food culture.

Very soon after the arrival of that latest influx of Jewish immigrants, East End locals, whether Jewish or not, could hold forth with authority on what made a good bagel: the correct size, the correct sweetness, the optimum chewiness. And all because they'd eaten an awful lot of them. Although almost certainly they would have called it a beigel, pronounced by-gull. Don't get involved. The rows, or broiguses, over the correct spellings and pronunciations of Yiddish words depending on location really should not detain us.

The point is that in a big city, and many smaller ones too, you can travel the world by knife and fork. The opening up of China and the massive influx of students into the UK's universities really did result in a huge wave of restaurants and cafés serving the food of previously obscure Chinese provinces and traditions. We became fluent in hot pot and bao. A restless, questing appetite for the new created a market for restaurants from the Indian subcontinent representing very specific regions like Goa or Rajasthan or whole countries like Sri Lanka or Pakistan, whose food previously had been grouped together under the bald heading 'Indian'. Courtesy of restaurants like Supawan Thai or Som Saa we came to understand that Thailand had huge regional differences; that the food went far beyond fish cakes and green curries. And yes of course, if you visited the actual countries, you would learn more, so much more. But as an education goes, these restaurants have never been a bad place to start.

Once, during a lengthy stay in Los Angeles, I fell into conversation with Jonathan Gold, the revered critic first for *LA Weekly* and then the *LA Times*. He was as much anthropologist as he was restaurant critic. Through him I came to understand that the interesting food was not to be found in the fancy gilded palaces of Beverly Hills. It was in the huge patchwork of ethnic communities which made up the city's seemingly endless sprawl: the superb taquerias of East LA, the izakayas in Little Tokyo Downtown, the terrific Chinese restaurants in the San Gabriel Valley. I was looking for recommendations in Koreatown. 'The thing you have to understand,' Gold told me, 'is that you can find more traditional Korean restaurants in Los Angeles than you can in Seoul, because in Seoul they're looking to the future. Here, the immigrants are remembering.' He sent me to Soot Bull Jeep, one of the last Korean BBQ restaurants which still used burning coals, where severe middle-aged Korean ladies treated you like you were an idiot if you didn't immediately know what to do with the flames and the platters of sliced meats and the dips. Guilty as charged: I was an idiot. I didn't know what to do. They showed me. I loved it.

Cities are always changing. People from all over the world find reasons to come. Those reasons may not always be good – civil unrest, natural disasters, wars – but the end result, a new community amid the city's clamour, can be. For just as my great-grandparents' generation did, they bring with them their food. And we get to eat the good things and educate ourselves.

Sometimes of course people come from other countries just because they hunger for something new. I knew nothing of Filipino food before I went to Sarap, a bistro run by chef Ferdinand 'Budgie' Montoya, who was born in the Philippines and grew up in Australia. He came to the UK with his wife in 2012 determined to make his way in the restaurant business. He worked his way up from the very bottom rung of the brigades in some serious London kitchens cooking in a bunch of styles, before realizing he missed the flavours of the home cooking of his upbringing. That led in 2021 to the opening, on a site in London's West End, of Sarap Filipino Bistro. If you know where to look in a city like London you will find a café or restaurant serving the food of even the most seemingly obscure of culinary traditions. Many of them have been there for a very long time. The late and very great Charles Campion, a restaurant critic and fellow judge with me on *MasterChef*, did a serious and thorough job long before the Internet existed, of chronicling those establishments in his regularly updated *Rough Guide to London Restaurants*. He ground down shoe leather traipsing through the suburbs to find the best hole-in-the-wall places serving communities from, say, Afghanistan, Kerala or Kurdistan. As a result I was aware there were a couple of restaurants serving the relatively small London Filipino community; I just hadn't visited them.

At Sarap, which means 'delicious', I ate tranches of seabass cured in a soft coconut vinegar, roasted aubergine with salted duck egg, and a crunchy, crackling-heavy pig's trotter stuffed with lemongrass and truffle rice. The latter was a consolation prize for not being able to order the famed lechon or suckling pig, because at that point in the restaurant's life you had to have the whole piglet, which required twenty-four hours' notice and at least six friends to help you eat it. But the dish which really caught my attention, because it immediately felt like something I could replicate at home, was the kale laing, or kale braised in coconut milk with chilli and ginger. It was intense and soothing; a cousin of many similar South East Asian vegetable dishes, but deeper and darker. I liked it so much I made a clumsy version for dinner a couple of nights later. I then set about making it less clumsy by looking up a few recipes, including Montoya's own. Many versions use shrimp paste to boost the umami in the dish. I favour Montoya's choice of miso. It very much does the job and also has the benefit of rendering the dish entirely vegan. You can of course add more or less fresh chilli according to taste.

Serves 4 as a side dish

Vegetable oil, for frying
3 cloves of garlic, finely chopped
1 tbsp finely chopped ginger
1 fresh red chilli, finely chopped
1 tbsp brown miso paste
300g kale, stripped from the stalks and washed (discard the
    stalks)
200ml coconut milk
1 tbsp soy

METHOD

1. Put a deep frying pan or wok over a low heat. Add a
   couple of tablespoons of the oil, then add the garlic,
   ginger and chilli and cook gently for a couple of
   minutes.

2. Add the miso paste and mix in with the other
   ingredients. Cook gently for 5 minutes so it starts to
   melt down in the oil.

3. Add the kale in batches, giving each handful a little
   time to wilt. Mix in with the aromatics and miso.

4. When all the kale is in the pan, add the coconut milk,
   stir to combine everything, then cook covered over a
   low heat for about 10 minutes, giving it a stir every
   now and then.

5. Cook uncovered for 5 more minutes. Add the soy
   sauce. If you want it saltier, add a little more. Serve.

Nasu dengaku or miso glazed aubergine

Inspired by the version served by Scott Hallsworth at
Kurobuta, Double Dragon and now the Freak Scene,
London

It's rare that we can identify the beginning of a food trend
with any precision. With miso glazes we can be very precise
indeed. It began in a modest, low-slung building at 129 N. La
Cienega Boulevard, Beverly Hills. Some time in the first three
months of 1987. Probably around 5pm. That was when, after
stints cooking in both Peru and Alaska, chef Nobu Matsuhisa opened the doors to his eponymous restaurant.
Matsuhisa would become the cornerstone of a forty-strong
restaurant empire spanning the globe. Amid the lists of lov-
ingly hand-tooled sushi and sashimi was a dish of black
cod, marinated for three days in a glaze of miso, sake and
sugar, and then grilled. In the early years it would often be
misnamed by both journalists and diners as 'blackened' cod,
because of the caramelization of those sugars. Its name
actually refers to the species of fish involved, also known,
depending upon where you are, as sablefish or butterfish.
After those three days in the thick, sticky marinade and then
a quick flash under the grill, it becomes an irresistible mix of
soft and crisp, of sweet and deeply, umami-rich savoury. A
picture of it is still used on the Matsuhisa website as the entry
point to the menu.

Matsuhisa did not invent the dish. The Japanese have been
curing fish in sake and miso as a way of preserving it for
centuries. All he did was add a little more sugar to meet western tastes. In 1988 a moderately successful film star by the
name of Robert de Niro ate at the restaurant. He became a

233

regular and eventually encouraged Matsuhisa to go into a partnership with the restaurateur Drew Nieporent to launch an outpost in New York. Nobu opened in 1994. The brand was born. And yes, the sushi and sashimi were great. But oh, the black cod. As Adam Platt, the former restaurant critic of *New York Magazine*, once put it: 'Certain dishes are like that famous obelisk in Kubrick's *2001: A Space Odyssey*. When it lands in their midst, the apes have never seen anything like it, and they are changed forever. Miso cod was one of those dishes.' I think Platt liked it.

I first ate miso black cod in late 2000 at Ubon, the second London restaurant from the Nobu group, located in a shiny space of hard surfaces and high ceilings above a health club in Docklands, where the money people worked and played. And yes, it was delicious. It managed that neat trick of appearing sophisticated and poised and elegant in a way we associate with a Japanese aesthetic, while also being the sort of massive flavour bomb that would appeal to almost anybody. It would crop up time and again both in ostensibly Japanese restaurants, and in those that had merely been influenced by them. Eventually it became an item trundling around the conveyor belt at the YO!Sushi chain of self-service quasi-Japanese cafés. Nobu's miso black cod had achieved ubiquity.

But that wasn't all. It introduced a generation of western chefs to the possibilities of the fermented soya bean wonder that is miso paste, dissolved into a bit of liquor with a few scoops of sugar. Oh, the things that could be done with a miso glaze. In 2011 at the Modern Pantry in London's Clerkenwell, chef Anna Hansen, known for her magpie-like way with ingredients from the global store cupboard, served me a grilled onglet first marinated in miso and tamarind. I liked it very much. A couple of years later I came across it as a glaze for raw scallop at the Raby Hunt, the highly ambitious restaurant of self-taught chef James Close, near Darlington in the English north-east. In a restaurant in Bath, it was used to perk up grilled salmon. In a Norwich restaurant called Farmyard it was the topping to a dessert of white chocolate ganache. It has cropped up in literally dozens of my reviews. I'm aware this makes it sound like I am jaded by miso glazes. Not at all. Miso is an extraordinary ingredient. Yes, it has a huge flavour of its own but yet somehow it manages not to completely overwhelm the ingredient it's been introduced to.

Which brings us to miso grilled aubergine, or nasu dengaku as it's known in Japan, where it's a familiar side dish. (As 'nasu' means aubergine and 'dengaku' refers to the miso glaze, it's a pretty literal title.) It was first served to me in 2014 at the Japanese-inflected Kurobuta. I immediately decided it was my favourite way with aubergine. The skin was smoky and slightly chewy and the flesh, creamy. Then over the top was a bubbled and blistered glaze the colour of antique amber, scattered with various crushed salty nuts and bits of foliage. The west London restaurant belonged to Australian-born chef Scott Hallsworth, who had worked his way through the brigade at Nobu in London to become head chef and therefore knew one end of a glaze from another. He moved on from Kurobuta, through various other ventures, and a few years later opened Double Dragon. Again, the aubergine was one of my favourite things on the menu. He now has the Freak Scene in London's Parson's Green.

This is the version I first came up with a few years ago to feed a vegan guest I wanted to impress. I think it did the job. It's a huge crowd pleaser, vegan or not. You may find, when you go looking for miso paste, that the names are less than revealing or that there might be a dizzying selection. If it's red or brown it is perfect for the job. Although this is a recipe for nasu dengaku the glaze described here can be used on frankly anything. It's terrific as a late addition to roasted meats and fish, especially to cuts almost finished on the barbecue. Add it right at the end and let the heat get to it. It works well with other vegetables too. Just experiment.

Serves 4 as a side dish or 2 as a main

INGREDIENTS

120ml mirin
120ml sake (or substitute with Shaoxing wine or dry sherry)
120g red miso paste
60g light brown sugar
2 tsp sesame oil
A thumb-size piece of ginger, peeled
2 sizable aubergines
Vegetable oil, for cooking
80g crushed peanuts
4–5 spring onions, finely chopped

METHOD

1. Put the mirin and sake (or substitute) into a saucepan and gently heat.

2. When it's just beginning to simmer, add the miso paste and the sugar. Continue to heat and stir until both the sugar and the miso have dissolved into the liquid. Allow it to come to just shy of boiling, then turn down the heat and simmer for 10 to 15 minutes, stirring every now and then, until it thickens.

3. Add the sesame oil and grate in the ginger. Stir again and then leave to cool.

4. Meanwhile, cut the tops off the aubergines, and slice them in two vertically. Now score the flesh quite deeply in long diagonal strokes a couple of centimetres apart. Then score them in the other direction, so that you have a square pattern.

5. Heat 3 tablespoons of vegetable oil in a frying pan over a medium heat. Place the first 2 aubergine halves skin side down in the oil and cook for 3 minutes, until the skin is starting to crinkle. Now put them flesh side down for 4 or 5 minutes, until deeply coloured, but do not let them burn. Turn them back skin side down. Cover the pan with a big enough saucepan lid, turn the heat down and leave them to cook for about 5 minutes. They should end up soft and slumped but in one piece, the square pattern still obvious. Transfer them to an oven tray and then cook the other halves. You can do this and make the glaze well in advance, leaving you only to finish the dish when it's time to eat.

6. Heat your grill as high as it will go. Slather the aubergines with the miso glaze, and grill. Keep an eye on them. You want them to bubble and brown, but not to blacken.

7. When done, scatter the aubergines with the crushed peanuts and the chopped spring onions. You can also add fronds of coriander if you fancy.

Potatoes and salsa verde

Inspired by the dish served by Jacob Kenedy at
Bocca di Lupo, London

Some of the things served in restaurants are less dishes than
ideas. Really good ones, but only ideas all the same. You just
have to see through the cheffy presentation to recognize it.
The first time this struck me was in May of 2007. I was in
New York at the start of a night out that I eventually came to
regard with both suspicion and shame. I was researching a
book about the rise of the luxe economy, through the high-
end restaurant sectors in seven of the world's big cities, the
likes of Dubai, Tokyo, Moscow and, of course, New York.
When I had proposed the idea to my wife, she had rolled her
eyes. 'That just sounds like an excuse to travel the world
eating expensive food.' To which I had replied, 'What do you
mean, just?'

Eventually, it would smother my appetite, both literal and
figurative, for the luxury restaurant experience, with its stools
for the lady's handbag and its torchon of foie gras and its
chandeliers like crystal tits. I had overdosed on luxe, which is
its own very special kind of obscenity. For now, though, here
I was in New York in the spring, and I was still very much up
for it. To kick off, I wanted to write about the newly emerging phenomenon of something called 'the food blogger',
whatever that was: something to do with people who went
out for dinner and wrote about it. Yes, that was what I did,
but I got a newspaper to pick up the bill and I knew who the
readers were. These people actually paid for their own dinners, and had to find their own readership. It seemed like an

odd hobby, and I wanted to understand it better. I had recruited a man called Steve Plotnicki, a wealthy and successful businessman regarded then as the king of the food bloggers. He ate out all over the world, photographed his dinner, and wrote about his experiences dish by dish. (He would eventually turn this into a high-end restaurant review site called *Opinionated About Dining*.)

I asked if I could accompany him on a restaurant meal in New York, and watch him do his thing. I would pick up the bill. He had suggested a high-end restaurant crawl: a couple of dishes each, taken in the biggest of big-ticket places across Manhattan. My bank account shuddered. I said sure, why not. We would end up eating our way through Thomas Keller's Per Se, Bouley, Eleven Madison Park and WD 50, all of them revered and garlanded in their own way. Don't ask me what we ate; the whole thing merged into a mess of duck this way, and scallop that way, and just look at this limpid jus. Oh, the humanity. As journalists are wont to say, it was good copy.

Our adventure started at Jean-Georges, the flagship Michelin three-star restaurant of the Alsatian-born chef Jean-Georges Vongerichten. It's located on the ground floor of a golden skyscraper at the south-west corner of Central Park named Trump International Hotel and Tower. Back then, when Trump was only a bright orange businessman rather than a bright orange political fraud, this seemed only vaguely ludicrous rather than deeply sinister as now. I have had a decidedly mixed set of experiences with Vongerichten's restaurant empire. His diffusion lines, places like ABC in New York as well as Spice Market and his brasserie at the Connaught, both in London, have always struck me as a masterclass in form over content. I hated Spice Market for its mediocre, grossly over-priced take on the laksa, and its tasteless short rib. I pointed and laughed at Jean-Georges at the Connaught for its tiny, £31 truffle pizza.

But I have always loved the mothership, in a high-ceilinged room flooded with light from the tall windows so it feels like eating at altitude. I have loved the parade of perfectly poised, Asian-accented dishes that come to the table: the tuna tartare in the spicy ginger broth; the egg shell filled with frothy scrambled white and yolk topped with caviar; the crisp, golden slices of fried brioche sandwiching a cured egg yolk, the whole topped with more caviar.

And then there was the sea urchin. It's very simple. A piece of black bread, perhaps pumpernickel or something similar, is spread with a thick, cold layer of the best salted butter. Placed on top of that is a sea urchin, the bigger the better. And on top of that is a single, crisp ring of pickled jalapeño pepper. That's all. It is possibly the single best mouthful I have ever eaten. There are the dark rye and treacle tones of the bread, the fat and salt of the butter, the creaminess and seaside umami of the sea urchin, and then the pinprick of heat and acidity from the jalapeño. Granted, if you don't have a taste for sea urchins you won't like it. Stay away. But if you do, oh boy.

I was going to include a recipe for this, but there really is no recipe. It is just bread, butter, urchin and jalapeño stacked one atop the other. If you attempt it at home, yours may not end up looking as perfect as the one coming out of the Jean-Georges kitchen for big bucks, but the essentials will be there. It's the same with the deep-fried prawn heads served as a snack at Mark Hix's Oyster & Fish House in Lyme Regis. It's a genius of a snack. By dint of what else they serve, they have a lot of small prawn heads. Instead of throwing them away they chuck them in the deep fat fryer. The prawn shells become friable, like fragments of fried filo, and the heads give them a sweet savoury burst. Again, I was going to include a recipe, but really, it's already there: get some prawn heads; throw them in the deep fat fryer.

And then there's this dish, which I first tried at Jacob Kenedy's Bocca di Lupo, the lovely Roman restaurant responsible for the sage and anchovy fritters on page 58. It was served to me as part of a ludicrous white truffle dinner: steak tartare with truffles, forty-egg-yolk tagliolini with truffles and so on, which Kenedy holds each year when the truffle season arrives. One year I made the cut. My life is awful.

This arrived as a mid-course, a rest from all the truffle action, and looked exceptionally precise. Thin slices of steamed potato had been formed inside a metal ring, a couple of layers deep, and the ring then removed. The disc had then been entirely covered by a deep green lawn of finely chopped herbs and salted anchovy. The chilled potato, with just a little bite, was sent on its eager way by what it transpired was simply a finely chopped salsa verde. It looked like the product of a very skilled kitchen and of course it was. But at its heart is that simple idea, one that is easily replicable: potatoes and salsa verde. I don't use a chef's ring for mine, opting instead for a freer family-style plating. But it still looks very pretty. For the potato I suggest using Maris Piper, because it's such a good all-rounder, but you could experiment. Both Charlotte and Anya would work well, although they might be a slight pain to slice because they are quite small. The cooks and writers Tim Anderson and Jeremy Pang, of *The Kitchen Cabinet*, once told me that an interest in potato varieties like this was a particularly British thing; that in the US, Japan, and China, which they know the most about, generally there are just potatoes. Obsessing over potato varieties seems to me a rather sweet obsession.

Serves 6 as a side dish or 4 as a starter

INGREDIENTS

A full portion of the salsa verde from page 22 (if you want to
make this dish entirely vegan, substitute the anchovies in the
salsa verde with a handful of chopped capers)
500g (peeled weight) medium-sized Maris Piper potatoes or
similar
Ground black pepper

METHOD

1. Make the salsa verde. Don't blitz it, but do hand chop
   it finely. Leave it to rest for a good couple of hours,
   while you deal with the potatoes.

2. Steam the peeled potatoes for 25 minutes or so.
   Check by sticking a sharp knife in. The knife should
   go in, but the potatoes shouldn't be too soft. (I really
   do advise steaming them, rather than boiling them,
   because the latter tends to leave them sodden.)

3. Let the steamed potatoes cool for 10 minutes, then
   put them into the fridge to chill for at least 2 hours,
   so that they firm up.

4. When the potatoes are completely cold, take a small
   slice off the bottom lengthways of each one to form
   a flat surface you can place it on. Then lie them on
   the flat side and cut them into thin discs, no thicker
   than a £1 coin.

5. On a standard 30cm dinner plate, arrange the slices in
   a circle around the edge, as if petals, then work your

Main

Halibut & Salmon en Croûte Served with a Pernod Sauce

Seabass Fillet Served with Sauce Vierge or Cooked to your Choice (please enquire)

Salmon Steak Grilled with Bearnaise Sauce or Poached with Hollandaise Sauce

Dover Sole Meunière or Grilled or to your Choice (£11.50 supplement)

Fillets of Dover Sole Veronique
Muscatel Grape Velouté Sauce (£11.50 supplement)

Fried Goujons of Dover Sole Served with Sauce Tartare (£11.50 supplement)

Fillets of Wild Devonshire Baby Turbot
on a champagne Velouté Sauce or with a Native Lobster Sauce (£7.50 supplement)

Wild Scottish Halibut Grilled or with a Langoustine & Fennel Sauce (£7.50 supplement)

Native Lobster Thermidor or Grilled to your Choice (£24.50 supplement)

Crispy Roast Duck Served with Orange, Cherry or Apple Sauce

Breast of Chicken Princess Fried in Bread crumbs

Chicken Princess Oslo Court Onions, Mushrooms, White Wine & Cream Sauce

Côte de Veau Served with a Lemon & Rosemary Jus

Veal Schnitzel Plain or Holstein with Fried Egg, Anchovies and Capers

Calves' Liver Pan Fried with Caramelized Onions

Fillet Mignon Sigano Shallots, Mushrooms, Red Wine and Cream

Steak Diane Flambé, Shallots, Mustard, Worcester sauce and Brandy

Roast Rack of Lamb New Season Served with Mint Sauce, Red Currant Jelly (£12.50 supplement)

French Trimmed Lamb Cutlets New Season Charcoal Grilled (£12.50 supplement)

Fillet Steak au Poivre Green Peppercorns, Brandy and Cream or Charcoal Grilled (£7.50 supplement)

Black Angus Rib-Eye Steak (300gr) Charcoal Grilled (£15.00 supplement)

Chateaubriand for two Served with Béarnaise Sauce (£12.50 supplement)

Beef Wellington Fillet Wrapped in Puff Pastry with a Truffle & Mushroom Duxelles (£7.50 supplement)

Accompanied by a Selection of Seasonal Vegetables

Sauté Potatoes, New Potatoes, Triple Fried Chips, Latkes
Spinach, Cauliflower Au Gratin, Fried Zucchini, Carrots, Mushrooms, Broccoli, Petit Pois,

PRICE PER PERSON: LUNCH £45.00   DINNER £55.00
Children under 12 years (1/2 portion): Lunch £23.50   Dinner £28.50
(A Discretionary 12% Service Charge will be added to your bill)

Oslo Court, St John's Wood, London NW8.
2023

Oslo Court, located on the ground floor of a mansion block, is famed for a menu of what many would call, always admiringly, retro classics. Or as my 2006 review put it, 'When it is lunchtime in London, it is 1977 at Oslo Court.'

Greggs

Blackett Street, Newcastle

Erst

Controcorrente Vermouth & Tonic   7
Controcorrente red vermouth, Fever Tree tonic & orange

Carlingford oysters   3

Grilled flatbread, beef fat & urfa chilli   6

Grilled flatbread, walnut tarator & sage   6

Cantabrian anchovies   9

Coppa d'Abruzzo   12

Bagna cauda & crudites   9

Fried potatoes, creme fraiche & three cornered leek   5

Delica squash, ricotta fresca & chilli   9

Beetroot, ajo blanco & green chilli   10

Cavatelli e ceci   13

Raw scallop, pink naval orange & bergamot   14

Cuttlefish, chickpeas & rouille   16

Plaice, clams & sherry sauce   18

Onglet tartare, bone marrow toast & egg yolk   15

Partridge in escabeche   16

Old spot pork chop, brown butter & lemon   25

St James, quince & lavosh cracker   9

Panna cotta & PX prunes   7

Pear frangipane tart & creme fraiche   8

Chocolate sorbet & olive oil   6

erst-mcr.co.uk   @erst_mcr

Erst, Murray Street, Ancoats, Manchester.
2023 / chef: Patrick Withington

This is quite a lengthy menu by Erst's standards, which styles itself as a bar offering a few plates of food. When I visited in 2021 there were just nine dishes available. I ordered them all. They were all brilliant.

way into the middle in concentric rings. Do a second layer and if you have enough potato, go for a third.

6. Cover with the salsa verde in a thick layer as if icing a cake. When spooning it out of the bowl, drain off some of the olive oil so you are using only the chopped herbs and anchovies (or capers). If you can see even the slightest white of potato, cover it up.

7. Place back in the fridge for an hour or two and take out half an hour before serving. Season with a good grind of black pepper. Serve as if cutting slices from a cake.

And while we're talking about Bocca di Lupo . . .

Charred courgettes

Inspired by the courgette trifolate served at Bocca di Lupo

I came across this method for cooking courgettes at home, during the first lockdown rather than at the restaurant. I had ordered the Bocca di Lupo At Home menu box, a delightful offering of tagliatelle al ragù, trofie al pesto and vitello tonnato which brought sunshine and variety into a house desperately in need of both. I confess I was quietly outraged by the bag of sliced raw courgettes. Had I really paid good money for something I could so easily do myself? I felt a bit of a fool. But it turned out that when combined with the olive oil with chilli and garlic, and the instructions that accompanied it, Kenedy had introduced me to something very special. I almost always cook courgettes this way now.

Serves 4 as a side dish

2 or 3 sizable courgettes, cut into discs each about the thickness
  of a pound coin
2 cloves of garlic, peeled and sliced
1 fresh red chilli, chopped (optional)
40ml extra virgin olive oil
Sea salt and ground black pepper

METHOD

1. Heat a cast iron pan, or better still a metal (not
   non-stick) wok, until smoking hot.

2. Add the courgettes in as much of a single layer as
   you can. Leave to cook in the dry pan for a few minutes
   until, when you lift them up, you can see they are
   browning. Don't be scared of a couple going
   properly dark. Courgettes can take it. Circulate the
   rest into contact with the hot pan. Then turn the
   slices over, and repeat.

3. While the courgettes are cooking, put the sliced garlic
   and chilli (if using) in the olive oil.

4. Once the courgettes are properly caramelized,
   take the pan off the heat and immediately throw in
   the olive oil/garlic/chilli mix. It will smoke
   furiously, so before you add the olive oil, turn your
   extractor fan to maximum, open your windows
   and expect your smoke alarm to go off. This too
   will pass.

5. Toss the courgettes in the oil. Season with salt and a good grind of black pepper.

6. You can serve this hot or at room temperature.

And while we're talking about charring vegetables . . .

Serves 4 as a side dish

Charred Tenderstem broccoli with fried breadcrumbs and anchovy sauce

Inspired by the side dish served at Origin City, Farringdon, London

Like courgettes, all the brassicas take very well to being charred. The two main varieties of broccoli are no exception. Yotam Ottolenghi's famed charred broccoli with chilli and garlic, from the first *Ottolenghi* cookbook, is a perfect example of this. The charred Tenderstem served at Origin City was the smallest detail of the great meal I ate there in 2023. I loved the smoked coppa and the salami Milanese, made on site, and their Morteau sausage with mustardy lentils. But it was their way with Tenderstem that came home with me. It goes very well with the anchovy sauce from page 24 but, as it says below, you can simply toss them in butter.

INGREDIENTS

300g Tenderstem broccoli (or thereabouts)
2 generous tbsp breadcrumbs (panko, if you have it)
¼ tsp garlic powder
Vegetable oil and salted butter, for frying
White wine vinegar (optional)
Anchovy sauce from page 24
Sea salt and ground black pepper

1. At least an hour before you want to finish the dish, blanch the broccoli in boiling water for 2 minutes. Drain and leave to cool, ideally in a single layer.

2. Mix the breadcrumbs with the garlic powder. Heat a glug of vegetable oil with a lump of salted butter until frothing. Throw in the breadcrumbs and fry until golden brown. Watch they don't scorch. Add more butter to the pan if it is drying out. Yes, this is the way to make a healthy vegetable dish far less healthy. Put the toasted breadcrumbs to one side.

3. As with the courgettes above, heat a cast iron frying pan or better still a metal wok (not non-stick) until smoking. Add the broccoli and allow to char, turning the vegetables around in the pan so they all get a chance to blacken at least in part.

4. I'm a strong believer that a little acidity helps everything along, and I do like to spritz the charring broccoli with a little white wine vinegar. If you do this, give the veg a good shake. Cook until dry.

5. When the broccoli is cooked, transfer to a serving dish. You can now dress with the anchovy sauce from page 24, then top with the fried breadcrumbs. Or if you want to keep it simple (and fully vegetarian), toss the broccoli in a good-sized knob of salted butter, add a good grind of black pepper and top with the breadcrumbs.

And while we're talking about charred brassicas . . .

Charred hispi cabbage topped with crushed Scampi Fries and Frazzles

Inspired by the dish served at XO Kitchen, Norwich

Some dishes start as innovations and end up as clichés. That doesn't mean they're bad. It just means there's a lot of it about. Across the past decade, charred hispi cabbage has become practically a required part of every side dish menu. I've certainly mentioned it in over thirty reviews going back over the past ten years, which clearly means each way of cooking it was of note. It started in 2014 at Plum and Spilt Milk, then the restaurant of the Great Northern Hotel at King's Cross, where the charred hispi came with bacon. In 2016 at the steak restaurant Hill & Szrok, just off London's Old Street roundabout, it was slathered in anchovy and chilli. In 2017 it turned up at Skosh in York, at Noble just outside Belfast and at Box-E in Bristol, where it was covered in anchovy butter and seaweed. In that review I described it as 'the rock god of the vegetable world right now'. The chef Gary Usher of the Elite Bistros group in the English north-west even named one of his restaurants Hispi.

I suspect it's so popular with restaurants partly because it portions up nicely. Half a hispi cabbage makes a good side dish. It can also take a spanking over the coals, which is helpful because live-fire grills have become increasingly popular. And once charred it proves a sturdy platform for huge flavours, smeared on the singed surface. Because it's such a ubiquitous dish I wouldn't have included a way with charred hispi. But this version, served at the boisterous XO Kitchen in Norwich, just made me laugh. It was described on the menu as BBQ Hispi with salad cream, black bean dressing and XO seasoning. On the night I tried it I asked the chef Jimmy Preston what the golden rubble of XO seasoning actually was. 'Well,' he said slowly. 'You need a pork element for XO, so that's crushed-up Frazzles. And then you need dried seafood so that's Scampi Fries.' He paused. 'Monster Munch might also have been involved.' If you're reading this outside the UK and have no idea what I'm going on about, you can look these great and vital snack products up online. Just know, it's genius.

Serves 4

INGREDIENTS

2 hispi cabbages cut vertically in half (if they're very large, slice them vertically in three, just making sure to keep each steak attached to the root. Sweetheart cabbage also works well)
Olive oil
100ml thick vinaigrette from page 26

For the black bean sauce
1 heaped tbsp preserved black beans
60ml light soy
50g caster sugar
½ tsp cornflour

For the XO seasoning
3 sheets of nori seaweed
1 packet of Frazzles
1 packet of Scampi Fries
30g Pickled Onion Monster Munch
2 tbsp crispy onions (of the sort sold in tubs for topping hot dogs)
1 tsp chilli flakes

1. Heat a cast iron skillet until smoking hot. Dribble the pieces of cabbage with a little olive oil, then place them flat in the skillet. Do not worry about charring. It's what you want. Turn them occasionally and check that the tight slabs of leaves are softening. It will take 15 to 20 minutes. You will need to do this in a couple of batches.

2. Meanwhile, make the black bean sauce. Put the black beans into warm water to soften. Put the soy sauce and sugar in a pan. Heat to dissolve the sugar, then bring to the boil. Mix the cornflour with a tablespoon or two of water to make a slurry and add that. Stir until the sauce thickens a little. Drain the black beans and add them. Stir and set aside to cool.

3. Now make the XO seasoning. Blitz the sheets of seaweed in a food processor until finely chopped. Smash up the Frazzles, Scampi Fries and Monster Munch. I find the best way is to open the bag a little to let out the air, then bash liberally with the end of a wooden rolling pin.

4. In a bowl mix the seaweed, crushed snacks, crispy onions and chilli flakes until they are a well-mixed rubble.

5. Dress each piece of cabbage first with a generous amount of the vinaigrette, then spoon over a quarter of the black bean sauce. Finally pile on the XO seasoning.

6. You will have more of the XO seasoning left. Experiment with using it to top other things. Or just eat it with a spoon in front of the telly.

Life lessons: learning to make spätzle

At the Spärrows, Manchester

It was when Franco Concli started whipping the batter for the spätzle, his rigid forearms becoming a blur, that the challenge really made itself obvious. There are some dishes that anybody can make if they can follow a recipe. This book is full of them. There are other dishes which require repetition and experience and a growing instinct built up over years, for when everything is right. Spätzle is very much the latter. The word is Swabian, or High German, for 'sparrows'. It's meant to describe what these mildly misshapen noodles look like when they are cut in ribbons and scraped off a board into a boiling pot: creamy little sparrows in flight, flapping away through the bubbling waters. Which explains the name of the restaurant inside this vaulting red brick railway arch, in the Red Bank district of Manchester, on the edge of the City Centre.

This is the restaurant's second incarnation. The first Spärrows was an accident. Polish-born Kasia Hitchcock and her partner Franco, originally from Italy's south Tyrol, had worked across the restaurant sector in London. After a business failure in the capital, they moved to Manchester to run a new venture importing sake. One of their clients, a lovely Japanese restaurant called Umezushi located a few minutes from Manchester Victoria station, offered them use of a tiny railway arch across the road. They were going to use it for a sake pop-up. 'We quickly realized that wasn't going to work,' Kasia says. 'So we started a café doing breakfasts for the local builders. That turned into doing lunches, and that turned into doing dinners.' There were just five tables but they managed to turn them five times a day to feed 100 people.

'At first we thought the food would be Italian,' Kasia says. Franco is classically trained and had cooked Italian food all over the world, including in Michelin-starred restaurants. 'But then we realized that the thing the two of us really had in common,' she says, 'was mountains.' They both grew up amid them. They went on road trips through them every year. If you live in the mountains, you need sustaining food. You need dishes loaded with carbs and fat. Franco came up with a menu of pastas and gnocchi; of pelmeni and pierogi, those stoutly-filled Russian and Polish dumplings. At the heart of it, though, were spätzle, the short, thick noodles a version of which, served with a variety of sauces, can be found from Alsace to the Tyrol, from Slovenia to Hungary to Switzerland, under various names. 'My grandmother lived in the Dolomites and I spent a lot of time with her as a kid,' Franco says. 'She showed me how to make them. Her name was Maria Monte.'

She was called Mary Mountain?

'Yeah, I know.'

The spätzle were a huge hit. Certainly, I adored them. It's probably best if I just quote myself. The Spärrows, I wrote, is 'one long middle finger thrust towards the entire keto diet lobby. If you don't do carbs, do not come here. If you think gluten is the enemy, do not come here. If you disapprove of cheese, do not come here. If you are joyless and miserable, with lips that are liable to fall into a fleshy knot resembling a puckered arse, definitely do not come here. The rest of you, get in.' I liked it. I especially liked the largesse of the braised onion and cheese sauce with which they were served. We'll come to that.

Eventually, Umezushi asked for their railway arch back, so Kasia and Franco moved to this new much bigger site, opening in the first week of the first lockdown. Happily, the restaurant is located opposite some large apartment blocks full of people who needed feeding. They offered takeaways to people in desperate need of serious Alpine comfort through the long empty days. People would come and sit on the bench outside so they were ready to grab their order the moment it was ready and could therefore guarantee to get their spätzle home in prime condition.

Now Franco is going to show me how to make them. 'I tried to do it once,' Kasia says, dryly. 'They ended up looking like fat pigeons.' I appreciate the encouragement.

In the kitchen Franco has laid out the ingredients. 'It's basically egg, water, flour and salt, the same as an Italian pasta. I also add a little bit of nutmeg.' The balance of the ingredients, however, is not like pasta. It uses equal volumes of dry ingredients to liquids, resulting in something much closer to a batter. We are making this in restaurant volumes, so for a kilo of flour I am asked to crack a dozen eggs, then add three extra yolks. 'Do not beat them. Just get your hand in the bowl and break the yolks.' I do as I am told. It's a little like dropping my hand into giant frogspawn. We then take that up to a litre of liquid by adding water.

The flour is poured on to the surface of the water where it rests, an unstable island, until gently mixed in, to make a paste. Now Franco starts to whip it with his rubber spatula.

'It's all about the glutens,' he says, as he works it. 'You need to be energetic. You don't want to overwork it or the glutens will be too strong and the spätzle will be hard. But underwork it and they will break.' I have a go with the spatula and realize that Franco has some serious arms on him. He's beating in air as well as working the flour. Most importantly, he knows when it is right. I do not know, not yet. I watch. I take notes.

Behind us is a large industrial-scale boiler, full of rolling, surging hot water. Laid out on a work surface opposite that is a set of what look like large pizza paddles. That's exactly what they are. 'You need a board with a handle,' Franco says. 'These are made of carbon fibre. They really are meant for putting pizzas into ovens but they are perfect for the job: light, sturdy. They don't get damaged by the water.'

He dollops a big pile of batter into the middle of the paddle then rests it on the side of the boiler. He dips a plastic spatula into the boiling water to get it hot, shakes off any excess water and uses it to smooth the batter into a relatively thin layer a few millimetres thick. It stretches right to the edges. I have a go. Immediately I can see the skill just this part of the process requires. If the spatula is too wet the batter will stick to it. You need to be able to skim across the surface.

Now the fun part. 'You need to rest the leading edge of the board with the batter just under the surface of the water.' Franco takes his spatula, and rests the edge at 90 degrees to the board, like it's a blade. 'And now you start to cut.' He slices away tiny ribbons of noodle which wriggle off into the water. He works from one side to another and back again, slowly at first to show me the action, and then much faster as he gets going. I take over and quickly see how this works;

how what looks like a slab of paste becomes sturdy noodles. He waits another 30 seconds or so after the last noodle has been cut in, then dredges them all out with a huge slotted spoon and into a metal tray dribbled with a little vegetable oil. They will hold like this for at least a day, although they need to be allowed to cool down before being put into the fridge. On service he simply takes a portion and reintroduces it to boiling water for about 40 seconds before adding it to the chosen sauce.

At the Spärrows, they offer them with a beef ragù, a straight tomato sauce, and a mess of cherry tomatoes, spinach and cream.

'But the classic is the Käse,' Franco says, bubbling up a snowy mess of braised onions, Emmental cheese and cream. He plates this up and we stand at the pass, forking it away. It happens to be a late summer's day, but here at the Spärrows the menu is written as if there is always a chance the cold winds might blow and the snows might come and something more sustaining might be called for. Now happily, I know how to make the right dish for that. I just need to practise.

Makes 4 portions of noodles (though you'll have to finish them with the sauce, 2 portions at a time)

INGREDIENTS

3 eggs + 1 yolk
A pinch of ground nutmeg
250g plain flour
5g salt

1. Break the eggs into a measuring jug, add the extra single yolk and then use your hands to pop the yolks. Add enough water to top up the liquid to 250ml, then transfer it all to a mixing bowl.

2. Add the nutmeg to the liquid, then pour in the flour and salt. Gently stir until it is incorporated into the liquid. Do not use an electric whisk. This requires physical labour. Enjoy the feeling of being an Alpine shepherd.

3. When it has formed a paste, whip it with a rubber spatula, pulling the batter towards you from the back of the bowl to incorporate air, until it is coming away from the sides. A couple of minutes should do it. If you've gone straight to this recipe, go back and read the description in the introduction above for a little more detail or, at the very least, a sense of the skill it requires.

4. Put a big pan of salted water on to boil.

5. Get a light chopping board with a handle. Yes, this recipe does require kit. Dollop the batter into the middle of the chopping board. Now perch it on the edge of the pan. Get a plastic spatula. Dip it in the water so it heats up. Shake off any excess water quickly – do all of this quickly – then use it to smooth out the batter. Keep doing this until the batter is in a layer not much more than ¼cm thick.

6. Lightly oil an oven tray, ready to receive your finished noodles.

7. Once again rest the chopping board on the edge of the pan of boiling water, with the leading edge just under the water. Now with your spatula at a 90-degree angle, cut ribbons the thickness of fat worms off the front of the batter, working from one side to the other. Watch them fly away into the water like sparrows. Move the board down into the water a little, as they come off.

8. Wait 30 seconds after the last one has gone in, then sweep them all up with a slotted spoon, drain them a little and then drop them into the oven tray. Once cool they can transfer to the fridge where they will be fine for at least a day.

9. When you are ready to serve them, give them another 40 seconds or so in boiling water, drain them with the slotted spoon and transfer to the pan of sauce described below. Do not worry if a little of the water comes with them.

And breathe. Are you going to give this a go? Are you really? If so, I'm very proud of you. Some skills are worth perfecting. You'll probably find videos online to help you with the various techniques described here. Consult them. That said, the two sauces listed below go equally well with gnocchi, which are much easier to make or which, whisper it, can be bought. For a good gnocchi recipe search up the great Felicity Cloake's method online.

Käse or Emmental and braised onion sauce

This is ludicrously delicious and stupidly rich. Tell yourself you'll go to the gym tomorrow. Or the day after. It is best to make no more than two servings in a single pan at once, so

I'm only giving volumes of ingredients for two servings. If making four servings you'll have to do it all again, and double up the ingredients.

Enough sauce for 2 servings

INGREDIENTS

1 large onion, roughly chopped
A little vegetable oil and a knob of butter
Sea salt and ground black pepper
A bay leaf
100g Emmental cheese, grated (though you can substitute with Gruyère or Comté)
200ml double cream

METHOD

1. Put the chopped onion into a frying pan with a little vegetable oil, a knob of butter and 3 tablespoons of water. Season generously with salt and pepper and add the bay leaf. Cook over the very lowest heat you have, for around 20 minutes until soft and translucent. Stir regularly to stop them caramelizing or burning.

2. For two servings of the finished dish, put 50g of cheese, 200ml of double cream and 4 good tablespoons of the onions into a frying pan. As I say, don't attempt more than two servings to a pan.

3. Heat gently, stirring occasionally until you can see that the cheese has melted. Turn up the heat a little so the cream starts to bubble, thicken and goes a deeper creamy colour. It should take no more than 5 to 7 minutes. Season with a little extra salt.

4. Add 125g of the reheated spätzle per person, so roughly 250g for two (or similar of gnocchi) to the pan, toss to incorporate, then portion up.

5. Top each serving with 25g more of the grated cheese, a few chopped chives if you're feeling fancy and a good grind of black pepper.

6. Repeat for the other two portions.

Butter and sage sauce

This is a very simple alternative, which works equally well with both spätzle and gnocchi. It's similar to, but not exactly the same as, the recipe to go with the flatbreads on page 118. Again, you should do no more than two servings to a pan at once, so I'm giving you ingredients for two servings. Just double up to make more.

For 2 servings

INGREDIENTS

50g grated Parmesan, plus a little more to garnish
70g salted butter
12 fresh sage leaves
Sea salt and ground black pepper

METHOD

1. Put 25g of the grated Parmesan on each plate.

2. Melt the butter in a frying pan. When it starts to foam, crush the fresh sage leaves in your hand to release the oils, then throw them into the

foaming butter and stir. Season with a little salt and pepper.

3. Add 2 portions – around 125g per person – of either the spätzle or the gnocchi. Toss in the butter and sage mix, then serve on top of the Parmesan already on the plates. Top with a little extra Parmesan and a grind of black pepper.

Intercourse: Whose body is it anyway?

Or: the war on fat. Mine

When I was eight or nine years old my mother told me I had 'the Greenspan arse'. I knew she meant it fondly, even if I didn't quite get the reference. I also knew who the Greenspans were. John Greenspan, who was stocky and bearded, was my mother's first cousin, the child of a great-aunt I had never met. He was a regular visitor to our house along with his brood; a sweet and funny man who treated us kids like people who were a part of the conversation. I liked him, which was good because he was also my childhood dentist, although I later concluded he was only marking time. John, who died in 2023, eventually moved from London to San Francisco, where he became an eminent professor of dental surgery and a world-renowned researcher into Aids/HIV. I did not share his academic prowess. Apparently, I only shared his arse.

My mother's point, it later turned out, was that a branch of our family, the Greenspans, of which I was clearly a part, had a genetic predisposition to hefty, tree-trunk thighs and magnificent bottoms. We were a tribe of Jewish immigrants who, through hard work possibly driven by a paranoia that our host country might not always be welcoming, had done well for ourselves. And yet for all that, like most British Jews, we were essentially peasants from the Russian Steppe, where the winters are hard and the pickings once meagre. Natural selection had favoured those of us with slower metabolisms and a tendency to store calories, in our case around our ripe apple middles. If I wanted to know who I was, I only needed to take my clothes off and stand before a mirror. Behold: the Greenspan arse.

I have never been thin, much as Elton John has never been understated and the Himalayas have never been flat. Like the Himalayas I am simply built that way. There have been moments when I have been thin-adjacent, achieved through quite monstrous effort, both in the gym and in the kitchen. Such achievements are meant, in our culture, to be celebrated, so hooray for me and all that. But generally, I have come to understand myself as a large man who will never buy slim-cut jeans or tight-fitting jackets. Those are for the others; for the ones whose bottoms were never named after branches of their family tree. There is no doubt that I have appetites. I was a hungry child and a hungry adolescent. The point I made to the editor of the *Observer Magazine* when I pitched for the restaurant reviewing gig, that I already spent my own money in restaurants, was absolutely true. I like my dinner. And my lunch. I firmly believe I would always be a large man whatever so-called career I stumbled upon.

The question is, does the job I now have contribute to my size? I really am adamant, often defensively so, that I do not eat for a living. That would be a stupid way to earn money. I am a writer, describing experiences. But to have something to write about I must first have the experiences, which means eating. From time to time people have asked me how I manage all those heavy-duty restaurant meals. I point out that I only review one a week. It's not as if I am Caligula, face down in a constant Bacchanalian orgy. I am not re-enacting *La Grande Bouffe*, the 1970s French movie about a group of men who meet in a country house and resolve to eat themselves to death.

This may be true, but it ignores two key points. The first is that my glib line about only reviewing once a week ignores the fact that restaurant critics treat as a routine occurrence that which for most people is a special occasion. Most people do not eat in a restaurant, fancy or otherwise, once a week. The food is engineered to reflect that. It's a treat. The old joke about the three secrets to French restaurant food being 'butter, butter and butter' is only funny because it's true. Yes, there are places offering options for those who do not wish to over-indulge, and we can have a long, discouragingly tedious discussion about eating regimes, like the carbohydrate-free rigours of keto, which are achievable in restaurants. Those, however, are simply dodging the point that restaurant meals are by their nature a carnival of largesse. Generally, we don't go out to eat to be healthy. We go out to eat to have a nice time. And even if some people do pick around menus in search of healthier options, that is not a route that's open to me. My job is to order all the pies. And all the chips. And all the cakes. No, not all of the time. But a lot of the time. A picky-eating, pernickety restaurant critic is of no use to anyone.

The second point is that whole 'I only go once a week' thing. It's an outright, filthy lie. Yes, I only *review* one restaurant a week, but these things are habit-forming. I go to many more restaurants than that. Sometimes, it is as part of my work, and boy do I put my back into it. Perhaps it's research for a feature rather than for the restaurant column. If I'm writing about a chef, I need to eat their food (although I do less of that these days than once I did). Or perhaps it's because I'm working away from home and need dinner. These, however, are just feeble excuses. The truth is I bloody love eating in restaurants, and I am lucky enough to be able to afford to do so. In a bad week, which is to say, a very good one, I might eat out three or four times. As a sweet soul once put it on Twitter, the question with me is not why am I such a big man? It's why am I not bigger?

The answer, I think, is that the job makes you very conscious of the process of eating and its impact upon you. Part of that is what euphemistically we might call the 'forward-facing' elements of the role. I do a fair bit of television. I am regularly asked if I will be photographed, perhaps to illustrate a piece I have written. This means I am required to look at myself, often in excruciating detail. Professional photographers shoot digitally to laptop, which means I get to examine how I look moment by moment. I like to think that I am now professionally vain, which is just a fancy way of saying that I am vain. I know exactly which positions I look thinner in, and which positions make me look especially huge. I do not leave a photographic studio without having first scorched the digital earth of all unflattering images.

There's also my email inbox, which fills daily with invitations to free meals. This is not a complaint, just a statement of fact. It is a privilege in all senses of the word to get invitations to try a restaurant's food before it opens properly, or to help launch a new cookbook or drink brand. I accept none of them. Partly it's because I am an anti-social scumbag who lives in rigid fear of being seated next to someone with whom I don't want to spend an evening making forced conversation. I'm sure they feel the same way. Partly it's because these events aren't of any use to me journalistically. But mostly it's because I'm terrified of the unwanted calories. There's already enough beautifully plated food in my life, much of which is unavoidable, without me inviting more. And yes, in an age when too many people in too many places struggle to put food on the table this complaint is an obscenity. We know this. But that doesn't change the fact that it is a feature of my life.

Over the years I have tried to alter my general diet, rather than follow formal diets. I hold to the view that none of those diets work. Or to put it another way, if a single one of them did, no one would ever publish another diet book again. They wouldn't need to. Almost all of them are some variant on making a calorie-restricted eating regime tolerable. At one point around 2008 a combination of low-carbing and excessive gym work, by which I mean five or six huge sessions a week, took a number of stone off me. But what people who run to fat know is that serious self-achieved weight loss is rarely sustainable. Not all of it went back on but quite a lot of it did. When the so-called fat injections like semaglutide, sold under the brand names Wegovy and Ozempic, came on the market, I considered them, but only in the way I might have considered skydiving or BDSM and then decided neither were for me. A drug that altered my metabolism so I turned into all those skinny people I have occasionally yearned to count myself among would be a fabulous thing, if you put aside the morality of a drug enabling you to eat whatever you want. But semaglutide operates differently. It interferes with your appetites, and my appetites are a profound part of me. I don't want to start jacking up with a drug which might mean I no longer recognized myself, even if it did give me a non-Greenspan-like arse.

What's the solution? I could stop reviewing restaurants. Eventually of course I will, whether it's my decision or that of a restless editor hungry for new voices. No journalist should assume a column is theirs by right. The thing is, even if I'm no longer reviewing restaurants, I'll still be me. I'll be eating in them, because that's who I am, and I'll still be of Russian peasant stock with a sluggish, indolent metabolism. My solution is to assume that if I can't be thin, I can at least be fit. At home I tend to avoid pasta and rice. The gym habit acquired around 2008 has never gone away. I'm in there three to five times a week, wearing a sweatband to keep my ludicrous hair out of my eyes, bashing away at the cross-trainer like 'a waxed Wookie giving it stacks' as one fellow gym-goer once observed. I do sit-ups. I lift weights. I sweat in the way large men are prone to do, and end up looking like I've just taken a shower with my clothes on. It's not a pretty sight, but then it's not meant to be pretty. It's meant to be a solution of sorts. While I'm doing all of this I'm thinking about dinner.

I like being alive. I've concluded that the best way to stay alive is by not dying and that's what I'm attempting to do. So far it seems to be working. Unless you're reading this after my death. In which case, boy did I have fun, Greenspan arse and all.

High Street Favourites

The Steak Bake

Inspired by the iconic item sold by Greggs,
the high street bakers

Am I a man blessed with exquisite and refined taste, or just a greedy bloke who happens to have an expense account? I'd go with the latter every time. Not that it's how people view those of us paid to review restaurants. They think it's all braised otter and roast swan, with a dollop of caviar on the side. And obviously there is a bit of that, or at least the legal equivalent. For the record I have never eaten otter or swan. But one of the qualifications for the job is certainly very broad tastes, encouraged by a healthy appetite.

There's one question I'm often asked which is related to

this. It's always put with a mischievous grin, as if the questioner imagines they're about to do something akin to asking a nun if they do a little stripping on the side to make ends meet. It's a variant on this: have you ever eaten McDonald's? Or Burger King? Or KFC? Oh, you dear sweet things. Of course I have, and many times over. I even reviewed McDonald's once, though only as an act of solidarity with an Italian counterpart who had been sued by the company for criminal libel and £15 million in damages. Edoardo Raspelli had published a disobliging review in which he called the food 'gastronomically repellent'. My review was hardly more positive. I deconstructed a Big Mac by laying into the 'slimy grey puck of a burger' and the way 'the thing leaked hot, greasy, salty water into my mouth'. I slagged off the 'fatty cardboard' of the chips, and the Chicken Selects which were 'a truly remarkable example of fast-food science. Although they are clearly pieces of breast, they taste of chicken not at all.' At the end I invited McDonald's lawyers to 'come and have a go if you think you're hard enough'. I never heard a word. They later dropped the case against the Italian critic.

This whole episode could be misconstrued. It was not an attack on fast food in general, only on McDonald's in particular. I loved a bacon double Swiss from Burger King and mourned its passing. I have been known to do serious damage to a lot of KFC's finest deep-fried hen. When my kids were small, we used to drive each year to East Anglia for an Easter break which required a stop at a motorway services. It had a KFC from which I would always order. So shoot me. My son, then nine or ten years old, joked that I should pay him not to reveal my KFC habit to the world. Sod that. I wrote a column about it. I wasn't going to be blackmailed by a child for being myself.

I really wasn't embarrassed. High street and fast-food

restaurants aren't inherently bad. Eating from them too much might well be, and sometimes too many of them in a row can force out smaller, independent restaurants who can't compete for the sites or afford the rents. Such is the way of high street economics. But there's a good reason why so many places have opened over the past couple of years doing apparently fancy versions of stacked burgers, fried chicken and wings. It is food with a clear purpose. Sometimes it is exactly the right thing at the right time, and it can be done well, even by vast corporate concerns.

Which brings me to Greggs. If you haven't heard of Greggs, perhaps because you are an elderly High Court judge or have just been roused from a decades-long coma, it is a 2,000-strong bakery chain. It was originally founded by baker John Gregg in Tyneside in the middle of the twentieth century, though, for the pathologically pedantic among you, the company carrying Mr Gregg's name does not boast a possessive apostrophe. It grew at first through acquisition, making much of its regional identity, until eventually coming together as one national chain in the noughties. For many decades it was indeed a bakery selling bread. Eventually, they concluded they couldn't compete with the supermarkets, and so focused on food to go, generally wrapped in buttery, flaky pastry: sausage rolls, pies, and of course, the mighty Steak Bake. They opened earlier to get trade from people on their way to work. By sticking tightly to a narrow repertoire and doing it exceedingly well, Greggs has become much beloved of the British, who have always been a total sucker for a well-made pie.

And so to that Steak Bake, a beguiling rectangular pocket of braised beef brisket and chuck in gravy, first launched in 1999. Greggs now sell over 45 million of them every year. Some of them to me. It is just a genius combination of flaky pastry and deep savoury filling. This is my home-made tribute. In truth, if they ever attempted to market my version, they'd very quickly go out of business. That's because it is undoubtedly the luxury steak bake, with the culinary equivalent of go-faster stripes, turbo injection and a ludicrous aerofoil. To make the money they need to cover their costs – production, shops to sell them from, staff, marketing and so on – and still turn a reasonable profit, most high street businesses need to calculate prices based on making a gross profit of around 70%. So, for 30p worth of ingredients they'd need to charge £1. I have calculated that this version of the Steak Bake would cost about £12 a pop, instead of the £2 charged by Greggs. That doesn't mean mine is necessarily better. The Greggs version has its place. Mine is just, well, different.

But then there are some serious ingredients in this. I recommend using real beef stock and veal jus, rather than stock from cube. There are some very good ready-to-use products on the market these days. I get mine from Truefoods in Yorkshire. You could of course do it with a stock cube or three. If you use enough flour the gravy will thicken, but honestly it won't have the same depth of flavour. I also advise you to get shop-bought puff pastry. It's what everyone else does. There are very few restaurants and bakeries these days that make their own puff. Most of them buy it in on a large roll. That includes some of the fancier places. If you want to make puff pastry from scratch and have the necessary half day to spare, I advise you get a copy of Calum Franklin's book *The Pie Room*, published when he was still doing lovely things with pastry at the Holborn Dining Room. He'll see you right. You'll also note that I recommend using a pressure cooker for the filling. If you have one, it is definitely the way to go. If you go so far as to buy one just for this adventure, your guide as to what to do with it afterwards is Catherine Phipps. She was certainly mine. Her *Pressure Cooker Cookbook* will be your bible. And you can use it for the spare ribs on page 89.

The key to this is making sure that everything is good and cold at each stage of the preparation, and then seriously hot for the baking.

Makes 6 steak bakes

INGREDIENTS

3 heaped tbsp plain flour, for dusting
A good tsp garlic powder
Table salt and black pepper
1kg braising steak or chuck, cut into 4cm cubes and trimmed of
    excess fat and connective tissue, so probably 1.2kg before the
    trim (you can also remove unwanted fat, etc. after it's been
    braised and chilled)
Vegetable oil, for frying
1 large onion, chopped
500ml beef stock
350ml veal jus
1 tbsp tomato purée
1 tsp Worcestershire sauce
2 x 320g packets of shop-bought puff pastry
1 beaten egg for egg wash

METHOD

1. Put the flour and garlic powder into a bowl. Add a generous amount of table salt and use your hand to stir the mix together. Put the cubes of beef into the seasoned flour and mix around until they are all well coated.

2. Heat a couple of tablespoons of vegetable oil in your pressure cooker or saucepan and brown the beef on all sides in batches, taking each batch out and putting it into a bowl to make space for the next. The flour will start to form a crust on the bottom. Watch the heat and make sure the flour crust doesn't burn. You may need to add a little more oil for each batch of beef, as it does get absorbed by the flour.

3. When all the beef has been browned, turn the heat down, add the chopped onion and cook for a few minutes until soft. Again, you may need to keep it moving to stop the crusted flour from burning.

4. When the onion is soft, add the stock and the jus and as it heats up, use your wooden spoon to scrape up any of the crust on the bottom of the pan. When it gets to a simmer, add the tomato purée and Worcestershire sauce and stir it all in. Finally put the beef back in, with any juices that have been released. Season with a little salt and cracked black pepper. If you're not using real beef stock and veal jus, use 850ml of beef stock from two cubes.

5. If you're not using a pressure cooker, you will now need to braise this in a pan, half covered on a very low heat. Give it a stir every now and then to make sure it's not scorching on the bottom. It should take about 2 hours for the meat to become tender, but it could need up to 3. Check by taking out a piece of beef and seeing if it will come apart easily when you pull at it with two forks.

6. If you are using a pressure cooker, put the lid on, bring to pressure and cook for 25 minutes. At the end

of that I use a fast pressure release by pressing on the valve with a folded tea towel so as not to burn my hand. Steam burns are nasty.

7. Use a slotted spoon to transfer all the beef to a dish which can take it in one layer. Allow it to cool for 10 or 15 minutes. Meanwhile reduce the gravy by about a third if using the real stocks and by half if using the stock from cube. If you're using the latter and it isn't thickening properly, take a couple of tablespoons of the gravy and put it into a mug with a teaspoon of flour. Mix it to make a slurry, then reintroduce it to the gravy and continue to reduce. If you have cooked your beef on the hob, you may find that you don't need to reduce the stock very much at all.

8. When the gravy is reduced, pour it over the meat. Allow that to cool for a further 10 minutes and then put it into the fridge for at least 3 hours. You want it all very cold and for the gravy to have turned into a jelly.

9. Two hours before you want to eat, make the steak bakes. The Greggs version measures 10cm × 12cm, so you need 6 sheets of pastry measuring roughly 10cm × 25cm. (The product I use, Jus-Rol, measures 23cm × 35cm, which allows for 3 per sheet of roughly these dimensions.) Spread them out across the greaseproof paper that the puff pastry comes on. Mark across the middle of each sheet, so you can see where the bottom half is.

10. Your beef should now be in a jellified gravy. If you want to take off any lumps of fat and connective

tissue do so now. They will come away easily. Use a spoon (or your fingers; I'm not watching) to take pieces of the meat out with just a little of the jelly attached and arrange in a tight square in the centre of the bottom half of the pastry, leaving a 1cm border all the way around. You want it to be a generous filling. Egg-wash all the way around the pastry edges, then fold the top half of the pastry sheet over the filling and press the pastry edges of both halves together. Remember this is a home-made steak bake, not a mass-produced version. It will end up looking a bit rough and ready.

11. Go around the edges with the tines of a fork, to make little indentations that will help seal them, just like on a Greggs Steak Bake. Then lightly score the bulging surface on the diagonal from one corner to the other, making sure not to cut through the pastry. Generously egg wash the top of the steak bake. Immediately put back into the fridge to chill again for 90 minutes. Reserve what's left of the egg-wash.

12. If making 6 small ones feels like a total faff, you can make 2 giant ones, using the whole 23cm × 35cm sheet. Follow the same instructions as above, only this time fill half the sheet with beef, but still leave the 1cm wide border. The key to either version is not to allow too much gravy in with the beef or it will leak. There will be enough with the jelly that's attached.

13. An hour before you want to eat, heat the oven to 220°C/425°F/gas mark 7. Lightly oil two baking

trays which are big enough to take the 6 steak bakes. Put them into the oven for 15 minutes until smokingly hot. Take the steak bakes out of the fridge. Egg-wash them again. Take the first oven tray out and put the steak bakes on, leaving the other one in there so it doesn't get a chance to cool down. Once the first is in the oven, take out the second and repeat. Using very hot oven trays guarantees the bakes will have crisp rather than soggy bottoms. If you've made the giant steak bake it will be a little hard to move it across from the fridge, but it is doable, because you've chilled it and it has firmed up.

14. Bake for 25 to 30 minutes, until golden and crisp. From about 20 minutes in you may have to swap the oven trays around so they get equal amounts of time at the top. Despite your best efforts they may still leak a little gravy. Don't worry. The Greggs ones do that too.

15. While they are baking, heat up the remaining gravy and any leftover beef in a saucepan.

16. Serve the steak bakes with extra gravy on the side.

Piri-piri sauce and piri-piri chicken livers

Inspired by the sauce and chicken livers served by Nando's

I am often asked what my favourite restaurant is. I understand the question. I also understand that once again my answer is infuriating: I don't have a favourite restaurant, or at least not in the way the questioner means. There is no single place to which, given the choice, I would always head. It depends on mood. I have the Chinese I love to eat in by myself (Four Seasons, Gerrard Street) and the one I like to go with others (Mandarin Kitchen, Queensway) and the one for Sichuan food (Barshu, Soho). If I want to go meat-free it's Bubala, for the haloumi with black seed honey, or the oyster mushroom skewers with tamari, just two of Helen Graham's inspired creations. There's the French place for when I want the rustic and the butter-laden (Bouchon Racine) and for when I want the fancy (the Ritz; come the revolution, I'll be hanging from a lamppost, probably the one next to yours). For small plates it's Erst in Manchester and for seafood it's Ondine in Edinburgh, unless it's Bentley's in London. And so on. I am polygreedy and unashamed of the fact. It's like being polyamorous, only with more napkins and calories.

And yet, if a simple criterion had been set, which is to say, if I had been asked to name my favourite restaurant as defined by the number of times I had eaten its food, that would at one point have been easy to answer. For the better part of a decade or more from the late 90s onwards, it was a Portuguese piri-piri grill house called the Gallery on Brixton Hill near my south London home. In the back was an utterly bonkers windowless dining room, its walls painted with romantic murals of Portuguese landscapes, where they served heaving platters of grilled meats, and pork with clams, with plentiful chips and salad. I ate back there a few times. But mostly I got a takeaway from the counter at the front, overseen by the two brothers. They were friendly, jowly men in their sixties from the old country who both looked a little like James Mason and who worked that grill at speed. For years I got one of those takeaways every two to three weeks, sometimes more often than that. I adored their lightly charred piri-piri chicken, which you could ask for with hot, medium or herb sauce, although what lightweight would ask for the latter? A bit of heat was the point of it. They also did fabulous pork ribs, which were dark and crusted, alongside great Portuguese chorizo, which is denser than the Spanish variety, the long sausage half sliced so it coiled on itself, leaking its orange paprika-boosted juices into its foil container. And of course, there were the chips, and the green salad, with thin ribbons of onion in a simple dressing of vegetable oil, vinegar and salt. I refused to think of myself as having a Gallery problem, but I was probably addicted. It really was my go-to takeaway.

One day I went in and learned that one of the brothers had died suddenly. The mood in the brightly lit space was quiet and dark. Unsurprisingly, shortly after that the remaining brother retired. He sold the business on, and it was never quite the same after that. It changed its name. There was a fire which closed the takeaway side for a long period. I never went back. I very much miss the Gallery. Although I live not far from Stockwell, the heart of London's Portuguese community, I've never quite found a takeaway replacement, although for eating in I've become a very big fan of Casa do Frango, literally chicken house. It's a small but expanding group which does terrific piri-piri chicken.

And then there is the mighty high street chain which is Nando's. It was born in South Africa in 1987 to serve a version of the piri-piri chicken that the founders had tried in a restaurant in Mozambique, a former Portuguese colony. There are nearly 500 branches in the UK and Ireland, making it the biggest market for the brand in the world. I like Nando's. The chicken is always reliable, as are the salad and chips. If it wasn't for the offer of bottomless fizzy drinks, it would be by far the healthiest chain restaurant on the high street. When the jazz sextet I lead is on tour, I always make sure that we eat well before a gig. We have been known to power our stunning musical performances on a delivery from Nando's.

Plus, they serve what they refer to as peri-peri chicken livers, using the alternative spelling for the name of the sauce favoured by the company. They have been on the menu since the earliest days in South Africa. As I was told via email by Fernando Duarte, Nando's co-founder, 'In Mozambique you'd go to a bar and order a beer, and they would offer you livers with peri-peri as an appetizer. It's always been part of Portuguese gastronomy, where I'm from, so it was a natural decision to include it on our menus from the beginning.' Given an often-pronounced resistance among the British public to offal of any kind, the presence of the dish on a high street menu like this has always struck me as a curious anomaly. But they wouldn't be there unless people liked them. Whenever I've written about them, I've received many messages from people thrilled that their virtues have been recognized and celebrated. People who love the Nando's chicken livers feel like they belong to a club. They arrive dark and spiced, and slightly crumbly and caramelized. Alongside, there's always a Portuguese crisp-crusted bread roll. You are meant to pile one on top of the other.

To make a version at home, it became clear to me that I would first have to come up with my own piri-piri sauce. This was no bad thing because, as well as being a vital part of the chicken liver recipe, it could be used as a general sprightly marinade for meat, fish and vegetables, or even simply as a dipping sauce. Of course, Nando's has a retail version available to buy in supermarkets but where's the fun in buying that? I am in no way claiming to have come up with a replica of the Nando's sauce, not least because that would be pointless. If you want that, buy it. Tasted side by side I'd say mine is a little sharper and fresher. The commercial version is also smooth, whereas mine is chunkier and rougher, which only adds to the texture when it's cooked out. There is, of course, the issue of heat. I use six of the small, red African bird's-eye chillies, which I think corresponds to hot in Nando's. You can vary that element according to taste. If you want what they call lemon and herb, leave out the bird's-eye chillies altogether. There are indeed herbs and lemon in my sauce. Although I would again argue that there's not much point making something called a piri-piri sauce if you use fewer than three.

Piri-piri sauce

Makes around 350g

INGREDIENTS

1 medium onion, roughly chopped
1 red bell pepper or long sweet pepper, deseeded and roughly
    chopped
6 bird's-eye chillies (or fewer, according to taste)
3 large cloves of garlic, roughly chopped
Juice of 1 lemon
40ml white wine vinegar
1 tsp salt
½ tsp cracked black pepper
1 tbsp tomato purée
1 tbsp dried oregano
1½ tbsp smoked paprika
30ml vegetable oil
1 tbsp sugar

1. Put all the ingredients into a blender and blitz until it's a loose purée. I found it helpful to blitz the onion and red pepper roughly first, before adding all the other ingredients and blitzing again, but that may depend on the power of your blender. Store in a jar in the fridge and use within 4 days.

Piri-piri chicken livers

Serves 4 as a starter

INGREDIENTS

6 tbsp plain flour
1 tsp garlic powder
½ tsp salt
½ tsp cracked black pepper
500g chicken livers, trimmed of any connective tissue, rinsed, patted dry and cut into bite-size pieces
Vegetable oil, for frying
4–5 tbsp piri-piri sauce (see above)
50g salted butter

METHOD

1. Mix the flour with the garlic powder, salt and pepper in a flat bowl big enough to take all the chicken livers.

2. Toss the livers in the seasoned flour so they are fully coated.

3. Use a frying pan big enough to take all the chicken livers without crowding them. Add enough vegetable oil to lightly coat the bottom of the pan and put over a medium to high heat.

4. When the pan is hot, add the chicken livers in a single layer and allow to sear on one side until starting to crisp. This will take a couple of minutes. Turn them over and do the other side.

5. When they are crisped, add 4 or 5 good tablespoons of the piri-piri sauce and mix to coat the livers liberally. Stir them around and let the sauce reduce down vigorously for a couple of minutes.

6. Add the butter and as it melts stir the livers in the now pleasingly messy sauce. Wait until the sauce has just started to bubble and darken. Serve immediately.

Spicy peanut sauce or pindasaus

Inspired by the satay sauce served with chips at FEBO, a Dutch fast-food chain (with help from Ravinder Bhogal of Jikoni, London)

It is common to talk about one's misspent youth. I did not mis-spend mine. I spent it wisely. Part of that was on summer backpacking trips; only vaguely planned, snaking journeys which always seemed to end with a few days in Amsterdam. While it is all now a long way in my past, I very much enjoyed the city's liberal approach to cannabis consumption. In retrospect I concluded this wasn't just because, at that time, it all seemed so well managed and so good-natured. It was also because Amsterdam had, and still has, a killer chain of fast-food restaurants called FEBO, which are perfectly engineered for stoned people. FEBO, which was founded in 1941 and now has over sixty outlets across the Netherlands, is an automat. The walls are lined with small transparent cupboards, each holding a freshly cooked burger or a croquette or a portion of chips. You put in a coin to unlock the door, and take out your high-fat, high-carb, deep-fried item of choice, without ever having to interact with a human being.

The croquettes, with their soft, meaty centres and crisp, breadcrumbed shells, were great. But what I really loved was the spicy satay sauce which went with the chips. In the 1980s, this struck me as proof of the sophistication at the heart of Dutch culture: here, they didn't eat their chips with anything as pedestrian as tomato ketchup. They ate them with a completely irresistible, sweet-salty peanut sauce with a seriously spicy end. Later, I would come to understand that this, along with the many Indonesian restaurants in the city offering a rijsttafel, was a legacy of the country's colonial history. A nation's relationship with its colonial history is always complex and rightly, often uncomfortable. Its relationship with the food that results from that history is often rather simpler. The Dutch really do like their satay or, as they call it, pindasaus.

The FEBO version is smooth and almost frothy, as you would expect of a commercial condiment. I prefer a rugged, crunchy sauce, with a proper, uncompromising whack of heat. Mine draws on a peanut sauce recipe by Ravinder Bhogal. We met in 2010 when we were both cast to present a weird factual Channel 4 series called *Food: what goes in your basket*. When giving people the name of the show I had to tell them it was blessed with a colon, or it sounded like I'd lost control of basic English grammar. That was the least of its problems. The show, quite rightly, didn't get recommissioned but the friendship endured. Ravinder had just left a job as a fashion journalist for one in food, after winning a TV cooking competition run by Gordon Ramsay. She could have settled for a comfortable career as a food writer but she was determined to make more of a mark and put herself through the hell of some often abuse-ridden restaurant kitchens to learn how to run her own. That led in 2016 to the opening in London's Marylebone of Jikoni, which is the Swahili word for kitchen. Ravinder was born in Nairobi and raised in London and her food draws on her East African Asian heritage but also on the influences of the world felt through the city around her. She has an acute understanding of how to balance spice and aromatics. She's also an inveterate feeder with an instinct for the irresistible. There's her prawn toast Scotch egg with banana ketchup. Or her crispy aubergine with Sichuan caramel, part of a repertoire strong on plant-based options. Or her fabulously named scrag end pie, with its turmeric-infused mash potato topping, which is a robustly spice-boosted take on a shepherd's pie. I recommend both her restaurant and her books, *Jikoni* and the vegetarian *Comfort and Joy*. You get the point. I'm a fan.

Her spiced peanut sauce was served at Jikoni with pork skewers. Frankly you could serve mine with almost anything, but it really does go very well with chips. The chips become a vehicle for the sauce, rather than the sauce being a mere condiment for the chips. I try not to be an ingredient snob, but sometimes a bit of that is necessary. While you can use any crunchy peanut butter for this sauce it is much better if you use a quality brand which contains only peanuts and salt.

INGREDIENTS

2 large cloves of garlic, finely chopped
1 heaped tsp finely chopped ginger
1 tsp chilli flakes
1 tbsp sesame oil
2 tbsp rice vinegar
1 tbsp caster sugar
100g crunchy peanut butter (the good stuff)
100ml full fat coconut milk (not light)
1 tbsp dark soy
1 tbsp fish sauce

METHOD

1. Over a low heat, gently fry the garlic, ginger and chilli flakes in the sesame oil for 2 to 3 minutes until it's all just starting to brown.

2. Add the vinegar and quickly scrape anything stuck to the bottom, then add the sugar and stir to dissolve. Let it bubble for a minute.

3. Add the peanut butter and coconut milk, and stir over the low heat until it is all mixed together and any lumps in the peanut butter have smoothed out. Carry on cooking until it's beginning to bubble and it all starts to pull away a little from the sides of the pan. Take off the heat and transfer the sauce to a bowl.

4. Give it a couple of minutes to cool, then add the soy and fish sauce and stir to fully incorporate. Store in the fridge for up to 5 days. If it lasts that long.

Rosemary salt

Inspired by the rosemary salt sprinkled on
chips at Honest Burgers

Honest Burgers now has dozens of outlets across England but it started in 2011 with a single tiny burger shop in the covered market known as Brixton Village, ten minutes' walk from my house. Throughout my years in the job I have been wary of reviewing restaurants too close to where I live. The owners will most likely be my neighbours and I didn't want to be buttonholed on the street by livid chefs and restaurateurs accusing me of favouritism or, perhaps worse, of cutting up rough on a local independent business. However, in the mid-noughties a concerted effort was made to revive the covered markets in Brixton and I simply couldn't ignore the sudden influx of small, independent restaurants and bars.

It has not been without controversy. The markets have long been home to grocers and speciality food shops providing local immigrant and ethnic communities with the specific produce they need at affordable prices. There were and remain reasonable concerns that those businesses would be forced out by restaurants catering to the often-white middle classes, even though some of the restaurants and cafés have been run by people with roots deep in the community. There were justified cries of 'gentrification'. It is a tension which continues to this day, as long-standing communities try to maintain a grip on the area, while money continues to flow in from outside. It is a pattern which has been repeated in inner-city areas across the country, but in 2011 it was novel and exciting and writing about those restaurants felt like an urgent and necessary thing to do. I shone a spotlight on a tiny family-run

Thai place called Kaosarn, from which we still occasionally get takeaways. There was a terrific Pakistani street food café called Elephant, and I really did go off on one about the menu at Honest Burgers. I described the chips as 'triple cooked, skin on, dusted with salt and rosemary and the edible equivalent of crystal meth'. Over a dozen years later that line about crystal meth is still on their website. It makes me cringe a little. It sounds like I am trying to be clever and edgy when I am the antithesis of edgy. But the rosemary salt is properly good stuff: fresh and aromatic without overwhelming the all-important chips it is there to serve.

When I asked the founders how it was made, I received a recipe which entailed beating up the ingredients for ten minutes in a mortar with a pestle. Have you ever banged away at anything in a stone bowl with a stone pestle for even two minutes? It's exhausting. It's why we gave up cave dwelling and invented kitchen equipment: because the good old days of banging at things with stone tools were a total pain in the arse. I'm suspicious that they hand out those specific instructions to stop people attempting to make their own rosemary salt at home.

All that really matters is the ratio of the ingredients, and those I have. What you do with them after that is so very much simpler.

Makes about 90g

INGREDIENTS

70g flaky sea salt
20g fresh rosemary leaves, stripped from the stalk
Zest of 1 lemon

1. Put all the ingredients into a small food processor and blitz for 30 seconds. Store in an airtight box.

Deep-fried apple pies

Inspired by the apple pies served at McDonald's
in the UK (but not in the US)

Sure, I may once have written a less than positive review of McDonald's, but that doesn't mean I have never eaten its food in my own time. As I've already said, that review was an act of solidarity with a fellow critic, rather than a forever condemnation. I don't hold with lying just to polish some fake gastronomic credentials, which in any case I do not possess. I've eaten almost everything voluntarily at one time or another.

McDonald's arrived in the UK in 1974 when I was eight. I first tried one of their burgers a couple of years later when my mother came home from an event at the US Embassy with a big box of them. McDonald's had catered it and there were leftovers. I say I ate one. I probably had three. Or four. They were small hamburgers. Later, when I was thirteen or fourteen years old, I became a Sunday evening regular at the branch of McDonald's in Marble Arch, which I frequented with friends after an hour or two at a Jewish youth club. We played games. We learned about the Holocaust. We went to McDonald's. At one point they ran a competition. You could win a T-shirt if you said their Big Mac sales slogan in the quickest time. Tragically, I can still recall the slogan without searching it up.

'Two-all-beef-patties-special-sauce-lettuce-cheese-pickles-onions-on-a-sesame-seed-bun.' I did it in under four seconds. I won the T-shirt.

I was a late convert to the McDonald's apple pie. Getting the apple pie as well as a Big Mac and fries felt like trying to turn a purchase from the Golden Arches into actual dinner. What, two courses? Don't be silly. You don't treat McDonald's like a restaurant. Next, you'll be suggesting I use a knife and fork to eat my Big Mac.

But eventually, after a couple of years, the apple pie did happen for me. I got to experience the joy of slipping it from its glossy cardboard sleeve. I thrilled to its explosive sweetness, the crisp, deep-fried pastry, and the occasional third-degree burns. God, but that filling could be hot. Which is what happens when you plunge a pie into bubbling oil. Only when I came to research this recipe did I learn that the McDonald's apple pie is no longer deep-fried in the US and hasn't been for decades. It was first introduced to the menu by a franchisee in Tennessee in 1968 and spread worldwide, until in 1992 McDonald's decided they should in future be baked because of health concerns. They also have a pastry latticework in the US. This makes them closer to a strudel. In the UK meanwhile, the deep fat frying carries on regardless. It almost makes you proud.

So why would you want to make one of these? Perhaps because, like me, you haven't had one in years and now you really want one, but you no longer see yourself as the sort of person who would step across the threshold of a McDonald's to place the order and pay up. The neighbours might see you. You're a snob. You have your dignity. You're also a hypocrite. All of that. Better then to make your own, which carries with it the thin, greasy patina of the artisanal. Also, it's kind of amusing. Look at me, making versions of classic fast food at home. Or it could just be that they really are delicious. Don't eat too many. Also, the method below extends to any other filling you might like to try. You are now in deep-fried pie heaven.

As with the Greggs Steak Bake, and most things involving pastry, the key here is to chill and, where necessary, freeze as you go. Freezing your apple pies helps give them a flaky crust when they cook, and means that the filling shouldn't be a vicious weapon of overheated torture when you come to eat it. Also, if you want, you can make a bunch of them in advance and leave them in the freezer for when the urge hits. As the recipe says, each sheet of shop-bought puff will make 4, so scale accordingly.

Makes 4

INGREDIENTS

3 crisp dessert apples, peeled, cored, and cut into 1cm dice:
  Braeburn, Pink Lady or Jazz work well for this
60g soft brown sugar
30g salted butter
Juice of ½ a lemon
A generous pinch of ground cinnamon (up to ¼ tsp if you really
  like cinnamon)
A grating of nutmeg
1 tsp cornflour
1 x 320g packet of shop-bought puff pastry
1 egg, beaten, for sealing the pastry
Vegetable oil, for deep-frying
Icing sugar, for dusting

METHOD

1. Put the chopped apples, sugar, butter, lemon juice, cinnamon, and a grating of nutmeg into a small pan

on a medium heat. Stir until the butter is melted, then turn the heat down low and cook, covered, for 15 to 20 minutes until the apples are soft but not falling apart.

2. Take the lid off, add the cornflour and stir until the liquid has thickened. This will take about a minute. Transfer the mix to a bowl. Allow it to cool for 10 minutes, then put it into the fridge for at least 2 hours.

3. Take the pastry from the fridge and give it 10 minutes to warm up a little. There are slight variations in the size of shop-bought puff pastry sheets, but they are all rectangles of roughly the same dimensions. Cut the pastry into 4 equal, rectangular pieces. Work out where the middle of each rectangle is. You will be folding from this point.

4. Put a quarter of the apple mixture on one side of the rectangle, close to the middle. Egg-wash the edges of the other side, then fold over and close up tightly. Crimp the edges with your thumb just to make sure the pies are as tightly closed as possible. Put into the freezer for at least 3 hours.

5. Heat a deep fat fryer (or a pan with a thermometer, if using) to 190°C. Fry the pies, 2 at a time, until a deep golden brown. This will take about 5 minutes.

6. Drain for a couple of minutes on kitchen paper. Dust with icing sugar. Serve with whipped, sweetened cream. Because you don't get that from bloody McDonald's.

Intercourse:
Cooking the food of the gods

The gods, in this instance, are a trio of the biggest and most enduring names in European gastronomy. All three of those names are French, although two of them have very much made their careers in the UK; all three of them are dripping in Michelin stars; all three of them are skilled in the business of using dairy fats to show people a good time.

Am I providing home recipes inspired by the originals? Am I hell. Partly that's because I suspect these chefs probably nailed it the first time. But it's also because all three of these recipes are very much in the public domain not just in books, but also online, both in text and as videos. If you want to have a go at them you can. That's the way with the recipes for hugely famous dishes: they become like religious scripture, heading out into the world to be studied by disciples and acolytes. The originating chefs know they don't need to guard the detail too jealously. They know that a recipe is all well and good, but that it's no substitute for the dish being cooked by the individuals who created it. That will always carry a premium.

I am lucky enough to have had all three of these dishes cooked for me by the people who wrote the recipes. But I'm enough of a chef nerd to want to know exactly what makes them tick. The best way to do that, the best way to get to grips with the haughtiest of haute gastronomy, is to cook the dish yourself. It's like popping the car's bonnet and having a really good look at the engine; a simile that would work if I had any interest in cars or for that matter, actually owned one, which I don't. But you get the general idea. So join me on my adventures cooking the food of these culinary gods. It's a rewarding if sometimes terribly messy business.

Joël Robuchon's pommes purée

By the time I became a restaurant critic in 1999 Joël Robuchon, once named 'chef of the century' by the revered French restaurant guide Gault & Millau, had been retired for three years. This made me unreasonably sad. It meant I would never get to experience the cooking of a man regarded by his fellow French Michelin three-star chefs as the very best of them all. Mostly it meant I would never get to try his mashed potato. This one dish, I had come to understand, was the true mark of his greatness: he had revolutionized the way high-end restaurants made mashed potato. He had done this by putting in less potato.

In 2004 fate smiled upon my already charmed life. The year before, Robuchon had decided the whole retirement thing really wasn't for him and had opened a restaurant in Paris, which would eventually become part of a global empire boasting over thirty Michelin stars. Now that he was back cooking, a couple of big wine businesses had joined forces – for which read, coughed up an awful lot of money – to get him to London to cook a one-off dinner for twenty people at the Connaught Hotel. I was to be one of just two journalists there. According to the organizers, the event was not without its complications. Robuchon's advance party of chefs, a notoriously flighty bunch, had insisted they be met at the Eurotunnel terminal because they wouldn't drive their vans loaded with ingredients on the left side of the road. Too stressful, they said. Later they wandered around the Connaught kitchens, then under the control of Angela Hartnett, barking at her commis chefs not to touch their cheese. French chefs can be quite intense about their stuff, apparently.

Still, they made it here along with Robuchon, and they cooked. It really was a hell of a dinner. There was caviar, set in a light shellfish gelée covered with the most delicate of cauliflower creams. There were 'ravioli' made with cabbage leaves stuffed with truffled chicken in a sharp vinaigrette. There were huge langoustine, wrapped in pastry and deep-fried before being draped in a garlicky basil purée.

And then there was the mashed potato or, to use its culturally appropriate name, the pommes purée. Cor. And blimey. In the world of high-end restaurants, where it often feels as if everything is about refinement and polish, it was mind-blowing to eat something built around just one word: comfort. It was smooth and luscious. It recalled the mashed potato of childhood, when a well-judged plate of food could be all the nurture and care you needed in a day, but it was also magnificently grown-up. It was a great chef's taste and technique brought to bear on just one question: how do you make something as simple as mashed potato so very much more than itself?

The Robuchon pommes purée recipe is available in his cookbook *The Complete Robuchon*, published in 2008. Plus, you really will find it in many places online. Cooks love showing people how to make it, possibly because there is something so outrageous about the whole business. It comes down to this: boil half a kilo of nutty Ratte potatoes in their skins. Once cooked, peel them, and press them through a potato ricer on its finest setting three times. Put that now fluffy mash into a dry pan on a low heat to drive off as much moisture as

possible. Then add half a kilo of cubed cold butter, in five or
so equal amounts, making sure each portion is incorporated
into the potato before adding the next. A little hot milk and
seasoning finishes the dish, but it really is this one-to-one
butter-to-potato ratio which makes it so astonishing. At
times Robuchon, who died in 2018, credited his grandmother
with the inspiration. Boy, did that woman love her grandson.
I have had a go at making it and I'll be honest: even with my
highly developed commitment to dairy, I still find it hard to
take it all the way. Adding that much butter feels utterly
wrong even though the end result is so completely right. For
an awful lot of restaurants, it has become the default recipe
for mashed potato even if many of them no longer acknowledge the chef who came up with it.

Robuchon's name lives on in the two dozen or so restaurants and bars which still carry his name. Doubtless, his biggest
fans will be able to talk breathlessly about his most intricate
creations. But it is testament to his true genius that the recipe
for which he will really be remembered is one for mashed
potato.

The Roux family's soufflé Suissesse

While I was writing this book Michel Roux closed Le Gavroche, the restaurant launched by his uncle and father, Michel
Snr and Albert, in 1967. It would be easy to shrug at the news
that a spendy restaurant in London's Mayfair was shutting its
doors after more than half a century. So what? The world
moves on. But Le Gavroche and the Roux family's impact on
the British restaurant world was so huge, the end couldn't
easily be dismissed. Le Gavroche means the urchin, which is
a humble name for such a flashy establishment. It was the

first restaurant in Britain to win one, then two, then three Michelin stars. It lit and then carried a flame for a kind of cream and butter-basted, lobster-rich, soufflé-happy classical cooking of which a lot of Britain was once deeply suspicious. Albert once told me a story about how his then wife would go off on shopping trips to France because many of the ingredients they needed, including certain cheeses, breeds of poultry and charcuterie, were impossible to get in Britain. If she was caught at the docks with a boot full of the stuff, she would be refused entry by British officials unless she allowed it all to be confiscated. She would simply turn around and head to the next port in the hope that this time she wouldn't be stopped. In those days in the late 60s and early 70s it must have felt as if eating well was literally illegal in the UK.

Le Gavroche also employed and trained brigades of cooks who went out into the world to open their own restaurants, and then trained others: everyone from Gordon Ramsay, Marco Pierre White and Pierre Koffmann to Monica Galetti, Jun Tanaka and Rowley Leigh. As a result, it was a major player in the restaurant revolution that swept the UK from the mid-80s onwards. The basement room, with its olive-green walls and button-backed banquettes and its peach-coloured chairs, could feel at times like a ludicrously plumped sofa of a place; a room untouched by the vagaries of fashion. That was part of the charm. Its regulars will tell you that it was at its very best not in the evening, when the most expensive menus were available and the biggest wines were being uncorked, but at lunchtime when they offered an extraordinarily good value set menu of classy bistro classics, the cost of which included half a bottle of great wine, mineral water and service. It was a lunch for which you cleared the diary.

In 1993 Albert Roux handed control of the restaurant to his son Michel. Some of the regulars feared it would become a very different place, not least because Michelin immediately took away one star. Michel declared himself untroubled. His Gavroche would not be the same as his father's. Shock, horror: the men would no longer need to wear ties. The food would be lightened. Even so, a few dishes had to stay. Think of them as delicious golden threads pulled through its many decades of history. One of those was the soufflé Suissesse, which went on the menu in 1968 and stayed there until the restaurant closed in January of 2024. It was, apparently, the Queen Mother's favourite dish, which says a lot for the old girl's appetite, given it is a soufflé based on a yolk-enriched béchamel, resting in a thick lake of cheese-enriched double cream, covered with more Gruyère, and then baked again.

For some reason during the first Covid lockdown, that reason probably being boredom, I decided it would be fun to attempt to make it, with Michel watching me via FaceTime on my phone. He told me the dish had been lightened over the years, which was remarkable because to make four servings, the recipe I was using from *Le Gavroche Cookbook* required 6 eggs, 600ml of double cream, 500ml of milk, 200g of Gruyère, a slab of butter and the equipment for a triple heart bypass. Again, if you go online, you will find many versions of the recipe including videos of Michel himself cooking it. He makes it look easy, because he is a multi-Michelin-starred chef who has been doing this for decades. Although it is basically only five ingredients it isn't easy. If the egg whites are over-whisked the soufflés won't hold. If you overcook it, the damn things will collapse. There's a lot of whisking and grating. All my work surfaces ended up lightly smeared in butter, cream and flour. Once out of the oven the soufflés must be upended into a dish, then covered in the cheese sauce. More cheese, indeed a snowfall of cheese, must be grated on to the top before it is grilled. I won't lie. Mine didn't end up looking anything like the suave and pert version served at Le Gavroche. It looked like a golden, butter-coloured undulating field. But it was delicious. That lunchtime the rest of the family joined me from the corners of our lockdown house and we stood around the kitchen happily spooning away the reason why eggs and dairy were invented.

Michel Roux gave a number of reasons for closing the restaurant. It wasn't financial. The place was still fully booked, even if Brexit and the fallout from Covid had proved challenging. It was more existential than that. Michel Snr died in 2020. Albert died in 2021. His son was now in his sixties and, given his commitment to being in his kitchen, he felt he had worked enough sixteen-hour days. There were a few other things he wanted to do with his life. His daughter Emily and her husband now have their own restaurant. She had no desire to take over the family business and without a Roux in charge, it simply wouldn't be Le Gavroche. However, the name would live on, he said. There would be pop-up versions of the old place on cruise ships. There would be special dinners. The dishes for which his family had become known would endure. It was, in short, very unlikely that he had cooked his last soufflé Suissesse.

Pierre Koffmann's pig's trotter stuffed with sweetbreads and morels

Some recipe words can be scary. Faced by the ingredient list for Pierre Koffmann's famed stuffed pig's trotter, in his book *Memories of Gascony*, I had good reason to be intimidated. The first line reads: '4 pigs' back trotters, boned'. The recipe for what is regarded by many as one of the most challenging of dishes is, hilariously, just one page long. It is very short on detail. There is, for example, no explanation of how you might go about boning said trotter, just the instruction that it should be done. One afternoon in that first Covid lockdown I found myself standing in my kitchen staring at a chopping board laid with a single trotter looking extremely foot-like, while my fist gripped the red plastic handle of the boning knife that my butcher, thoughtfully, had added to the order he had delivered to my doorstep. I didn't have a clue where to begin.

I did what I always do in these circumstances: I searched YouTube. It doesn't matter what the task is. There is always a video. A few minutes later I finally understood what I was being asked to do. I wasn't boning anything out. I was skinning the trotter, which was a much simpler task. Kinda. It was time to get to work.

Pierre Koffmann first came to Britain in 1970 to work at Le Gavroche. When the Roux brothers opened the Waterside Inn at Bray, just outside London, he became its head chef. He left in 1977 to set up his own Chelsea restaurant, La Tante Claire, which would go on to be the second British restaurant, after Le Gavroche, to win three Michelin stars. Koffmann has said that he knew he would have to come up with a menu of new dishes for his restaurant, rather than 'borrow' any from the Roux brothers. The pig's trotter, boned-out, filled with a stuffing of cream-bonded chicken mousseline with morels and sweetbreads, and glazed with veal jus, was one of those dishes. 'The pig's trotter was there long before me,' Koffmann once told me. 'My part was to bring in the sweetbreads, the morels.' It represented a certain 80s excess and became such a hit that Marco Pierre White, who worked briefly at La Tante Claire, put it on the menu of his flagship restaurant at the then Hyde Park Hotel in the early 90s, as Pig's Trotter Pierre Koffmann.

I first tried it in 2009 when Koffmann came out of retirement to stage a pop-up on the roof of Selfridges department store on London's Oxford Street. It was meant to last for a week but instead, due to demand, went on for eight. The plan had always been to serve his greatest hits, including the trotter, but he had underestimated the hunger for them. He had to buy the trotters in batches of 500 and employ two cooks whose only job was to debone them, leaving just the little toe-bones intact. By the end of the pop-up, they had sold 3,200 of them. That success led in turn to Koffmann at the Berkeley, a last restaurant from a legendary chef, which ran from 2010 until 2016.

It is not a dish for everyone. It is not a dish for vegetarians, or perhaps even for meat eaters who prefer that their food not look too anatomically like part of an animal. It really is a foot on a plate. It is also soft and gelatinous, again in a way some people find disconcerting. I do not find either of these challenging. It is a delightfully old-fashioned dish; a reminder of the engrossing virtues of classical French cooking, before a new wave of chefs thought it was time to go easy on the cream and the sticky demi-glace. Koffmann used to serve it with a dollop of Robuchon-style pommes purée, mined with shards of crackling, as if saying: there are no half measures here. The soft, sticky, melting long-braised skin gives way to the smoothness of the cream-boosted mousse and the bite of the morels and the sweetbreads. For dessert, may I recommend a lie down?

My advice for anyone who wants to have a go at cooking this dish is to clear a couple of days in the diary and seek a little therapeutic support. You will, as ever, find endless versions of the recipe online, along with instructive videos. Watch them. Watch them again. Once you've skinned the trotter, which would apparently take Koffmann about 90 seconds and genuinely took me 2 hours, the skin, with those toe-bones attached, must be braised in veal jus for 3 hours. The skin should then be put into the fridge to chill for at least a few hours, or perhaps overnight. You may wish to make yourself a cup of tea at this point and stare into the middle distance, while considering your life choices. Next, you'll have to work out how to prep the sweetbreads, probably by looking up another recipe in *Le Gavroche Cookbook*, which is very good for those sorts of basic skills. You'll then have to make the chicken mousseline, by blitzing the raw chicken breast with large amounts of double cream. Sauté the sweetbreads with the morels. Make yourself another cup of tea while all this cools. Again, question the point of it all. Introduce the ingredients of the stuffing to each other and then introduce the stuffing to the trotter. Roll it all up into a cylinder, wrap it in foil, put it into a steamer and pray to whichever deity you think appropriate that the whole damn thing doesn't fall apart.

I did two trotters. One did fall apart. It was wreckage, albeit delicious wreckage. The other one, however, startled me by looking and tasting not unlike the original. It was rough around the edges. Koffmann would never have let it off his pass. But it wasn't a total, unmitigated disaster, and for a recipe of this complexity that felt very much like a win. It is worth pointing out, if only as a matter of personal pride, that, while this is Koffmann's dish, he would have had a kitchen full of skilled professionals to help him execute it: one on the trotter, one on the stuffing, one on the sauce and so on. As a cook it is always good to know your limits and I found mine: it's the Pig's Trotter Pierre Koffmann.

Dessert

A Snickers or Marathon pot (depending upon your age)

Inspired by desserts served at both the Wheatsheaf near
Cheltenham and the Alan, Manchester

The vast majority of restaurant chefs would rather saw off the
fingers of their dominant knife-holding hand than serve
savoury dishes which in some way aped or recalled high street
branded foods. In the last quarter of a century, I can't recall
ever being served a kitchen's witty take on the Findus Crispy
Pancake or the Vesta Curry. It may have happened but if so,
it never came my way. (And if you're too young to know what
these products are, or you're not from the UK, oh what irre-
sistibly ultra-high-processed food joys you have been denied.)

Dessert is different. Dessert is a place which positively

encourages nostalgia both for the high street and for child-hood. The fact is nobody needs dessert. Nobody runs into a restaurant shouting, 'I'm hungry, bring me the dessert menu,' unless they are completely devoid of shame. Dessert is an unnecessary treat, just as the sweets of childhood once were. There is a shiny golden thread that links the restaurant dessert of adulthood, and the bag of sweets you practically inhaled when you were a kid. Which explains, I think, why so many chefs have referenced specific sweet brands and items over the years. Heston Blumenthal of the Michelin three-star Fat Duck in Bray long ago came up with a way to pump air into milk chocolate to make his version of the finely bubbled Aero. Gary Rhodes put a giant Jaffa Cake on his dessert menu. Meanwhile, when the Hawksmoor steakhouse group opened their curving Air Street restaurant overlooking London's Regent Street, the dessert menu included chocolates with a soft salted caramel centre, which they described as their version of the Rolo. Later, they came up with a sizable hazelnut-crusted chocolate ball filled with ganache, a dessert they decided to call the Ambassador's Reception so as not to upset the multinational confectionery giant Ferrero. The title referenced the company's advertising campaign, in which a platter of gold-foil-wrapped hazelnut chocolates is passed around at a party, to such rapturous delight that one guest gushes to the host that, 'with these Ferrero Rocher you are really spoiling us'. What a diminished life she must have led.

One of my favourite examples of this didn't reference high street confectionery. It simply used them. In 2008, during his relatively short-lived tenure at the Angel, a bare-bones Manchester pub that smelt lightly of damp dog, the Lancashire chef Rob Owen Brown served a Cadbury's Miniature Heroes terrine. It was exactly what it sounded like: a slice of a chocolate terrine made from melted-down miniature versions of Cadbury classics, like the Double Decker, Wispa Bar and Twirl. It came topped with pieces of Mars Bar and Crunchie. I laughed all the way through eating it. If you like the sound of this, do seek out Owen Brown's marvellously titled cookbook, *Crispy Squirrel and Vimto Trifle*.

One high street chocolate bar, which involves a winning combination of chocolate, caramel and peanuts, has inspired two desserts I have been served and, in turn, this recipe, although the name has changed depending on the age of the people involved. In 2014 at the Wheatsheaf, a pub just outside Cheltenham, a chef called Antony Ely served me what he called a Marathon pudding. It was a large chocolate fondant, but when you broke through the hot, dark wobbling surface you found not liquid chocolate but a heart of dulce de leche, that lovely South American caramel made from milk cooked down with sugar, along with crushed peanuts. It was a jolly riff on the Marathon Bar, as it was called in the UK until 1990, when it was renamed Snickers to bring it into line with the rest of the world. Which tells us just how much of a nostalgic Ely was when he named his dessert. (Snickers was apparently the name of a favourite Tennessee racehorse owned by the Mars family.)

Fast forward to April 2022 and dinner at the Alan, a new boutique hotel in Manchester. The first chef, Iain Thomas, clearly had a thing for nostalgia because his dessert menu included both Nana Betty's rhubarb and custard and an Arctic roll. But there was also a dessert simply called Snickers. His was a fat disc of a light chocolate mousse, again with a centre of dulce de leche, scattered with chocolate shavings and caramelized peanuts. Thomas had the time and equipment to make his dessert stand alone on the plate. Mine uses the time-honoured virtues of the chocolate pot. And if you're frowning at the page and muttering, 'But a Snickers bar also includes nougat,' I'm aware of that and I'm sure the chefs were too. Let's not complicate things. What matters here is a take on the flavours of the Marathon/Snickers, albeit a slightly grown-up one courtesy of the dark chocolate.

Makes enough for 6 x 200ml pots or 8 x 150ml pots. They are pretty full on.

INGREDIENTS

For the caramel
175g light brown sugar
300ml double cream
50g butter
1 heaped tsp cornflour
¼ tsp sea salt

For the caramelized peanuts
300g raw, skin-on peanuts, sometimes sold as red peanuts (this will make more than you need, but the peanuts tend to come in 300g bags, and nobody will hate you for making too much of this)
220g caster sugar
85ml water

For the chocolate mousse
200g 70% dark chocolate (or a mixture of 70% and 85%)
120ml water
3 medium eggs, separated (as ever, when beating egg whites make sure not to get any yolk into the whites)
50g caster sugar

METHOD

1. First make the caramel. Combine the sugar, cream and butter in a saucepan over a low heat. Stir until

all the sugar has dissolved. Take a couple of tablespoons of the liquid out of the pan into a mug, add the cornflour to make a slurry, and then add back to the warm but thin caramel. Turn up the heat and let it bubble gently for 3 minutes, stirring now and then, until it has thickened a little. Add the sea salt and stir again. Take off the heat and leave to cool for about 10 minutes. Don't worry if it's not very thick. It will thicken up later.

2. You may find it easier to decant this into a measuring jug, so you can now pour it into the 200ml ramekins to a depth of about 1½cm. Put them into the fridge to chill for 2 hours.

3. While the caramel is chilling and solidifying, caramelize the peanuts. Put all the ingredients into a frying pan. Cast iron is best if you have it, but it's not vital. Heat the ingredients over a moderate heat, stirring all the time. The sugar will dissolve into the water. Bring the mix at the sides into the middle and repeat. Keep it all moving.

4. After about 10 minutes the sugar will start to crystallize. It will look like everything has gone terribly wrong but it hasn't, because the crystallized sugar will remelt. Keep stirring, scraping at the bottom so that the peanuts get coated in the sugar as it melts. If you think there's any chance it will burn, especially if it starts to smoke, take the pan off the direct heat and continue to stir, then return to the heat. You may find yourself taking it on and off the heat repeatedly. This will probably be a nightmare if you have induction, but then I didn't design your

kitchen. Eventually after about 10 minutes all the peanuts will be covered in caramel. Scrape on to an oven tray and leave to cool. (If it's winter and dry and you have an outside space, pop them there for 10 minutes.)

5. When they have cooled, the peanuts will have properly hardened. You will need to break up slabs of what is essentially peanut brittle into individual peanuts. Eat a few as you go, as a reward. As I say, you'll have far more than you need.

6. When they have cooled and the caramel in the ramekins has set, put a thick layer of the peanuts on top.

7. Now to make the mousse. Make a bain-marie by sitting a glass bowl over a pan containing a few centimetres of simmering water, then break the chocolate into the bowl and add the 120ml of water. Making sure the simmering water in the pan doesn't touch the bottom of the glass bowl, leave everything to melt for 5 minutes, stirring the chocolate and water together until it forms a thick, dark chocolatey soup. Take off the heat and leave it to cool for 10 minutes.

8. Give it a good stir, then hand-whisk the egg yolks into the chocolate until smooth and glossy and set to one side. This should only take a minute or so.

9. Now use an electric whisk to beat the egg whites. As they firm up, add the sugar and continue to whisk to medium stiff peaks.

SIX

OMNIVORE

298

sea trout crispy sushi*
sea urchin, salted butter and yuzu*
herbal leek velouté

EGG TOAST
caviar and herbs

DIVER SCALLOP
cured fresno pepper, citrus marinade and shiso

KING CRAB
nishiki rice, vermouth fondue and nori

BLACK SEA BASS
glazed cabbage, sauerkraut and dill

WAGYU BEEF TENDERLOIN
smoked black garlic, endive and bergamot jus

RHUBARB
rice croquant, rhubarb compote, matcha pistachio sorbet

TEN

OMNIVORE

398

sea trout crispy sushi*
sea urchin, salted butter and yuzu*
herbal leek velouté

CAVIAR SALAD
smoked egg yolk emulsion

DIVER SCALLOP
cured fresno pepper, citrus marinade and shiso

YELLOWFIN TUNA RIBBONS
avocado, radish, ginger dressing and chili oil*

KING CRAB
nishiki rice, vermouth fondue and nori

BLACK TRUFFLE
mushroom dumpling, potato consommé

BLACK SEA BASS
glazed cabbage, sauerkraut and dill

MAINE LOBSTER
spaghetti squash, cashew, guajillo chili infusion

HUDSON VALLEY FOIE GRAS
chestnuts, mulled brandy and vanilla

CHARRED DUCK
parsnip, bacon marmalade and horseradish butter

CHOCOLATE
passion fruit, bitter caramel, cocoa

**Consuming raw or undercooked meats, poultry, seafood,
shellfish or eggs may increase your risk of foodborne illness*

...ean-Georges, 1 Central Park West, New York, New York, USA.
...2023 / chef: Jean-Georges Vongerichten

...ean-Georges is the Michelin three-star flagship of the Alsatian-born
...hef's 40+ strong global empire. In my 2005 review I described a meal
...n the high-ceilinged dining room as like 'eating at altitude'. The price for this
...asting menu is in US dollars and excludes service, which is usually at least 20%.

Russ and Daughters

E. Houston St, New York

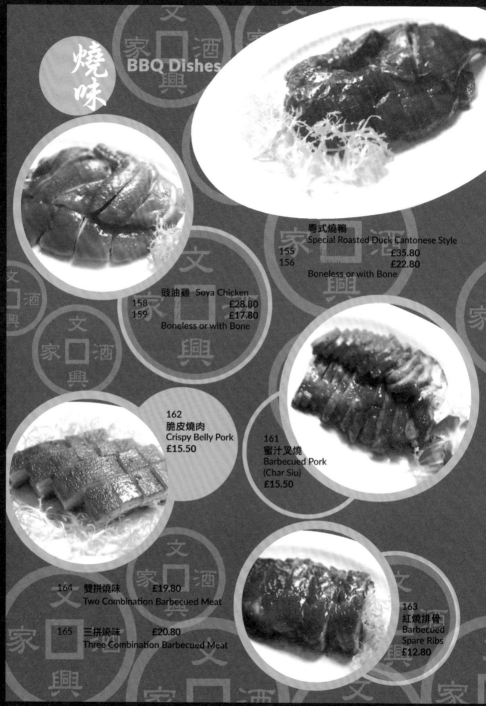

燒味

BBQ Dishes

粵式燒鴨 Special Roasted Duck Cantonese Style
155   £35.80
156   £22.80
Boneless or with Bone

豉油雞 Soya Chicken
158   £28.80
159   £17.80
Boneless or with Bone

162
脆皮燒肉
Crispy Belly Pork
£15.50

161
蜜汁叉燒
Barbecued Pork
(Char Siu)
£15.50

164   雙拼燒味   £19.80
Two Combination Barbecued Meat

165   三拼燒味   £20.80
Three Combination Barbecued Meat

163
紅燒排骨
Barbecued
Spare Ribs
£12.80

Four Seasons, 12 Gerrard Street, London W1.
2023

It's important to give the full street address because the company has a number of businesses in London's Chinatown. The branch at number 12 is prized for its roast meats, especially the Special Roasted Duck Cantonese Style, which chef and writer Simon Hopkinson has described as the best in London. I agree.

10. Mix a third of the egg whites through the chocolate mix to loosen it up. Now, bit by bit, fold the rest of the egg whites through the chocolate, making sure to break down any lumps of egg white that form.

11. Portion up the chocolate mousse mix over the layer of peanuts almost to the top, and return to the fridge for at least 3 hours. Once the mousse has firmed up, top with a second layer of the peanuts.

If you prefer you can make a single large 'family style' dish of this in a bigger bowl, though the layers may take slightly longer to set.

Iced berries with hot white chocolate sauce

This is not inspired by the dessert served at Le Caprice and the Ivy. It simply is that dessert.

There are two reasons for including this very familiar dessert. First, it was another of those early dishes that I reverse-engineered. I scooped a plate of it away gleefully one night at the original Ivy, and a few weeks later made it at home, because how hard could it be? Not very, is the answer. I reckoned there were three ingredients: frozen berries, white chocolate and cream. I was right. Like so many great dishes, it's more of an idea than a recipe. And second, I've included it to make sure the right chef got the credit. If you search up the title online you will get literally millions of results. Seemingly every recipe website and every big-name chef offers a version. Some do reference the Ivy, although it is very much a minority. None mention a pastry chef called Jayne Kress, then of Le Caprice, who was responsible for refining it. The idea was suggested to her in the early 90s by Jeremy King, then owner of the restaurant. He had got it from a friend who had been served a plate of it on a trip to Denmark.

It's rather fun spooling through all the other uncredited recipes, looking for the details which chefs have added in an attempt to make the recipe their own and therefore claim authorship. This is a popular, if little mentioned, wheeze in the recipe-writing world. The fact is that truly original dish ideas can sometimes be hard to come by. I was struck by this one year while making a report for the BBC's *One Show*, for whom I covered food stories. We had brought together a panel of viewers in Bristol to test various celebrity chefs' Christmas recipes against each other: it was Delia's roast turkey against Mary Berry's roast turkey; it was Nigella's roast potatoes against the Hairy Bikers' version and so on.

As part of the research for the report, I thumbed my way through piles of Christmas cookbooks. What was most striking was how similar all the recipes were, bar a detail here and there to set them apart. Perhaps a different herb turned up in the turkey stuffing, or a different fat was used to get the spuds crisp. But the underlying recipe? There was nothing that could be done to alter that or the dish simply wouldn't work. The same is true of this dessert. Some versions add vanilla extract (unnecessary; there should be more than enough vanilla in the white chocolate). Others add rum or, god help us, limoncello, which I think smells like toilet cleaner. The most hilarious adaptation in pursuit of authorship came from an otherwise extremely skilled and well-known chef who will remain anonymous to protect the guilty. To be fair he doesn't mention the Ivy or Le Caprice, so perhaps we should just give him sole credit. His version removed one of the three ingredients, which is to say the cream. It simply suggested pouring melted white chocolate over frozen berries. Two issues. First, it's cloyingly sweet, and second, the white chocolate just sets solid again very quickly, whereas with the addition of cream it stays liquid.

Here, then, is the original version which is now on the menu at Arlington, Jeremy King's reborn version of Le Caprice (only under a new name), which opened in the spring of 2024. When scaling, keep in mind that you need equal amounts of sauce to berries per person, and that the sauce is half chocolate, half cream. A single serving of the frozen berries should be around 100g, so you need 50g of white chocolate and 50ml of double cream per serving. You can make more of the sauce if you like, but just make sure it's on a ratio of one to one.

Serves 6

INGREDIENTS

300g good quality white chocolate
300ml double cream
600g frozen berries (you can, of course, freeze them yourself in a
    single layer on a tray, but you'll find a bunch of options in the
    freezer section of your local supermarket. Avoid large fruit
    like strawberries. Favour blueberries, as well as red, black and
    white currants and smaller blackberries)

METHOD

1. Break the chocolate up into small pieces and place in
   a glass bowl with the cream. Put the bowl over a pan

of simmering water, but not in contact with the water. Leave on a low to medium heat for around 20 minutes, stirring occasionally to mix the melting chocolate with the cream.

2. Five or so minutes before you want to serve, portion out the frozen fruit on to plates.

3. Although the chocolate and cream will be incorporated by now, you do want it good and hot. You can put it on high in the microwave for 45 seconds if you feel it's a little tepid to the touch.

4. Pour the hot white chocolate sauce on to the berries and serve immediately, while telling the hilarious story about Gordon Ramsay's cream-less version.

Baked chocolate puddings with cherries

A response to the sad decline of the restaurant dessert menu

In early 2023, in a moment of madness, I agreed to compete in a special episode of *MasterChef* in which the show's regular critics would cook off against each other. I say a moment of madness. It was my mad idea. I bumped into the executive producer of the show in our local park, because we live near each other. Making chit-chat, as you do, I suggested that what the audience would really love to see is an episode in which the various restaurant critics, who regularly held forth on the contestants' cooking, showed off their own cooking chops. He said it was a good idea, and got it commissioned. That was the episode for which, in the guilty pleasures round, I cooked the spare ribs with cumin and chilli on page 89.

Various terrors haunted me in the small hours of the night as the contest approached. Would I accidentally open a vein on camera through some less than deft knife-work? Some people might enjoy that. I wouldn't. I knew I could cook but would I be able to cook under pressure? Would I, indeed, generally make a total arse of myself, thus in one short hour of high-def television undermining any meagre gloss of authority or reputation I had somehow managed to acquire over the previous twenty-plus years of reviewing?

Key among my concerns was dessert. I had to come up with a proper one which I could execute fully in the limited time, and it had to be good. Which is to say, it couldn't just be a bunch of creamy things in a bowl. Ah, creamy things in a bowl. For years on the critics' round of *MasterChef: The Professionals*, I had been whining about creamy things in a bowl being passed off as a sophisticated dessert. Faced by the need to prepare two courses, one of which should be a dessert, too many contestants defaulted to a mousse, or a posset or a panna cotta. There would, of course, be bells and whistles. There might be some sort of fruity sauce. Maybe they'd melt a bit of chocolate and drizzle that on top. For texture, perhaps they'd throw on a biscuit crumb or the dreary tooth-clogger that is granola. Then they'd decorate the dish with a few edible flowers to make it look pretty. But it didn't change the reality of a seemingly endless parade of panna cottas, those vanilla-flavoured creams set with gelatine which are one of the very first desserts taught at catering college. Finally, you can grasp the true grinding hell of my working life.

I fully understand the time constraints. Generally, the contestants have only ninety minutes in which to produce two courses, sometimes just seventy-five. Even so, I did think they could do better. And, to be fair, a few did. Over the years I would be introduced to an impressive rhubarb tarte Tatin by Marianne Lumb, and a lovely sugar and cinnamon-dusted log of deep-fried bread and butter pudding. But they seemed to be the exceptions, not the rule. *MasterChef* desserts rarely shone. Then again, the performance of the contestants on the TV cooking show only mirrored what I was seeing in the restaurant sector from which the competing chefs came. For years, restaurant dessert menus seemed to have been in decline. Since the 2010s I had been pointedly commenting on restaurants which, instead of serving tarts or savarins, a sticky toffee or bread and butter pudding, dishes which required skilled pastry and baking work, instead went for a lemon posset or a chocolate mousse or perhaps a combination of the two.

Anecdotally, it seemed there were two causes. First, the economic climate within which restaurants operated had become so tough, so grinding, that having dedicated pastry chefs in the kitchen had become a luxury that only the biggest and best funded could afford. That meant having a small, tight brigade of generalists with perhaps an equally small repertoire of dessert techniques to call upon. As a result, there also seemed to be a growing shortage of classical pastry section experience available for young up-and-coming chefs. It was a self-fuelling problem.

Intriguingly, however, great pastry, baking and patisserie work hasn't been in total decline. It has simply been happening less inside restaurants than outside of them. In 2011 the French-born pastry chef Dominique Ansel left the world of New York's Michelin-starred restaurants and opened his own bakery on Spring Street in Manhattan's SoHo. There, in 2013, he launched the crème-filled cronut, the now much imitated cross between a donut and a croissant in flavours from rose vanilla to peach bourbon, roasted pecan maple caramel to banana and toasted oats. It inspired queues down the street of up to an hour or more, one of which, against my better judgement, I joined in late 2013. I'm not a patient man. The idea of queueing for a must-have bakery item does not sit well with me. It makes me feel like a wet-lipped fan boy. Still, I did it. I liked my cronut.

Dominique Ansel's bakery, which soon spread to Hong Kong, Las Vegas and, until the pandemic, London, was an early example of the growing trend for stand-alone dessert-orientated bakeries, like Rebecca Spaven's Toad in London's Camberwell, famed for its iced fingers flavoured with liquorice and orange blossom, or Gooey in Manchester which offers a brick of French toast filled with sweet-salty caramel. Pastry chefs often told me that in restaurant kitchens they felt like second division cooks, tasked with finishing off the meal after the important savoury stuff had happened. Why put up with that when they could open a place dedicated to their craft, only with better hours and working conditions?

Certainly, for *MasterChef*, I needed to bake something. We would have just seventy minutes in which to sort the first savoury course. I chose to do Francesco Mazzei's seafood fregola from page 193. There would then be another twenty minutes in which to complete the dessert. I would clearly have to start work on it before I started the fregola. I decided to adapt a previous recipe of mine, featured in my book *The Ten (Food) Commandments*, for individual baked chocolate puddings with cherries. It's a huge crowd pleaser: the dark chocolatey centre which should be wobbly towards the bottom gives way to soft sweet cherries in syrup. All it needs is dollops of fridge-cold whipped cream, perhaps slightly sweetened with a little of the cherry syrup to send it on its way.

This recipe isn't inspired by a restaurant dish like all the others. It qualifies for inclusion because it's a response to what's been going on in restaurants, albeit a slightly feeble one. That said, it's lovely. Look, I won the critics' episode of *MasterChef* so this recipe is literally a winner.

Originally, I made this with fresh cherries, but for *MasterChef* I convinced the production team to let me use cherries in syrup. They are just sweeter and richer, and you can use the syrup to flavour the accompanying cream. There are a few products on the market but the best by far are those by Fabbri Amarena, which come in 600g jars and are available online.

Makes 4

INGREDIENTS

250ml red wine
140g caster sugar, plus 3 extra tbsp
A 600g jar of cherries in syrup
150g plain chocolate, broken into pieces
115g butter
2 large eggs
1 tsp vanilla extract
25g plain flour
300ml double cream

1. Put the red wine, 3 tablespoons of the sugar and 2 dozen of the cherries into a small pan and heat gently. When it starts to boil, turn down and simmer for 20 minutes.

2. Strain the cherries, reserving the wine. Let the cherries cool and dry in a sieve. Meanwhile, put the wine back into the pan and reduce by half until it's starting to go syrupy. Allow to cool.

3. To make the pudding, melt the chocolate and butter together in a bowl over a pan of simmering water. When melted, give the ingredients a good stir to mix them all together fully.

4. In a mixing bowl, whisk together the rest of the sugar and the eggs with the vanilla extract until thick and foamy.

5. Carefully fold the chocolate mix into the egg mix.

6. Now sieve the flour over the chocolate mixture and fold in carefully.

7. Set the oven to 190°C/375°F/gas mark 5. Butter the inside of four ramekins.

8. Put 6 of the cherries in the bottom of each ramekin. Add a little of the reduced red wine sauce, to come halfway up the cherries. Pour over the chocolate pudding mix.

9. Bake in the oven for 20 to 25 minutes, until there is only a slight wobble in the middle.

10. While they are baking, whip the cream and then gently fold in 2 or 3 tablespoons of the syrup from the cherries, just to lightly flavour.

11. Serve the puddings immediately with the whipped cream and the remaining red wine sauce.

Individual baked custard tarts

Inspired by the custard tart served by Gary Rhodes,
at his many restaurants including Rhodes in the Square
and City Rhodes

The problem is, one baked chocolate pudding does not a pastry chef make. I have always been a little intimidated by the precision required by pastry work. At the savoury end of the meal there is a lot more space for improvisation and free-styling. But with pastry and baking if you don't get the essentials right, it risks being a total disaster. It's chemistry. During the various Covid lockdowns I decided to face my fears by having a go at the custard tart in *New British Classics*, the indispensable cookbook by Gary Rhodes, who died in 2019. I often thought the perky, bright, engaging TV persona could sometimes obscure what a truly marvellous and serious chef he was. Although Fergus Henderson at St John has long been credited with inspiring a renaissance in British dishes, Rhodes really should be given an awful lot of credit too. At the Castle in Taunton, he brought dishes like pork faggots to the table, and served an outrageously good omelette Arnold Bennett. His cooking was never over-adorned. It was all about the central idea. I loved his restaurants Rhodes in the Square, at Dolphin Square close to the House of Commons, and City Rhodes, in the City of London. Two dishes were always guaranteed to be on the dessert menu: that witty, indulgent take of his on the Jaffa Cake, which celebrated the happy communion of sponge, orange and dark chocolate, and his custard tart.

There was nothing different about Rhodes's custard tart. It was just very, very good. The pastry was crisp, the filling creamy. The grated nutmeg added a little punch. Each slice was so perfect, it looked like you could prick your finger on its tip.

My attempt at home really wasn't bad. I was pleased with it. But as with all my efforts involving making pastry from scratch, it felt like a fluke or at best a disaster averted. If I now offered you a recipe which encouraged you to make your own pastry, it would be dishonest of me. Elsewhere, with recipes involving pastry, I have encouraged you to buy the ready-made stuff. Why should it be any different here? If you want to make Gary Rhodes's original custard tart, I urge you to get hold of a copy of *New British Classics*. It is one of the great cookbooks and will be a good friend to you in the kitchen. It will probably have to be second-hand because sadly it is out of print.

This recipe uses shop-bought all-butter puff and a clever way of working with it popular in Portugal which, appropriately enough, I picked up from the Portuguese chef Nuno Mendes, who proposed it in a recipe for making pastel de nata, or Portuguese custard tarts. The custard filling belongs firmly to Rhodes.

Makes 12 individual custard tarts

(Halve the ingredients if you only want to make 6, but muffin tins generally have 12 cups and it seems a shame to leave any of them empty)

INGREDIENTS

Butter, for melting
2 x 320g packets of shop-bought all-butter puff pastry (brands
    differ and Jus-Rol does work best)

For the custard filling
8 egg yolks (keep the whites for the Mont Blanc recipe on
    page 324)
75g sugar
500ml double cream
A whole nutmeg, for grating

For the glaze (optional)
3 tbsp honey
Juice of ½ a lemon

METHOD

1. Heat the oven to 220°C/425°F/gas mark 7.

2. Liberally brush the inside of a 12-muffin tin with
   melted butter, and put the tin into the fridge to chill.

3. Take the packs of puff pastry out of the fridge 10
   minutes before you need them so they warm up a
   little. Unroll them on their greaseproof paper, then
   roll them out with a rolling pin so the sheet increases
   in size by about 10%. (The pack's instructions will tell
   you not to roll it because it will compress the
   laminations. Don't worry. That's exactly what we
   want. It will still be flaky.)

4. Starting from the short side of the sheet, roll the
   blocks of pastry up into two tight cylinders. With a
   sharp knife, slice off the ragged ends, then cut the

long cylinders into smaller 3cm cylinders. If you have any left over, freeze for later.

5. Using your thumbs on the flat ends of the cylinder, press each one into a disc, and then press into the tins by hand, so that the pastry just comes up over the lip of each cup. Put back into the fridge for 15 minutes to chill.

6. Cut squares of greaseproof paper big enough to fully line each cup, then fill with ceramic baking beans or dried beans to bake the pastry blind. Bake with the beans in place for 15 minutes, then take out the beans and paper, brush the inside of the tarts with a little of the leftover egg white to seal, and bake for a further 5 minutes. Once they have had a couple of minutes to cool, gently hold the rim of each one between thumb and index finger and lightly turn them in their cups. They should release. It's easier to do this now when they are unfilled, rather than when they are completed. Turn the oven down to 150°C/300°F/gas mark 2.

7. While the tart cases are blind baking, whisk the egg yolks with the sugar. Bring the cream to the boil. Take the pan off the heat, let the boiling subside, then pour it over the egg and sugar mix and stir to incorporate. Pour the mix through a sieve into a bowl, ideally one with a lip.

8. Pull the shelf out of the oven, place the muffin tin on it and then pour the custard into each one. (You can do it on the kitchen work surface if you think you can get the muffin tin back into the oven without spilling anything. Good luck with that.)

9. Grate nutmeg over the top, then bake the tarts for 20 minutes. When done the custard should be firm with a slight wobble.

10. Allow them to cool for 5 minutes, then lift them out on to a rack.

11. If you want to glaze them, make sure the rack is over an oven tray to catch the drips. Gently heat the honey in a saucepan so it goes liquid, and mix in the lemon juice. Brush the pastry rim and sides generously with the glaze. Don't worry if it gets on the surface of the custard. It just adds to the flavour.

Treacle tart

Inspired by the treacle tart served by chef Mary-Ellen McTague at the Creameries in Chorlton, Manchester

Recipes can be venerable. They can have longevity and be passed hand to hand, like pieces of holy scripture. There is, for example, a dark, dense chocolate terrine, with a biscuit element, a recipe for which first appeared in Elizabeth David's book *French Country Cooking*, published in 1951. It's called St Émilion au chocolat. I was served a lovely version of it in the autumn of 2023 at a Cirencester restaurant called Sam & Jak. The eponymous Sam Edwards and Jak Doggett had been introduced to the recipe by a chef called Bob Parkinson when they worked for him at Made by Bob, another Cirencester restaurant. Bob Parkinson will in turn have met it when he worked at Bibendum on London's Fulham Road, where the founding chef in 1987 was Simon Hopkinson, who included a recipe for it in *Roast Chicken and Other Stories*, the book he wrote with Lindsey Bareham first published in 1999. Hopkinson made his name in the early 80s at a restaurant in Fulham called Hilaire, where he cooked for one Elizabeth David. That one dessert pulls like another of those golden threads through the history of all those restaurants.

I first encountered Mary-Ellen McTague's fabulous treacle tart in 2018, when she served it at the Creameries, a one-time bakery located in a renovated dairy, where the menu had expanded so it was now a small but perfectly formed full-service restaurant. The tart's pastry was crisp, and there was a distinct citrus burst to the light, almost fluffy filling, echoed by the bowl of lemon jelly served alongside it. I said in my review that it tasted like a treacle tart baked by someone who had made an awful lot of them. McTague, who came to prominence through her restaurant the Aumbry in Prestwich, confirmed this was so. She had been making them since 2004 when she helped develop the recipe with Heston Blumenthal at the Fat Duck, where she eventually became a sous-chef. Every Blumenthal dish went through endless incremental changes and development, she told me, including this treacle tart. If you want to make the original, you will find a detailed recipe in Blumenthal's 2009 book *In Search of Total Perfection* (originally published in two volumes in 2006 and 2007) as a tie-in to the BBC series of the same name.

McTague's version was another of my lockdown projects. In his book Blumenthal admits that the pastry is probably the most challenging part of the process and he wasn't wrong. I got it done, but as ever it felt like a fluke rather than the product of a recipe followed. And so, once again, I'm telling you not to bother. Buy ready-made shortcrust. It does the job very nicely. Don't worry about it being unsweetened, because what matters here is that light breadcrumb and syrup filling, with the burst of lemon and an edge of salt. It's plenty sweet enough. You could also make individual tarts using the shop-bought puff pastry method detailed for the custard tarts. It would work very nicely for that too.

INGREDIENTS

1 x 320g packet of ready-made shortcrust pastry
2 medium eggs (plus egg white for sealing up the tart case)
60g double cream
7½g salt
85g butter
675g golden syrup
Juice and zest of 1 large lemon
115g fresh brown breadcrumbs

METHOD

1. Heat the oven to 200°C/400°F/gas mark 6.

2. Take the pack of shortcrust pastry out of the fridge 45 minutes before you want to cook with it. Once it's come to room temperature, roll it to make the sheet a little thinner.

3. Butter and flour a tart tin with a removable base generously. The tart tin should be 22–25cm across and roughly 3½cm deep. Line the tart tin with the pastry, then trim it back leaving a little excess over the rim. You can fully trim it later. Hold on to some of the raw pastry.

4. Line the pastry case loosely with parchment or greaseproof paper, fill with ceramic baking beans (or dried pulses) and blind bake it for 20 minutes. Take it out of the oven and remove the parchment and

baking beans. Check for any holes and fissures. Seal them up with tiny pieces of the retained scraps of pastry. Brush the entire inside of the tart case with egg white, then return it to the oven for 10 minutes. When it's done, remove the tart case from the oven and turn the temperature down to 150°C/300°F/gas mark 2. Leave it in the tin.

5. For the filling blitz together the 2 eggs, cream and salt, and pour into a large mixing bowl.

6. Now make a beurre noisette. Heat the butter in a saucepan over a medium flame. Once it stops foaming you will see it go from yellow to light brown. Allow it to go to a dark brown (but keep an eye on it, so it doesn't go black). Strain the beurre noisette through a muslin into a bowl. (I substituted with a new J-cloth).

7. While that is cooling, heat the golden syrup gently in a saucepan until it liquefies. Once that's happened, add the beurre noisette and use a stick blender to emulsify the two liquids. It will go a cloudy, creamy colour.

8. Pour the butter-golden syrup mixture over the egg and cream mixture. Blitz that together with the stick blender. Stir in the lemon juice and zest and then the breadcrumbs. Do this by hand rather than with the stick blender. Leave to stand for 5 minutes, then stir again.

9. Put the blind baked tart case, still in its tin, on a tray on the oven shelf, and pour in the mixture. You may have a little more than you need, depending on the depth of your tin.

10. Bake for 45 minutes, then carefully turn the tray around and bake for another 10 minutes. You want the top a lovely golden brown and set. If it looks wobbly and bulbous in the middle, put it back in, until it has subsided. Check every 10 minutes. It could take up to 75 minutes to bake. Don't worry if the excess pastry starts to singe. You can trim that off later.

11. Let the tart cool completely before trimming off the excess pastry and releasing it from the tin. (Place it on an upturned bowl, so that when the edges are released from the tin, the rim will drop down leaving it on the base. Then use a sharp knife to work your way around the bottom. A little of the syrup might have leaked, creating a chewy caramel. As long as you've let it cool you will be able to unstick it with the knife.)

12. If you decide to make individual puff pastry tarts, using the method in the previous custard tart recipe, give them 30 minutes at 150°C/300°F/gas mark 2, and then check the filling has set fully.

13. Serve with chilled cream.

Mont Blanc

Inspired by the version served by Henry Harris at Bouchon Racine, London

Curiosity can be exhausting. All that newness. All that originality. All those thrilling first-time experiences. They can really take it out of you. Sometimes in a restaurant, often in fact, we don't want new experiences. We want the specific thing we've gone there for. We might fight a small battle with ourselves about it; tell ourselves that we shouldn't just order the same things again and again. Then we'll do exactly that, for the simple reason that we know it's good and that it satisfies a particular need. This is very much me, when I'm not eating out for work.

When I go to Richard Corrigan's seafood restaurant Bentley's, just off London's Piccadilly, I will try not to order the spicy coconut and mussel soup with big wafts of lemongrass and chilli. Then I'll order it. No trip to Tayyab's in Whitechapel is complete unless I've ordered those lamb chops. At Ravinder Bhogal's Jikoni I find it very hard indeed to resist the scrag end pie. And at Bouchon Racine, it has to be the Mont Blanc. There are always other great desserts scribbled up on the blackboard menu: the perfectly wobbly crème caramel with prunes drenched in Armagnac, the plum and almond tart with its pastry shell like the crispest of biscuits, the strawberries with white port and white pepper. But if the confection of crisp-shelled and gooey meringue with whipped cream and boozy chestnut purée that is the Mont Blanc is there, then that's what I have to order. It's a pavlova without fresh fruit pretensions to healthiness. In *My Last Supper*, my book about my last meal on earth, it was the dessert course. In this, it was an outlier. All the other choices in the book had a strongly defined origin story. I chose oysters because I adore them but also because of the strong memories I have of eating them for the first time with my mother. I chose snails in their shells with garlic and parsley butter because of my childhood memories of almost burning down an Alpine hotel during a school skiing trip by turning up the burner they sat upon too high. Salad was in there because of my emotional associations with Kressi, a brand of Swiss vinegar to which I was introduced by my mother-in-law.

But the Mont Blanc? I just like it. Done right, it's a winning combination of sugary and crisp, chewy and lightly boozy. It's all the good things, with a light gloss of the adult. For *My Last Supper* I travelled around trying to find perfect examples and discovered that the term Mont Blanc has become a catch-all for a bunch of desserts which might feature meringue, cream and chestnut in some formation, but also biscuit bases, and chocolate coverings and pastry cases and basically a load of things that I regard as entirely superfluous. At the end of the book, I staged the meal I had devised in a room above a west London pub. It was cooked for me by Henry Harris because I really couldn't think of anyone who could do it better. Naturally, it ended with his Mont Blanc. At the original Racine in Knightsbridge he served individual portions, but by this point he was going large and plating them up to be shared. That's what I've done here.

It's worth saying that as long as you've got the meringue right, and this method is the best I've ever used, you could also push it into service for a fruit version. Or you could break up the meringue and mix it in a bowl with whipped cream and fruit to make an Eton Mess. In so doing you will have created dessert options from about 98% of British restaurants operating in the 2020s. The meringue recipe comes from Jeremy Lee, who is famed at Quo Vadis in Soho for ending special dinners there with 'tumbles' made up of individual meringues, piled on top of each other with fruit curds and coulis, custard and cream and all the good things. They are the Jackson Pollocks of dessert: a seeming plate of chaos, from which order quickly emerges. (For an alternative way with this fabulous dessert, the baker Dan Lepard has a recipe online for a triple-tiered Mont Blanc cake, using layers of meringue, cream, chestnut purée, and dribbles of dark chocolate. I made it one year for Christmas and it made my family love me more than they already do.)

You'll see I'm advising you to make two individual portions, each of which serves two. This is because, if I gave you the instructions to make one, that would require the whites of 1½ eggs, and any cookbook that suggests doing something as annoying as using one and half egg whites would deserve to be thrown against the wall.

Serves 4

INGREDIENTS

Whites of 3 medium eggs
300g caster sugar (approximately; the seeming vagueness is
    explained below)
300ml double cream
160g chestnut purée (don't worry if you can only get whole
    pre-roasted chestnuts; I have a tip for that below)
2 tbsp icing sugar, plus more for dusting
1 tbsp Cognac or similar (optional)

METHOD

1. Heat the oven to 180°C/350°F/gas mark 4, and line a
   tray with greaseproof paper.

2. Separate the eggs, making sure not to get any yolk in
   the white, because that will stop them whipping
   properly. Now weigh the whites. Depending on the
   size of your eggs it will probably come to anywhere
   between 90g and 130g because eggs can differ hugely.
   Now weigh out exactly double the weight in caster
   sugar and separate it out into two equal parts.

3. Start whipping the whites either in a scrupulously clean mixing bowl with an electric hand mixer or in a food processor. Just as the whites are starting to get to stiff peaks, stop mixing and sprinkle in the first half of the sugar. Mix again until you get to stiff peaks. Now fold in the second half of the sugar, making sure not to knock out the air.

4. Spoon the mixture on to the paper-lined tray, in two separate rounds. Put the tray into the oven and immediately turn it down to 120°C/250°F/gas mark ½. Bake for 1 hour.

5. At the end of the hour turn off the oven and leave the meringues in there with the door ajar for 30 minutes. Then remove them from the oven and let them cool.

6. Whip the double cream and add a good tablespoon of caster sugar.

7. Blitz the chestnut purée with the icing sugar and the Cognac or similar, if using.

8. That tip: if all you can get are whole, peeled and roasted chestnuts, blitz them to a crumb. Then add 20ml of water per 80g of chestnuts. (They often come in 80g pouches.) Blitz again until it becomes a smooth purée. Then add the icing sugar and booze, if using, and blitz again.

9. Now build the Mont Blancs. Put the meringues on large plates and top with half the lightly sweetened cream and half the chestnut purée each. If you have a potato ricer, use that to turn the chestnut purée into strands or noodles. But really you can just dollop it on. Finally, dust with icing sugar.

Intercourse:
I love my family. Most of the time

Every morning, I rise with the dawn, pull on a sturdy pair of walking boots, a rugged jumper against the chill, and a thick waxed jacket. Then I stride out into our smallholding. I adore this part of my day: the thick quiet, broken only by the birds greeting each other, or the rustle of squirrels chasing each other up branch and down. I have a routine. I check on the state of the apple and pear trees and then, if it's the season, the soft fruit. Next, I head to the rows of beans and tomatoes, the aubergines and courgettes, and the old iron bath which is now home to our herb garden. Bit by bit, almost unconsciously, I start to pick this fabulous bounty, filling the frayed but sturdy trug on my arm, which once belonged to my dear mother. In this way, a plan for the meals for the day ahead forms. And soon I am back in the kitchen, perhaps absent-mindedly pulling tarragon leaves from their stalks to fill the dainty ceramic bowl I picked up on a trip to Corsica many years ago, while I dream about a Béarnaise sauce to go with the rare-breed bavette currently sitting in my fridge, wrapped in a piece of paper tied twice with twine. This isn't as self-serving as it sounds, for I will be feeding my lovely family too.

Or not as the case may be because, to use a technical term, this is all total bollocks. It's a complete fiction. I live in Brixton in south London, which is not known for its smallholdings. People grow things here. There are inner-city allotments. But as described? No. Plus I hate getting up at dawn. There were various reasons for not filling this book with beautiful colour

photography. As described so many pages ago in the introduction, it really was partly because of my resistance to overly
art-directed food photography, presenting an unattainable
ideal of a dish. I didn't want to invite you to fail. Partly it was
because it kept the price of this book down. But it was also
because it removed even the slightest of temptations to
idealize my family life. You know the kind of thing: the perfectly coiffured cook in unstained apron looking blissfully
unflustered while stirring a bowl or chopping an onion in a
spotless kitchen, as sunlight fair gushes through the window;
a table laid with fourteen separate dishes, all of which seem
to have been completed miraculously at exactly the same
moment; sweetest of all, the rest of the beloved cook's
white-toothed family, smiling adoringly at the edible joy
which surrounds them.

Enough, already. It is hardly a searingly insightful analysis
to point out that a lot of modern cookbooks aren't just selling you a collection of recipes, but also a completely fictional
lifestyle. I should be careful not to roll my eyes at that too
much. I've spent a lot of my working life involved with
colour magazines, all of which have been flogging a fictional,
idealized lifestyle. People like looking at pictures of how life
could be and imagining themselves a part of it, me included.
Courtesy of the image, we fantasize about a different, more
honed and exuberant version of ourselves. It's fun. In this,
fashion and food have a lot in common. Inside this man in a
2XL shirt is a slim-hipped chap in a delightful Paul Smith
suit just fighting to get out.

But sometimes it's worth knowing how things really are.
While I have published a few recipes before, this is my first
full-length cookbook, and the reality of its preparation was a
source of endless amusement to me. And irritation. And
occasional despair. A lot of the time it was a controlled and

ordered process. I love a spreadsheet, me. But sometimes it really wasn't. I'm sure old hands at this cookbook business have the whole thing nailed; that their kitchens are never chaotic, and their family members are always genuinely delighted to be the guinea pigs. To be fair, my lot were often utterly thrilled. The first time I made the Wigmore toastie on page 48 was a good day. Everybody huddled in the kitchen to celebrate the virtuous interplay of aged dairy fats, mustard, pickled gherkins, bread and fizzing, melted butter. The work that went into the sweet soy-braised pork shoulder from Kushi-ya on page 157 was greeted with quiet murmurs of delight, which were their own reward. I have made that a couple of times for my lot, not to test it, just to eat it. The quietly muttered words 'This should be illegal' from my older child, Ed, as he practically inhaled my take on the McDonald's deep-fried apple pie really came as no surprise. It is very good indeed. One day it probably will be illegal.

But some things took more work than others. The Snickers pudding on page 301 was a case of multiple trial and error. I tried at first to make it with a milk chocolate mousse, but the lower cocoa solid content in milk chocolate meant it didn't quite set. Which is to say, it was a chocolate and caramel soup bobbing with abandoned caramelized peanuts. 'This is like a child was let loose in a kitchen and told to make dessert with whatever they liked,' Ed said. 'And they just decided to throw lots of soft things in a bowl.' I thanked him for his support. The second attempt wasn't much better and was met with quiet eye-rolling. When on the third attempt I got it right, his praise was effusive. Possibly too effusive. As any parent will tell you, there is nothing so humbling, so bittersweet, as being patronized for your achievements by your twenty-something progeny. How clever of me to notice.

Some of the responses to the dishes being tested were, of

course, down to personal taste. There are over sixty recipes in this book. Everything has been included because I think it's absolutely delicious. There's not a single herb or spice, fruit or vegetable that I do not think is anything short of fabulous. This should not come as a surprise. You can't do a job like mine for so many years if you are a picky eater or have dietary foibles. I'm always amused when I'm asked if I have any 'dietaries'. I'm a restaurant critic. We don't do dietaries, or at least we shouldn't. For the record, I do have one foible, but just one. I hate Heinz baked beans, and the supermarket own-brand versions thereof. Too sugary. Too slippery. Too soft. But it's only those. I do love the sort of baked beans you get from American BBQ places. As you can imagine, a dislike of Heinz baked beans is not exactly a problem for a restaurant critic. They do not appear in any of the recipes.

My daughter Taiga has an uncontroversial aversion to too much chilli heat. The Malaysian chicken curry on page 133 was very much not her favourite. She barely touched it. Meanwhile, my wife is wasted on me. Pat does not like hazelnuts or dill. She's not keen on certain fattier cuts of meat. There are some desserts she will eat, but really, she's just not that into them. There were a bunch of things in this collection she didn't much like. I adore the seaweed and sesame crackers with anchovy mayo on page 54, inspired by those served at the Suffolk in Aldeburgh. So did Ed. Pat was unimpressed. I'd spent serious time gluing sheets of seaweed to sheets of spring roll pastry and then pressing them in the fridge, before covering them in sesame seeds, cutting them up and deep-frying them. And her response was: 'Nah, not feeling it.' Same with the sage and anchovy fritters on page 58. She is wrong. Both are fabulous.

But the best response, which is to say, the very worst, came from Ed when presented with the late Esra Muslu's wonderful rice-stuffed globe artichoke on page 209. It's an extraordinary combination of soft aromatic spicing, fragrant fresh green herbs, lemon juice acidity and nutty rice. I was properly proud of that one. It had taken a lot of work to come up with a dish which drew on the fundamentals of the original and was achievable at home. Ed ate a lot of his then looked down at his plate.

'It would have been better if the rice hadn't been stuffed between the leaves of the artichoke,' he said.

'What do you mean?' I said, baffled. 'That's the whole point of it. The spiced rice brings its flavour to the artichoke.'

'That's what I'm saying. It would have been better if the rice was separate and not spiced. And was fried and had some egg in it.'

'Are you telling me that you would have preferred it if I'd made you a bowl of egg fried rice?'

'Yes. That would have been nice.'

It was a wry and humbling moment. I really do spend a substantial amount of my working day mentally planning what I will cook for dinner when the work is done. I know I am not alone in this. Perhaps, as someone who now has a copy of this book, you are the same. I often claim I put my back into it simply to serve my own appetites. I'm greedy. I want to eat the good stuff. If other people get to eat it too, then all to the good. But it's only partly true. I do like feeding myself. At the risk of suddenly turning into some unlikely and awful earth mother, it's the best kind of self-care. But cooking really is very much about feeding others. The process of writing this book has also been about feeding my family. It has been about listening to the satisfied silence as they empty their plates, or watching them nod approvingly or sometimes simply telling me the latest creation has hit the mark. And even when they didn't like it, when there was too much chilli in the Malaysian chicken curry for one, or another felt the rice would have been better without the spice and instead fried with an egg, well, that too has been fun. The great thing about dinner is there will always be another one along soon enough. There will always be another chance to cook, another chance to win their approval. Or not, as the case may be.

I still adore going to restaurants. I push through each new door into each new dining room with anticipation. After twenty-five years in the job, I still find the sight of an unfamiliar menu utterly thrilling. But staying in my own kitchen, putting effort into dinner, can be very special too.

There's no other way to put it. I simply love my nights out at home.

The Restaurants

This is a list of every restaurant mentioned in the text which was trading at the point of publication. Although this book celebrates the restaurants I've most loved and enjoyed over the past quarter of a century, their inclusion in this list doesn't necessarily mean it's one of the ones I loved. It just means it was mentioned. After all, Le Cinq is in this list and I didn't have a good word to say about that. Those that I have reviewed or written about are marked by an asterisk* after the name. If you want to read what I've written about it online, you can search using my name and that of the restaurant.

Acme Fire Cult,* The Bootyard, Abbot Street, London, E8 3DP | acmefirecult.com

The Alan,* 18 Princess Street, Manchester, M1 4LG | thealanhotel.com

Allard, 41 Rue Saint-André-des-Arts, 75006 Paris, France | restaurant-allard.fr

Amaya,* Halkin Arcade (Entrance via Lowndes Street), Belgravia, London, SW1X 8JT | amaya.biz

Barshu,* 28 Frith Street, London, W1D 5LF | barshurestaur ant.co.uk

Benoit, 20 Rue Saint-Martin, 75004 Paris, France | benoit-paris.com

Bentleys,* 11–15 Swallow Street, London, W1B 4DG | bentleys.org

Bocca di Lupo,* 12 Archer Street, London, W1D 7BB | boccadilupo.com

Bouchon Racine,* 66 Cowcross Street, London, EC1M 6BP | bouchonracine.com

Box-E,* Bristol Unit 10, Cargo 1, Wapping Wharf, Bristol, BS1 6WP

Brasserie Zedel,* 20 Sherwood Street, London, W1F 7ED | brasseriezedel.com

Bubala* Spitalfields, 65 Commercial Street, Spitalfields, London, E1 6BD | bubala.co.uk/spitalfields

Bugis Street Brasserie,* Millennium Gloucester Hotel, London, SW7 4LH | thebugisrestaurant.com

C & R Café,* 4 Rupert Court, London, W1D 6DY | cnrcafe restaurant.com

Café Murano, 33 St James's Street, St James's, London, SW1A 1HD | cafemurano.co.uk

Casa do Frango,* 32 Southwark Street, London, SE1 1TU | casadofrango.co.uk

Cervo's,* 43 Canal Street, New York, NY 10002, United States | cervosnyc.com

Checchino dal 1887,* Via di Monte Testaccio, 30 00153 Rome | checchino-dal-1887.com

Chez Georges,* 1 Rue du Mail, 75002 Paris, France | restau rantsparisiens.com/chez-georges

Chez Panisse,* 1517 Shattuck Avenue, Berkeley, CA 94709, United States | chezpanisse.com

Chishuru,* 3 Great Titchfield Street, London W1W 8AX | chishuru.com

Chop Chop,* The Hippodrome Casino, Cranbourn Street, Leicester Square, London, WC2H 7JH | hippodrome casino.com/chopchop

Climat,* Blackfriars House, Manchester, M3 2JA | restaurant climat.co.uk

Colbert, 50–52 Sloane Square, Chelsea, London, SW1W 8AX | colbertrestaurant.com

Coppi,* Saint Anne's Square, 11 Edward Street, Belfast, BT1 2LR | coppi.co.uk

Cornerstone,* 3 Prince Edward Road, Hackney Wick, London, E9 5LX | cornerstonehackney.com

Dominique Ansel, 189 Spring Street (btw Sullivan & Thompson), New York, NY 10012, United States | dominique anselny.com

Double Red Duke,* Bourton Road, Bampton, OX18 2RB | countrycreatures.com/double-red-duke/

Eleven Madison Park, 11 Madison Avenue, New York, NY 10010, United States | elevenmadisonpark.com

Erst,* 9 Murray Street, Manchester, M4 6HS | erst-mcr.co.uk

The Fat Duck,* High Street, Bray, Berkshire, SL6 2AQ | thefatduck.co.uk

FEBO, branches across the Netherlands| febo.nl

Four Seasons,* 12 Gerrard Street, London W1D 5PP | fs-restaurants.co.uk

Freak Scene, 28 Parsons Green Lane, London, SW6 4HS | freakscenerestaurants.com

French Laundry, 6640 Washington Street, Yountville, CA 94599 | thomaskeller.com

Gloriosa,* 1321 Argyle Street, Glasgow, G3 8TL | gloriosa glasgow.com

Gooey Café, 103 High Street, Manchester, M4 1HQ | Kiosk: Ducie Street Warehouse, Manchester, M1 2TP | thegooey.co

Greggs, branches nationwide | greggs.co.uk

Guinea Grill,* 30 Bruton Place, Mayfair, London, W1J 6NL | theguinea.co.uk

Haenyeo,* 239 Fifth Avenue, Brooklyn, New York, NY 11215, United States | haenyeobk.com

Hawksmoor,* 5a Air Street, London, W1J 0AD | thehawks moor.com/locations/airstreet/

Hispi, 1C School Lane, Didsbury, Manchester, M20 6RD | hispi.net

Hix Oyster & Fish House, Cobb Road, Lyme Regis, DT7 3JP | theoysterandfishhouse.co.uk

Holborn Dining Room,* 252 High Holborn, London, WC1V 7EN | holborndiningroom.com

Honest Burgers,* branches nationwide | honestburgers. co.uk

The Ivy, 1–5 West Street, London, WC2H 9NQ | the-ivy. co.uk

Jean Georges,* 1 Central Park West, New York, NY 10023, United States | jean-georges.com

Jikoni, 19–21 Blandford Street, London, W1U 3DH | jikoni london.com

Joe Allen,* 2 Burleigh Street, London, WC2E 7PX | joe allen.co.uk

Kaosarn,* 96 Coldharbour Lane, Brixton Village, London, SW9 8PR | kaosarnlondon.co.uk/

Kushi-ya,* 1A Cannon Court, Long Row W, Nottingham, NG1 6JE | kushi-ya.co.uk

Lamplighter Dining Rooms,* High Street, Windermere, Cumbria, LA23 1AF | lamplighterdiningrooms.com

L'Ami Louis, 32 Rue du Vertbois, 75003 Paris, France | paris bymouth.com [no official website]

L'Atelier Robuchon, 6 Clarges Street, London, W1J 8AE | jrobuchon.com

L'Escargot,* 48 Greek Street, Soho, London, W1D 4EF | lescargot.co.uk

La Petite Maison,* 53–54 Brook's Mews, London, W1K 4EG | lpmrestaurants.com

Le Cinq,* Four Seasons Hotel George V, 31 Avenue George V, 75008 Paris, France | fourseasons.com/paris

Leibhaftig, Metzer Strasse 30, 10405 Berlin | leibhaftig.com

Le Relais de Venise l'Entrecôte, Marylebone, 120 Marylebone Lane, London, W1U 2QG and 5 Throgmorton Street, London EC2N 2AD | relaisdevenise.com

Lisboeta, 30 Charlotte Street, London, W1T 2NG | lisboeta.co.uk

Mandarin Kitchen,* 14–16 Queensway, Bayswater, London, W2 3RX | mandarin.kitchen

McDonald's,* branches nationwide | mcdonalds.com

Mr Mackerel,* Market Kitchen, Leeds Kirkgate Market, Leeds, LS2 7BR | facebook.com/MrMackerelLeeds [no official website]

Nando's, branches nationwide | nandos.co.uk

Noble,* 27 Church Road, Holywood, Belfast, BT18 9BU | nobleholywood.com

Note,* 26 Fenian Street, Dublin, D02 FX09, Ireland | notedublin.com

Ondine,* 2 George IV Bridge, Edinburgh, EH1 1AD | ondinerestaurant.co.uk

Origin City,* 12 West Smithfield, London, EC1A 9JR | origincity.co.uk

Oslo Court,* Charlbert Street, St John's Wood, London, NW8 7EN | oslocourtrestaurant.co.uk

Per Se,* 10 Columbus Circle, 4th Floor, New York, NY 10019, United States | thomaskeller.com/perseny

Persian Cottage,* 2 Benson Street, Middlesbrough, TS5 6JQ | persiancottagetakeaway.com

Polpo,* 41 Beak Street, London, W1F 9SB | polpo.co.uk

Quo Vadis,* 26–29 Dean Street, London, W1D 3LL | quovadissoho.co.uk

The Raby Hunt,* Summerhouse, Darlington, DL2 3UD | rabyhuntrestaurant.co.uk

Red Chilli,* 403–419 Oxford Road, Manchester, M13 9WG | redchillirestaurant.co.uk

The Ritz, 150 Piccadilly, London, W1J 9BR | theritz
london.com

Rochelle Canteen, 16 Playground Gardens, London, E2 7FA
| rochellecanteen.com

Rules,* 34–35 Maiden Lane, London, WC2E 7LB | rules.
co.uk

Russ & Daughters, 127 Orchard Street, New York,
NY 10002, United States | russanddaughters.com

Salt,* 8 Church Street, Stratford-upon-Avon, Warwickshire,
CV37 6HB | www.salt-restaurant.co.uk

Sam & Jak,* 2 Cricklade Street, Cirencester, Gloucestershire,
GL7 1JH | samandjak.co.uk

Sanxia Renjia, 29 Goodge Street, Fitzrovia, London,
W1T 2PP | sanxia.co.uk

Sargasso,* Margate Harbour Arm, Stone Pier, Margate,
CT9 1AP | sargasso.bar

Sartoria,* 20 Savile Row, London, W1S 3PR | sartoria-
restaurant.co.uk

Seahorse,* 5 South Embankment, Dartmouth, TQ6 9BH |
seahorserestaurant.co.uk

Sichuan Folk,* 2 Hanbury Street, London, E1 6QR |
sichuanfolk.co.uk

Som Saa,* 43A Commercial Street, London, E1 6BD |
somsaa.com

Soot Bull Jeep, 3136 W 8th Street, Los Angeles, CA 90005,
United States | places.singleplatform.com//soot-bull-
jeep/menu [no official website]

The Spärrows,* 16 Red Bank, Green Quarter, Manchester,
M4 4HF | thesparrows.me

The Sportsman,* Faversham Road, Seasalter, Whitstable,
Kent | thesportsmanseasalter.co.uk

St John,* 26 St John Street, London, EC1M 4AY | stjohn
restaurant.com

St Moritz,* 161 Wardour Street, London, W1F 8WJ | stmoritz-restaurant.co.uk

The Suffolk,* 152 High Street, Aldeburgh, IP15 5AQ | the-suffolk.co.uk

Supawan Thai,* 38 Caledonian Road, London, N1 9DT | supawan.co.uk

Tayyabs,* 83–89 Fieldgate Street, London, E1 1JU | tayyabs.co.uk

Toad Bakery, 44 Peckham Road, Camberwell, SE5 8PX | toadbakery.com

Toups Meatery, 845 North Carrollton Avenue, New Orleans, LA 70119, United States | toupsmeatery.com

Tsiakkos & Charcoal,* 5 Marylands Road, London, W9 2DU | tsiakkos.co.uk

Waterside Inn, Ferry Road, Bray, Berkshire, SL6 2AT | waterside-inn.co.uk

The Wheatsheaf,* Wheatsheaf Inn, West End, Northleach, Gloucestershire, GL54 3EZ | cotswoldswheatsheaf.com

Wheelers,* 8 High Street, Whitstable, CT5 1BQ | wheelers oysterbar.com

The Wigmore,* 15 Langham Place, Regent Street, London, W1B 3DE | the-wigmore.co.uk

The Wolseley,* 160 Piccadilly, St James's, London W1J 9EB | thewolseley.com

XO Kitchen,* 13–15 St George's Street, Norwich NR3 1AB | xokitchen.uk

Zahter,* 30–32 Fouberts Place, W1F 7PS | zahter.co.uk

Zuni Café,* 1658 Market Street, San Francisco, CA 94102, United States | zunicafe.com

Bibliography

Bhogal, Ravinder, *Comfort and Joy: Irresistible Pleasures from a Vegetarian Kitchen*, Bloomsbury Publishing, 2023.

Bhogal, Ravinder, *Jikoni: Proudly Inauthentic Recipes from an Immigrant Kitchen*, Bloomsbury Publishing, 2020.

Blumenthal, Heston, *In Search of Total Perfection*, Bloomsbury Publishing, 2009.

Brown, Robert Owen, *Crispy Squirrel and Vimto Trifle: Fifty Great Recipes from the Extraordinary Culinary Adventures of Award-Winning Chef Robert Owen Brown*, Manchester Books Ltd, 2013.

Carrier, Robert, *Great Dishes of the World*, Mitchell Beazley, 1968.

Cloake, Felicity, *Perfect: 68 Essential Recipes* for Every Cook's Repertoire, Fig Tree, 2011.

David, Elizabeth, *French Country Cooking*, Macdonald, 1958.

Dunlop, Fuchsia, *The Book of Sichuan Food*, Bloomsbury Publishing, 2019 (reissue).

Franklin, Calum, *The Pie Room: 80 Achievable and Show-Stopping Pies and Sides for Pie Lovers Everywhere*, Bloomsbury Publishing, 2020.

Gott, Huw and Beckett, Will, *Hawksmoor: Restaurants and Recipes*, Preface Publishing, 2017.

Harris, Stephen, *The Sportsman*, Phaidon Press, 2019.

Henderson, Fergus, *Nose to Tail Eating: A Kind of British Cooking*, Bloomsbury Publishing, 2004.

Hopkinson, Simon and Bareham, Lindsey, *Roast Chicken and Other Stories*, Ebury Press, 1999.

Kenedy, Jacob, *Bocca: Cookbook*, Bloomsbury Publishing, 2011.

Koffmann, Pierre, *Memories of Gascony*, Mitchell Beazley, 1990.

Lascelles, Alice, *The Cocktail Edit*, Quadrille, 2022.

Lee, Jeremy, *Cooking Simply and Well, for One or Many*, Fourth Estate, 2022.

Norman, Russell, *Brutto: A (Simple) Florentine Cookbook*, Bloomsbury Publishing, 2023.

Norman, Russell, *Polpo: A Venetian Cookbook (of Sorts)*, Bloomsbury Publishing, 2012.

Oakes, Amoul, *Amoul: Some Family Recipes*, Amoula Ltd, 2008.

Ottolenghi, Yotam and Tamimi, Sami, *Ottolenghi: The Cookbook*, Ebury, 2008.

Phipps, Catherine, *The Pressure Cooker Cookbook: Over 150 Simple, Essential, Time-Saving Recipes*, Ebury, 2012.

Rhodes, Gary, *New British Classics*, BBC Worldwide Ltd, 1999.

Robuchon, Joël, *The Complete Robuchon*, Grub Street, 2008.

Roden, Claudia, *The Book of Jewish Food*, Viking, 1997.

Roux, Michel, *Les Abats: Recipes Celebrating the Whole Beast*, Seven Dials, 2017.

Roux, Michel Jnr, *Le Gavroche Cookbook*, Cassell & Co, 2001.

Sifton, Sam, *The New York Times Cooking: No-Recipe Recipes*, Ebury Press, 2021.

Slater, Nigel, *Real Fast Food*, Michael Joseph, 1992.

Tram, Van and Vu, Anh, *The Vietnamese Market Cookbook*, Square Peg, 2013.

The Zuni Cafe Cookbook: A Compendium of Recipes and Cooking Lessons from San Francisco's Beloved Restaurant, W. W. Norton & Company, 2003.

Wells, Patricia, *Bistro Cooking*, Kyle Books, 1990.

Acknowledgements

Many people made this book possible, among them a lot of chefs and restaurateurs who, despite what I do for a living, were willing to help me. Some simply gave me their blessing to come up with a recipe inspired by their dish. Others shared details of their restaurant method. A few reviewed my recipes in detail and gave me their thoughts. The vast majority are already name-checked in the text, but a few aren't. Therefore, for the sake of completeness, I would like to thank: Tom Barton, Will Beckett, Ravinder Bhogal, Chloe Burrows, Simon Carlin, Graham Chatham, Andrew Clarke, Franco Concli, Fernando Duarte, Fuchsia Dunlop, Philip Eeles, Helen Emler, Liz Falshawe, Alex Fane, Mohsen Geravandian, Huw Gott, Annie Gray, the Greggs Press Office, Scott Hallsworth, Henry Harris, Stephen Harris, Lawrence Hartley, Rosie Healey, Tim Healey, Thom Hetherington, Kasia Hitchcock, Mark Hix, Simon Hopkinson, Jacob Kenedy, Chris King, Jeremy King, Alice Lascelles, Gary Lee, Jeremy Lee, Rowley Leigh, Francesco Mazzei, Ricky McMenemy, Mary-Ellen McTague, Salvatore Megna, Nuno Mendes, Ferdinand 'Budgie' Montoya, Esra Muslu, the Nando's Press Office, Amoul Oakes, Jeremy Pang, George Pell, Adam Platt, Jimmy Preston, Stuart Proctor, Benoit Provost, Chris Rhodes, Michel Roux, William Tiger Sin, Crispin Somerville, David Stafford, Dave Strauss, William Sutton, Wasim Tayyab, Iain Thomas, Mitch Tonks, Choy Tran, Josh Russ Tupper, Elvira Tynan, Marcus Wareing, Marc Webbon, Cathie Winn, Patrick Withington and Christine Yau.

All recipes are mine as, of course, are any mistakes.

However, I was grateful to have on my side the marvellous and extremely experienced food stylist and home economist Pippa Leon, who tested a slab of them, marked my homework and kept me on the straight and narrow. In addition, I would like to thank various friends who tested recipes and gave me feedback. They are: Sarah Baker, Glen and Honor Blackman, Charlie Codrington, Catherine Kanter and Melissa Thompson. Fliss Freeborn provided superb research support, which made certain lengthy tasks much quicker and simpler. Huge thanks to the various shopkeepers in my corner of London, who kept me supplied with vital ingredients and sorted special orders: in Herne Hill, both Neil and Rosie Dugard of the butchers Dugard & Daughters and Gary Fox and family of the much-missed greengrocers Seasons of England; in Nunhead, the fishmongers F. C. Soper; in Clapham, Gary Moen of the butchers M. Moen & Sons.

Statement of obvious: I wouldn't have been in a position to write this book at all had I not been fortunate enough to hold the privileged position of restaurant critic on the *Observer* these past twenty-five years. I am therefore indebted to all the editors of the paper who allowed me to keep my job, namely Roger Alton, John Mulholland and Paul Webster. And of course, there are the editors of the *Observer Magazine* in its various incarnations across that period. They are: Sheryl Garratt, Justine Picardie, Allan Jenkins, Ruaridh Nicoll and latterly Harriet Green. In addition, I must thank my colleagues Eva Wiseman, Steve Chamberlain and Martin Love, who have variously overseen my column and kept me from making a total arse of myself.

I was very lucky indeed to find a home at Fig Tree with the wise, calm and incisively brilliant editor Helen Garnons-Williams, and her superb team, including Ella Harold, Olivia Mead, Annie Lucas, Annie Moore, Richard Bravery and

Annie Lee. I am thrilled that the huge talent that is Jack Martindale agreed to provide the beautiful illustrations for this book. At my agents Curtis Brown, Jonny Geller and Sabhbh Curran shepherded this project into life with care, attention and customary professionalism and reassurance.

But the last word of thanks must go to my family: my wife Pat Gordon-Smith, and Ed and Taiga who, by dint of being in the house and needing to be fed, got to taste every single dish as it went through its various incarnations, and gave me detailed and focused feedback, and rarely complained. I am, as ever, eternally grateful for their forbearance. I'd be nothing without them.

Index

While *Nights Out At Home* does not include full colour photography, throughout the research and writing of this book, I did photograph each dish as it was prepared, just for my own reference. You can access all of those images by visiting jayrayner.co.uk/noah or via the QR code on this page. Be aware: I am not a professional photographer and I make no great claims for the quality of the pictures. But some people might find a visual reference useful as they follow the recipes. Happy cooking.

Credits

Commissioning Editor	:	Helen Garnons-Williams
Assistant Editor	:	Ella Harold
Consulting Editor	:	Pat Gordon-Smith
Home Economist	:	Pippa Leon
Illustrator	:	Jack William Martindale
Art Direction	:	Richard Bravery
Design	:	Chris Bentham
Editorial Manager	:	Emma Brown
Copy-editor	:	Annie Lee
Production Manager	:	Annie Underwood
Press	:	Olivia Mead, Annie Lucas
Marketing	:	Annie Moore

The Hi[?]
Lei[?]

T

683 W[?]

*** BILL ***

[?]ble: 3

[?]ck - [?]   2

[?]hul[?]

Restaurant

Bicyclette
Rocroy Pastis 50ml
Jambon Noir
Bread & Butter
6 Oysters
Brains
Hareng
Chicken Liver [?]
Cote de Boeuf
Tete de Veau
Rabbit
Chips
French beans
Green Salad
Tarte Vaudoise
Mont Blanc
Creme Caramel with Prune
Cheese
Gavi di Gavi
Cote du Rhone

[?]TAL

[?]rvice charge 12.5% on
[?].00

due

[?]eceived

£ 420.78
ZOO

Division hint
420.78 / 6 = 70.13
[?]0.13 x 2 = 140.26
[?].13 x 3 = 210.39
[?]3 x 4 = 280.52
[?]T:4094[?]

---

iPad9/327456-L11/327415-Dav
Statement N771604.420

* DRAFT RECEIPT *
Lyon Pub Cor[?]

9   Item(s)

Service Charge

Amount Due

Rate 20%	Net £144.91	Tax £28.99	
	£144.91	£28.99	Gr[?] £17[?]
		VAT No. 409 0939 87	£17[?]

32.50

374.00

46.78

£ 420.78
ZOO

THREE
COMPAS[?]

1. Main Floor / 17[?]
AR-230845

1 Baby scallop with romes[?]
1 Vitello tonnato Frankie G[?]
1 Prawn Rice for 2 @76.00
1 -Prawn Rice
1 Spicy sausage fritter 2 un...
May 23
1 Water Sparkling
1 Henners Vintage Glass
1 Lemon Pie
1 Chocolate souffle

Bill [?]

Marlish
Hummus
Crispy Beer
Mackerel Soy
Curried Lamb
Monkfish Khol[?]
Beef Fillet
Isle of Wight Tomato[?]
Apple Terrine
Duck Egg Custard
Discretionary Service

Sub-Total

Total

44 Main St. Sedbergh LA10 5[?]
015396 20264
theblackbullsed[?]
VAT [?]